*Oxford Modern Languages and*
*Literature Monographs*

VOLTAIRE: Historian
By J. H. BRUMFITT. 1958

THE PETRARCHAN SOURCES OF
*LA CELESTINA*
By A. D. DEYERMOND. 1961

THE TRAGEDIES OF
GIAMBATTISTA CINTHIO GIRALDI
By P. R. HORNE. 1962

PONTUS DE TYARD AND HIS
*DISCOURS PHILOSOPHIQUES*
By KATHLEEN M. HALL. 1962

PIERRE BAYLE AND VOLTAIRE
By H. T. MASON. 1963

THE GENESIS OF *LE COUSIN PONS*
By DONALD ADAMSON, 1966

# RILKE AND FRANCE

## A STUDY IN
## POETIC DEVELOPMENT

BY

K. A. J. BATTERBY

OXFORD UNIVERSITY PRESS

1966

*Oxford University Press, Ely House, London W. 1*

GLASGOW NEW YORK TORONTO MELBOURNE WELLINGTON
CAPE TOWN SALISBURY IBADAN NAIROBI LUSAKA ADDIS ABABA
BOMBAY CALCUTTA MADRAS KARACHI LAHORE DACCA
KUALA LUMPUR HONG KONG

PRINTED IN GREAT BRITAIN

# PREFACE

FOR those who love the magic of words it is difficult, knowing him, not to fall under Rilke's spell. My own capitulation and, with it, the hope that I might sometime undertake a more extensive study, was immediate. If, however, this has made the task of writing this book a congenial one, it would be arrogant to underestimate the dangers of partiality or to ignore the difficulties awaiting those who enter the field of lyric poetry. To this extent, the quest for a suitable critical approach, in the opening chapter, has been an attempt to apply a corrective self-discipline. If this book does something to stimulate objective thinking on Rilke, while at the same time seeking not to intrude on the reader's personal response to the poetry, it will have achieved its purpose.

I have been more than fortunate in the help given me by many, not all of whom can be mentioned. My greatest debt is to Professor E. L. Stahl on whose advice I have been able to call from the beginning. Over a long period, he has given ungrudgingly of his time and interest, and without his patient counsel and encouragement the book would never have reached its present form. I would also thank Professor James Boyd with whom, in the difficult stages of planning and early writing, I was able to have frequent discussions and through whom many pitfalls were avoided. I am indebted, too, to Dr. Enid Starkie and to the late Mr. D. Garabedian for their advice in matters pertaining to French literature, which inevitably looms importantly in this study. Acknowledgements would not be complete without reference to the Committee for Advanced Studies, which has made publication of the book possible, and to the members of the Monographs Committee for their painstaking reading of the script and for their many helpful suggestions—my thanks are due particularly to Mr. A. D. Crow, Dr. R. A. Sayce, and Professor T. B. W. Reid. Finally, I would gratefully mention the staff of the Taylor Institution, and especially Mr. R. C. Maasz, whose help has always been so willingly and promptly given.

K. A. J. B.

*December 1964*

# CONTENTS

# ABBREVIATIONS

The following abbreviations have been used:

      *G.W.: Gesammelte Werke.*
      *A.W.: Ausgewählte Werke.*
      *G.B.: Gesammelte Briefe.*

Owing to their greater availability, the *Ausgewählte Werke* have, where possible, been used for reference in preference to the *Gesammelte Werke*.

# I

# THE PROBLEM OF CRITICAL APPROACH

I F the great mass of differing, and often contradictory, estimates
and attempted elucidations of Rilke leaves the reader bewildered,
one fact at least clearly emerges: that Rilke is one of the most
provocative and most discussed figures in modern literature.
Equally undisputed—and of this the great volume of Rilke criticism is a symptom—is the exalted place he occupies, not only in
German literature, but in the world of European letters as a whole.
His reputation, already considerable in his lifetime, reached new
heights within a short time of his death.

Even more remarkable, perhaps, is the fact that his achievement
has been in the field of lyric poetry, in an age that is commonly
adjudged hostile and unresponsive to poetry in general and to
lyrical expression in particular. If the dictum that the artist is the
product of his age be held in part to mean that he gives the public
what it wants, that he at once reflects and feeds the artistic needs of
the period in which he lives, then evidently Rilke's case presents
a paradox: that, while representing values seemingly diametrically
opposed to those of his time, he has yet succeeded in conquering
indifference and wresting unstinted acknowledgement. Rilke was,
like Baudelaire and Nietzsche before him, destined for conflict and
paradox. All three were products of an age of spiritual dispossession
and bankruptcy, an age when the values and ideals which had stood
firm and serene for centuries were being challenged and rocked,
when the things of the spirit were being attacked at their founda-
tions. And yet all three possessed, in abundant measure, precisely
those qualities of the spirit and the imagination which were now in
jeopardy. Each, in his different way, had the task of transplanting a
sensibility, an idealism, and a creative organization which belonged
to the benevolent past into an environment of spiritual winter,
and of keeping them alive.

We are therefore confronted at the outset by a poet whose fame
has been remarkable for the extent and rapidity of its growth; by
a poet, moreover, who has won his position when many would

B

regard contemporary conditions and taste as being against him. And we are further faced by a body of writing on Rilke which is, with some notable exceptions, as confusing and unsatisfying as its proportions are daunting. If it is true that only now, nearly forty years after his death, are we reaching a point of historical distance and detachment when we can begin to make a balanced and unimpassioned assessment, it is still noteworthy that so many of Rilke's commentators have not been content to treat him for what he is: a poet. It is obviously necessary, against this confused background, to seek to establish a valid approach. It is necessary to consider why and in what way so much Rilke criticism has failed. And it is, above all, necessary to examine the primary question: What is the nature of Rilke's art, and how has he achieved his effect? At this point, and as a salutary caution, it is interesting to recall what Rilke himself said of criticism, as early as 1898, in the *Florenzer Tagebuch*: 'Solange die Kritik nicht Kunst neben den anderen Künsten ist, bleibt sie kleinlich, einseitig, ungerecht und unwürdig.'[1]

These words, which might profitably be adopted by the literary critic as the perfect textbook principle, may in fact be written up as the epitaph on many of Rilke's expositors. The responsibility which lies on critics of lyric poetry is particularly heavy, since, of all literary forms, it is the one most dependent on immediacy of impression[2] and therefore the one most vulnerable to damage by preconceived or second-hand notions and by ill-judged commentaries. The harm done to the appreciation of Rilke's poetry has not been due to any unwillingness to praise him—Rilke has never lacked superlatives—except in so far as excess of enthusiasm may have contributed to the blinding and distortion of critical faculties. The real fault has been in the recurrent failure to treat him as an artist. Rilke has been variously heralded as a prophet, seer, thinker, the man with the solution to the problems of the twentieth century, a kind of literary Messiah. Such extravagant terms as Rilke's 'philosophy' and Rilke's 'message' are constantly met and are indicative of the care and reserve with which much of the writing on him should be approached. R. Guardini, for instance, makes the ominous statement: 'Was endlich den Inhalt der Elegien angeht,

---

[1] *Tagebücher aus der Frühzeit*, p. 48.
[2] The term 'immediacy of impression' is here used to mean the direct relationship between the reader and what is written, without the intervention of external elements.

so erhebt Rilke eindeutig den Anspruch, damit etwas Tiefes und Neues, eine metaphysische, genauer gesagt, religiöse Botschaft auszusprechen, die sorgfältiger Auslegung bedarf.'[1] E. Heller justly remarks: 'Around Rilke . . . a vast body of literature has grown up that appears to aim not at gaining comprehending readers for the poet, but at making proselytes.'[2]

Thus, if many of the great company of Rilke's commentators have done him the doubtful service of making him an almost legendary figure, they have achieved this by performing the far greater disservice of diverting attention away from his true qualities—qualities which are, in their own right, quite sufficient to ensure his reputation without the addition of fictions. As for the philosophical and metaphysical interpretations of Rilke, their most remarkable feature is not that they endow him with attributes which he does not possess. It is the much more radical contradiction, which has escaped notice by all but a comparative few, implicit in these interpretations: that these attributes of analysis and deductive thought are those which are most destructive of the creative artistic impulse. Rilke has therefore not merely been misinterpreted; he has been gratuitously saddled with just those qualities which, had he possessed them, would probably have prevented him from writing poetry at all.

It is useful to investigate the causes of these errors, not only as a means of clearing the ground, but also in so far as they may indicate certain difficulties and dangers which are particularly relevant to modern literary criticism. It is worth noting at this stage, especially remembering Rilke's own estimate of what criticism should be, that the problems which confront the artist confront his critics as well, in the sense that they must be able to project themselves into his work and not remove it from the context in which it has been brought forth. And this, in turn, involves the ability to modify one's approach in relation to the changed conditions of the time.

The peculiarity of the development of Western society since the industrial revolution, and particularly in the present century, has been not only the extent of the changes in ways of life and thought, with the consequent impact on art; it has been, even more, the pace

[1] *Rainer Maria Rilkes Deutung des Daseins. Eine Interpretation der Duineser Elegien*, p. 14.
[2] *The Disinherited Mind*, p. 123.

at which change has taken place. So, to the inevitable task of modification and reappraisal has been added the compulsion of time. Artist and critic have had to carry out the process of readjustment whilst being deprived of the freedom from temporal duress and of the more benevolent cultural climate which prevailed in the leisured past. In the case of Rilke, it is fair to say that the artist has succeeded in resolving this problem where the majority of his critics have failed. This question will come under consideration later.

Some of the shortcomings of Rilke criticism are necessarily interrelated, initial mistakes often setting up a chain reaction of cause and effect. The first factor which militated against a fair and sober appreciation of Rilke's poetry has already been hinted at, namely, the extraordinary promptitude and unquestioning certainty with which the world of Western letters allotted him his place among the immortals. That is not to say that this place is not deserved. In so far as the judgement of literary circles was a spontaneous reaction to merit, it was understandable and can be defended. But it had the unfortunate result of touching off prematurely the spate of critical writings. Rilke, in fact, never suffered the period of temporary eclipse after his death which is frequently the lot of even the greatest writers and which is usually, in the long run, of immeasurable benefit to their artistic health. Without this twilight period the chances of balanced and unprejudiced assessment are small. The natural, unhurried process of critical gestation, the gradual maturing of ideas before utterance, is telescoped, with consequent distortion. Already some time before his death, writings on Rilke began to appear, and shortly afterwards they became a flood which has continued ever since. There was no pause to consider; and inevitably, such has been the injudicious critical haste, these early writings, many of them by noted and respected authors, had their effect on those which followed, in that opinions and judgements, which in more leisurely procedure would have been subjected to investigation, remained unquestioned and were accepted as genuine currency.

Closely associated with this lack of perspective are the numerous memoirs written by people who knew Rilke personally. The circle of Rilke's friends was large, as reference to his letters will show, and as the greater part of them came from the nobility or near-nobility of Europe or were leading literary figures—in other words, they belonged to the cultural élite—a series of personal tributes and reminiscences was only to be expected. It is evident from the copious correspondence between his friends and himself, from his mode of life, which depended almost entirely on the good offices and patronage of other people, and from his unfailing ability to secure concessions and benefactions wherever he went, that Rilke exerted a remarkable—almost, one might say, hypnotic—influence on those who knew him. Personal contact always carries with it the danger of partiality; in the case of Rilke, with his exceptional powers of captivating and endearing himself to those around him, such partiality was certain.

Had these writers confined themselves to factual record and biographical detail, there would be little cause for complaint; but, almost without exception, they have been unable to resist the temptation to enter the lists of literary criticism and to comment on Rilke's function and his 'mission'. As a result, the undoubted validity of objectively recorded events and the considerable prestige attaching to personal acquaintance with the poet have lent a spurious authority to their critical opinions and judgements. These writings, more than any other single factor, have been responsible for the creation of the Rilke legend and have been the progenitors of the line of hagiographical evaluations. It is significant that not even those among Rilke's friends whom one would think most capable of a dispassionate estimate have been entirely free from fault. Those who come most readily to mind are Lou Andreas-Salomé,[1] Katharina Kippenberg,[2] and the Princess Marie von Thurn und Taxis.[3] All three knew the poet over a long period of years, and the length of association might reasonably have been expected to dispel any illusions created by the first flush of emotion. Lou Andreas-Salomé, in particular, understood Rilke better than anyone and was, moreover, a disciplined thinker. Katharina Kippenberg's views might also have been expected to be tempered by the impersonal commercial logic and business acumen of the great publishing house with which she and her husband were associated. And the Princess von Thurn und Taxis was a person whose wide range of cultural interests and talents and liberal approach would tend towards moderate and balanced judgement. Yet none of the three works mentioned is completely free from hagiographical taint or emotional distortion, although the last named is

[1] *Rainer Maria Rilke.*          [2] *R. M. Rilke, ein Beitrag.*
[3] *Erinnerungen an R. M. Rilke.*

on the whole a sober appraisal. We may agree with E. M. Butler's conclusion:

> The correspondence, the monographs and the biographies of Rilke's contemporaries must all be scrutinised with the care and scepticism with which medieval scholars interpret the lives of saints, or with which members of the distinguished Society for Psychical Research investigate the claims of mediums.[1]

Mention must also be made of the part played by Rilke's family. Some tolerance may perhaps be allowed on the grounds that they had a vested interest in Rilke's reputation; it is at least intelligible that they should have taken certain measures which they conceived necessary to preserve the poet—and themselves—from reproach or stigma. Certainly the biographical study by Carl Sieber,[2] Rilke's son-in-law, must be read against the background of family *esprit de corps*. But in matters of public concern there is a limit beyond which even the most legitimate private interests cannot creditably operate. The most serious indictment against Rilke's family arises from the degree to which they have utilized the absolute control they have possessed over the publication of almost all the writings which did not appear during the poet's lifetime. It is difficult to regard the slow, piecemeal release of letters and notebooks over a period of three decades as defensible. Even more unsatisfactory is the extensive censorship to which those documents which have appeared have been subjected; the *Gesammelte Briefe*, the principal collection of letters, is punctuated by frequent excisions. Since we have Rilke's poetry, this withholding of other documentary evidence may seem, in the context of seeking a valid critical approach to Rilke's art, of lesser importance against the more positive confusion resulting from exegetical malpractices. Nevertheless, although the biographer may be the chief sufferer, such a policy of suppression has had an inevitable, if indirect, effect on critical thought, in that it has helped to maintain the Rilke legend and has deliberately created a background of false values.

More harmful, perhaps, and more numerous than the hagiographies are the attempts, already referred to, to interpret Rilke according to philosophical systems of thought. There is the

[1] *R. M. Rilke*, p. 9. This critic, however, pertinently reminds us that 'the mistake would be gross indeed if, in exploding a mere legend, one should overlook a miracle'.

[2] *René Rilke. Die Jugend Rainer Maria Rilkes.*

reasonable probability that, as Rilke recedes more and more into historical distance, the influence of the hagiographers will dwindle proportionately. There is, however, no certainty that the abstractions and intellectual disquisitions on Rilke will cease, and it is appropriate to consider whether there are not certain besetting dangers threatening modern literary criticism as a whole, and in particular the criticism of poetry.

It has been suggested earlier that the swiftness with which the far-reaching changes in the pattern of modern life have occurred has placed artist and critic, in their constant need to adjust themselves to altered conditions and values, under a compulsion of time without precedent; art, if it is to live, must keep up with the times. It was further suggested that the greater number of Rilke critics have not succeeded in solving this problem of adaptation.[1] Side by side with this speed of change has come the great growth in productivity, and in so far as this has affected the field of writing, with the enormous increase of printed matter, this growth has subjected the literary critic to a second compulsion: that of much greater competition. The quest for originality becomes more difficult and strained, and normal receptivity and the open mind come under stress.

In addition, the problem of the nature of modern conditions cannot be ignored or underestimated. It is an age of science, of the machine, of technical progress; an age in which material values have gained the ascendancy. It is therefore not surprising that a series of thought-disciplines have emerged, the aim of which is to reduce everything to terms of factual and intellectually assimilable explanations. This has resulted in the tendency, so noticeable in the works on Rilke, to approach a subject with preconceived notions.[2]

Thus, a great body of Rilke's expositors, unable or unwilling to make the necessary self-adjustment to fit changed conditions and to fit the poet working in those conditions, have done the easier opposite of adjusting the poet to fit themselves, and this is probably the main cause of the stream of philosophical and metaphysical interpretations. Rilke has been made the vaulting-horse to display the particular brand of intellectual acrobatics in which the critic is proficient. No amount of academic ability, of close and careful reasoning, and of intellectual profundity on the part of a critic will

[1] p. 4.
[2] Cf. F. W. van Heerikhuizen, *Rainer Maria Rilke, His Life and Work*, p. ix.

compensate for what is fundamentally a wrong starting-point. On all sides Rilke's commentators have committed the unpardonable error of applying the principles of discursive thought to his art. This problem will be discussed more fully later, but it must be realized at the outset that such an un-rational field as lyric poetry demands its own special approach, an approach which acknowledges the empirical and subjective nature of poetic appreciation. Not only are we still without a genuine artistic and aesthetic study of Rilke on any scale, but we are confronted with the contradiction that whereas, of all literary forms, lyric poetry is least susceptible of treatment by any systematized or discursive method, this method has repeatedly been applied to Rilke's poetry. As E. M. Wilkinson pertinently reminds us, 'There is some element which marks off experiences produced by art from those produced by, let us say, dialectic reasoning, moral or political exhortation, or a quarrel with a friend.'[1] It is the task of the critic to recognize and isolate this element.

We may profitably recall, for our guidance, Goethe's words to Eckermann, on 6 May 1827:

> Die Deutschen sind übrigens wunderliche Leute! Sie machen sich durch ihre tiefen Gedanken und Ideen, die sie überall machen und überall einlegen, das Leben schwerer als billig. Ei, so habt doch endlich einmal die Courage, euch den Eindrücken hinzugeben, euch ergötzen zu lassen, euch rühren zu lassen, euch erheben zu lassen, ja euch belehren und zu etwas Großem entflammen und ermutigen zu lassen; aber denkt nur nicht immer, es wäre alles eitel, wenn es nicht irgend abstrakter Gedanke und Idee wäre![2]

And again on July 5 of the same year:

> Wenn durch die Phantasie nicht Dinge entständen, die für den Verstand ewig problematisch bleiben, so wäre überhaupt zu der Phantasie nicht viel. Dies ist es, wodurch sich die Poesie von der Prosa unterscheidet, bei welcher der Verstand immer zu Hause ist und sein mag und soll.[3]

A great part of Rilke criticism, therefore, belongs to one of the two extremes of hagiography and rationalism. It also appears that the modern age presents special difficulties for the critic of poetry. Commenting on the problem of art and life, which is, after all,

[1] *Johann Elias Schlegel*, p. 119.
[2] *Goethes Gespräche* (F. W. von Biedermann, Leipzig, 1910), Bd. III, p. 394.
[3] Ibid., p. 408.

a root problem for the literary critic, S. K. Langer defines these difficulties in even broader terms:

The problem of 'Art and Life', which is only of secondary importance for the other arts, becomes a central issue in literary criticism. It troubled Plato, and it troubles Thomas Mann; and at the hands of less profound theorists, it promises well to throw the whole philosophy of art into a welter of morals and politics, religion and modern psychiatry.[1]

This last thought leads to a consideration of one of the more recent works on Rilke. It is by E. Simenauer, and he significantly entitles his book *Rainer Maria Rilke: Legende und Mythos*. It is worth examining this work in some detail; not only because it is a completely new approach to Rilke; and not primarily because of its main thesis, which is not directly relevant in the artistic and aesthetic context, though its indirect implications will be discussed; but chiefly because it contains, beyond its central purpose, much that is of interest and value at any level of criticism. The author is a doctor, and, with the expert knowledge of his profession, he subjects Rilke to a searching and lengthy psychological analysis. There are certain general qualifications which must be applied to this modern branch of medicine. It is by its nature an experimental science; it makes its own premises, largely suggests its own data, and draws its own, often seemingly arbitrary, conclusions; it is concerned predominantly with the subconscious and unconscious mind. To the extent of all this it has to be taken on trust, though it is frequently convincing and its therapeutic application is becoming increasingly accepted. It must further be conceded that Dr. Simenauer argues his case skilfully and persuasively.

This said, the first question which arises is whether the result justifies a study of this nature and magnitude. Allowing the claim that many important aspects of Rilke's personality may have been overlooked or disregarded in the past; allowing that it is common practice, in examining any literary figure, to employ to a limited extent and in lay fashion some of the principles of psychology; and even allowing that Rilke was patently a psychopathic case, some doubts remain. The crucial question is whether this work is intended as a contribution to medical science or to literary criticism. Quite clearly, as it stands, it belongs more properly to the library of a medical institute. Yet equally clearly this is not the author's sole nor even, perhaps, his chief aim. His choice of subject, his

[1] *Feeling and Form*, pp. 234–5.

monumental feat of documentation, embracing almost all the available critical studies of Rilke, and, above all, his obviously intimate and discriminating knowledge of Rilke's writings, are eloquent of the duality of his interests. There can be no escape from the fact that Rilke's importance will always be as a poet; nor from the contradiction that while, on the one hand, Simenauer has written a work of medical science, he has, on the other hand, by choosing Rilke as his subject, ensured that it will be read primarily by those whose interests are literary. There must always be something equivocal in selecting an artist for a medical case-history.

Inevitably the psychological approach is of only limited value to those whose first interest is Rilke's poetry. The most it can do is to indicate and motivate some of the peculiarities of his life and personality, and perhaps, though not always conclusively, account for the occurrence or recurrence of certain themes and symbols in his writings. It can really tell us nothing about his art. This Simenauer himself admits, in one of the many passages which show his penetrative insight beyond his own specialized field. After pointing out that Rilke's work is not to be elucidated from rational, philosophical, or religious points of view, and that we still possess scarcely the beginnings of an aesthetic-literary appreciation, he continues: 'Die Interpretationen seiner Dichtung, zu sehr beschäftigt mit der Ausdeutung seines Bewußtseinsraums und mit Spekulationen über seine Gedankenwelt, haben die wesentlichen Fragen der Ästhetik unbeantwortet gelassen. Die psychologische Betrachtung kann diese Lücke nicht füllen.'[1] That this must be so is inherent in the function of psychology: for it is prevented, by its very nature, from accepting as its starting-point the fundamental fact that as soon as a product of the creative imagination is completed, that work of art acquires a separate and independent existence of its own.

If the psychological approach is at best of little help in the literary context, there remains the question whether, in the extreme and specialized form of this treatise, it may not militate against artistic appreciation. Here, again, we may take note of a comment by Simenauer. Rilke was himself acquainted with and interested in psychology, and this interest increased in the years of acute crisis which followed the completion of *Die Aufzeichnungen des Malte Laurids Brigge* in 1910. In 1912, when the crisis was at its peak,

[1] Op. cit., p. 661.

Rilke considered submitting himself to psycho-analytical treatment under Dr. Gebsattel, with whom he was in correspondence on the subject. In the event, Rilke decided against this treatment, fearing the consequences for his art. In reference to this decision Simenauer says: 'Es ist letzten Endes ein Kampf zugunsten seines Genius. Im Hinblick auf ihn war sein Entschluß der richtige. Wir und die Nachwelt müssen ihm dafür dankbar sein. Denn seine Vorstellung von der Wirkung der Analyse auf ihn war durchaus nicht "eine ganz falsche und alberne".'[1] In view of this significant admission, we are at least entitled to wonder whether such an exhaustive psychological treatment as this, *post mortem*, is not potentially as destructive of the aesthetic values and artistic appreciation of Rilke's poetry as psycho-analysis, during his lifetime, would have been of its creation. This is, after all, the technique of the hospital dissecting-room applied to the mind. If the poet is reduced to a nexus of neuroses, psychoses, and repressions, one is left with no more than a piece of mechanism, shorn of its mystery and working according to calculable laws. If the magician is explained, the magic is destroyed.

There is, however, much in this work of general value and importance, and this is in no way vitiated by any doubts as to the contribution of its main thesis. Simenauer has a keen critical perception, and there are many shrewd and revealing passages which can be welcomed unexceptionably by the student of Rilke's poetry. Of particular application to the present discussion of the critical approach is the useful service he performs in exploding so many of the misconceptions surrounding Rilke. He devotes some sixty pages at the beginning of his work to supplying the wholesome corrective of a penetrating and comprehensive analysis of Rilke criticism. This clearly reasoned exposure of the confusion and limitations of previous exegetical practices does in itself represent a major advance, and can profitably be used as a section of reference by all concerned with the problem of evolving a valid method of appreciating Rilke's poetry and of achieving truer perspective.

In view of the support it gives to the present discussion, one extract is particularly noteworthy for its illumination of the inadequacy and obscurity of so many of the writings on Rilke. Simenauer reproduces a series of interpretations of the 'Engel' of the *Duineser Elegien*:

[1] Op. cit., p. 194.

Der Engel—ein Pseudonym Gottes (Dehn).

Der Engel—das ist Orpheus (Angelloz und Bäumer).

Der Engel ist der Dämon der dichterischen Berufung (Mason).

'These angels were sexless beings, divine anthitheses to the natural man' (Butler).

Die Engel sind selber irgendwie Götter. In ihnen fühlt man das Olympische; die Gleichgültigkeit des übermenschlich strahlenden Daseins gegen die Not der Erde. Der Engel ist im Raum der Elegien die bestimmende Erscheinung des Numinosen. Er ist der Partner des Weltganzen. . . . Die Engel sind bei Rilke bloße Weltwesen, sind Garanten der Ganzheit einer Welt, welche das Sichtbare zur großen Einheit zusammenfaßt (Guardini).

Der Engel ist eine aus Not geschaffene Idee von unnahbarer Vollkommenheit und unerreichbarem Glück (von Jan).

Der Engel ist also gewissermaßen die Arbeitshypothese, die es erst ermöglicht, die menschliche Wirklichkeit zu erkennen (Bassermann).

Die Engel sind die symbolischen Wesen des Gesamtbereichs alles Seins (Rosteutscher).

Für den Engel gibt es weder das Diesseits noch das Jenseits, sondern das Ganze als Ganzes (E. Kretschmar).

'Der Engel ist die Gestalt der andern Seite des Diesseits. . . . So sind die Engel Gestalten der Unsichtbarkeit des Sichtbaren selbst' (F. J. Brecht).[1]

It is hardly surprising that Simenauer speaks of 'Verwirrung und Hilflosigkeit'. This selection is a representative cross-section of the manner of approach which characterizes a great part of Rilke criticism, and, in demonstrating the critical shortcomings which have been the subject of discussion, it provides powerful confirmation of the need to consider afresh the problems of poetic commentary.

The perplexity which this bewildering array of 'interpretations' must produce in the mind of the reader is obvious and is in no way lessened by the fact that among their originators are some of Rilke's generally most able critics. At worst, the above examples are meaningless; at best, they in no way help artistic appreciation. Such diffuse, contradictory, and elaborately barren explanations are the inevitable result of applying the methods of discursive thought to a literary form which is not amenable to this treatment. Any attempt to compress Rilke's poetry within the mould of any rational or logical system must fail, or at least misses the mark. Simenauer rightly sums up: 'Das Suchen nach philosophischen Hintergründen

[1] Op. cit., pp. 70–71.

kann im besten Fall nur einen Teil seiner Gestalt erfassen, der andere, wichtigere, um den es vor allem gehen sollte, muß so unbeachtet bleiben; das eigentlich Dichterische wird dabei ver-fehlt.'[1]

It is fair to add, as Simenauer also points out, that Rilke himself has been in part responsible for much of the critical confusion which followed. Great as was his creative imagination—and prob-ably, as was earlier implied, because of it[2]—he lacked a disciplined intellect; he was neither a deep nor an original thinker. E. M. Butler remarks that 'Rilke's doctrine about death, his repeated affirmations of its greatness and glory show less inspiration and vision than poets like Plato, Shakespeare, Goethe and Tolstoy....'[3] Thus, at moments when Rilke lapses into oratory and rationalizing, he is obscure and unconvincing and, above all, swings away from lyricism. The fault of so many of his critics has been their failure to recognize his limitations and their consequent unquestioning ac-ceptance of utterances which masquerade as genuine expositions of his life and work and appear on the surface to be the result of con-secutive and trained thought-processes. Rilke's letters contain many passages which purport to explain his art, and these have been invested with the authority of infallibility and have formed the basis of subsequent approaches.

One letter must be singled out for mention, in view of its dis-proportionate and far-reaching effect on Rilke criticism. It is the famous letter to his Polish translator, Witold von Hulewicz, dated 13 November 1925,[4] in which Rilke impetuously undertakes an explanation of the Elegies. Despite the fact that it reveals to the full the insufficiency of Rilke's intellectual pronouncements, the im-portance which has been attached to this letter cannot be over-estimated; it has become the oracle informing the majority of would-be expounders of these poems. If Rilke was himself con-scious of his deficiencies, it is, nevertheless, probable that he was flattered at being consulted on these, his greatest poetic creations. His first mistake was to enter into a discursive examination of the Elegies at all, a mistake implicit in his own words: 'Und bin *ich* es, der den Elegien die richtige Erklärung geben darf? Sie reichen unendlich über mich hinaus.'[5] The passages which follow have been

---

[1] Op. cit., pp. 71–72.       [2] p. 3.
[3] Op. cit., p. 421.      [4] *G.B.*, Bd. V, pp. 369–77.
[5] Ibid., p. 371.

echoed ever since; they have become the familiar pattern of interpretation of the Elegies:

In den 'Elegien' wird, aus den gleichen Gegebenheiten heraus, das
Leben wieder möglich, ja es erfährt hier diejenige endgültige *Bejahung*,
zu der es der junge Malte, obwohl auf dem richtigen schweren Wege
'des longues études', noch nicht führen konnte. *Lebens- und Todes-*
*bejahung erweist sich als Eines in den 'Elegien'.* . . . Der Tod ist die uns
abgekehrte, von uns unbeschienene *Seite des Lebens.* . . . *es gibt weder*
*ein Diesseits noch Jenseits, sondern die große Einheit*, in der die uns
übertreffenden Wesen, die 'Engel' zu Hause sind. . . . Die Vergäng-
lichkeit stürzt überall in ein tiefes Sein. . . . Die Natur, die Dinge
unseres Umgangs und Gebrauchs, sind Vorläufigkeiten und Hinfällig-
keiten; aber sie sind, solang wir hier sind, *unser* Besitz und unsere
Freundschaft, Mitwisser unserer Not und Froheit. . . . *Wir sind die*
*Bienen des Unsichtbaren. Nous buvons éperdument le miel du visible, pour*
*l'accumuler dans la grande ruche d'or de l'Invisible.* Die 'Elegien' zeigen
uns an diesem Werk, am Werke dieser fortwährenden Umsetzungen
des geliebten Sichtbaren und Greifbaren in die unsichtbare Schwingung
und Erregtheit unserer Natur, die neue Schwingungszahlen einführt
in die Schwingungs-Sphären des Universums. . . . Die Erde hat keine
andere Ausflucht, als unsichtbar zu werden: *in* uns, die wir mit einem
Teil unseres Wesens am Unsichtbaren beteiligt sind, Anteilscheine
(mindestens) haben an ihm, und unseren Besitz an Unsichtbarkeit
mehren können während unseres Hierseins. . . . Die *Elegien* stellen
diese Norm des Daseins auf. . . . Der 'Engel' der Elegien hat nichts mit
dem Engel des christlichen Himmels zu tun (eher mit den Engelgestalten
des Islam) . . . Der Engel der *Elegien* ist dasjenige Geschöpf, in dem
die Verwandlung des Sichtbaren in Unsichtbares, die wir leisten, schon
vollzogen erscheint. . . . Der Engel der Elegien ist dasjenige Wesen, das
dafür einsteht, im Unsichtbaren einen höheren Rang der Realität zu
erkennen. . . . *einige Sterne steigern sich unmittelbar und vergehen im*
*unendlichen Bewußtsein der Engel —, andere sind auf langsam und mühsam*
*sie verwandelnde Wesen angewiesen, in deren Schrecken und Entzücken sie*
*ihre nächste unsichtbare Verwirklichung erreichen. Wir sind*, noch einmal
sei's betont, *im Sinne der Elegien, sind wir diese Verwandler der Erde,*
*unser ganzes Dasein, die Flüge und Stürze unserer Liebe, alles befähigt*
*uns zu dieser Aufgabe* (neben der keine andere, wesentlich, besteht). . . .[1]

The limitations of this exposition are obvious, despite the illusory
weight produced by a pretentious style and by the repeated italics.
And even had Rilke been a philosopher as well as a poet, he would
have done no service to himself by attempting to superimpose

[1] *G.B.*, Bd. V, pp. 371–7.

a 'logical' explanation on to what are essentially great imaginative writings. It is with unconscious irony that Rilke closes with
the words: 'Möchten Sie, lieber Freund, hier einigen Rat und
Aufschluß erkennen und, im übrigen, sich selber weiterhelfen,
Denn: Ich weiß nicht, ob ich je mehr sagen könnte.'[1] This 'Rat
und Aufschluß' is, in fact, a disastrous legacy bequeathed to his
interpreters. For this letter, containing the substance of what was
to follow, set the standard for subsequent critical essays of every
trend, and even provided the catch-phrases.

In epitomizing the failure of a large section of Rilke criticism,
this letter also underlines the caution with which one must approach any statement by Rilke relating to his own writings. (He
was, on the other hand, frequently perceptive in appraising the
works of others.) There can be no progress in an examination of
Rilke without the realization of his intellectual circumscription,
the more so in view of the easy credence that has been given to the
numerous sections of his correspondence which claim to offer enlightenment on his art. He was, predominantly, a creature of
impulse and intuition, and these dictated and controlled in a large
measure his activity. His approach was inductive, not deductive,
his reasoning *a posteriori*. It was only *after the event* that he set
about supplying a 'logical' explanation. This was, as it were, grafted
on, and inevitably, after the principle of Procrustes, the argumenta-
tion was mutilated in being made to fit—a process which, as
Heller points out, has its origin in self-deception, but which is no
less dangerously persuasive for not being deliberately fraudulent.[2]
But if Rilke was neither a trained nor a consecutive thinker, he was,
like most intuitive personalities, very complex, and clearly many
have been deceived into mistaking complexity for intellectual accomplishment. This is the negative side of Rilke's thought. There
is, however, the positive side: for there can be little doubt that
this equivocation, this capacity to manipulate words and ideas, this
technique of 'Umschlag', what, in short, E. C. Mason[3] calls his
'Nuancierung', is one of the secrets of Rilke's greatness as a lyric
poet.

It is not, of course, suggested that there is no thought-content in
lyric poetry.[4] But the function of the intellect in Rilke's poetry is

[1] Ibid., p. 377.                    [2] Op. cit., p. 138.
[3] *Lebenshaltung und Symbolik bei R. M. Rilke.*
[4] Cf. E. Heller, op. cit., pp. 119–26.

not to initiate, but rather one of selection and arrangement. Commenting on the Elegies, van Heerikhuizen makes a useful contribution to this discussion when he stresses that 'Between the whole-hearted reader and the Duino Elegies there is soon established . . . a clear and human confidence . . .' and: 'Their "difficultness" is not an intellectual matter, though interpretations of them have often led to intellectual inhibitions . . .'[1] He goes on to define the function of the intellect in these poems.[2]

Having surveyed the unacceptable features of much previous Rilke criticism, and having set out the principal external reasons why such criticism misses the mark, it is opportune to direct attention to a question of more intimate concern. This is the problem of language, which, however much the fact may be overlooked, is an intrinsic element in all literary estimation. It is a large subject on its own, and it is not proposed to do more than touch briefly on those aspects of it which are germane to the present examination. But some consideration of it is indispensable if a valid critical method is to be attained. In helping the present study forward, moreover, it will also uncover the fundamental cause of past errors.

It is not superfluous to remind ourselves of the truism that the artist is confronted with the limiting discipline of his medium. E. M. Wilkinson points out: 'Medium, its treatment, its limitations, its fusion with the artist's vision, is one of the chief factors in artistic creation.'[3] Discussing Mallarmé, Sir Maurice Bowra puts this truth into the literary context:

> He believed that in poetry he might produce an effect so absolutely aesthetic that the understanding would almost be in abeyance. The sounds and associations would do all the work; the mere meaning of the words would not matter. But words are concerned with ideas, and poetry is made of words. It can never have the unlimited breadth of pure vision.[4]

The recognition of the particular restrictions imposed by language as an art medium is of radical importance, especially in contrast with music, with the analogy of which Mallarmé was so preoccupied. In music a purely aesthetic effect is possible to a degree that can never be in poetry. Words, with their ideas, automatically become the property of the intelligence, or, as Bowra succinctly

[1] Op. cit., p. 307.     [2] Ibid., p. 308.
[3] Op. cit., p. 1.       [4] The Heritage of Symbolism, p. 14.

expresses it, 'Words are limited by their meanings.'[1] It can therefore be seen that the peculiar nature of language, as the medium of
poetry, presents a challenge both to artist and critic. There must be
a compromise between the operation of the creative imagination
and the realm of ideas, through which that imagination must be
filtered and with which it must make shift if it is to come to utterance, if it is to exist at all in perceptible form.[2]

The difficulty for the critic of poetry, which is our particular
concern here, arises out of the many purposes which language ful-
fils as an instrument of communication, with the related problem of
distance between content and medium. This last does not trouble
the critic of music, in which content and medium are in effect one
and the same; neither does it trouble the critic of the representational arts, in which the distance between content and medium is
always sufficiently great for the danger of confusion to be eliminated. But in language we have a medium which covers a wide range
of functions, employing for each similar words and phrases, and
thereby encouraging the easy and erroneous assumption that the
same methods and standards of evaluation may be applied to all.
The primary differentiation of language into two kinds is made by
C. K. Ogden and I. A. Richards: 'the division between the *symbolic*
use of words and the *emotive* use. The symbolic use of words is
*statement*; the recording, the support, the organization and the
communication of references. The emotive use of words is a more
simple matter, it is the use of words to express or excite feelings
and attitudes.'[3] This unexceptionable definition, however, has to
be qualified, as its authors acknowledge, by the recognition that it
is not always possible in practice to draw a hard and fast line
between these two uses of language. What at first sight may
appear to be statement is frequently found to be emotive in its

[1] Ibid.
[2] E. Heller, commenting on Karl Kraus, adds an interesting gloss to this
discussion: '. . . For Karl Kraus all thoughts are in the world even before they
are thought. They are dispersed among the elements of language. The artist
gathers them together and welds them into his thought. He once said: "Language
is the divining-rod which discovers wells of thought." Thus language, for him,
is a means not so much of communicating what he knows, but of finding what
he does not yet know. Words are living organisms, not labels stuck to objects.
They are at home in a cosmos of the spirit, not in a chance assembly of "atoms of
perception". Each of them has a range of its own, and once struck up, opens up
numberless trains of thought. The greater the number of associations into which
the word enters, the greater its value in a piece of writing.' (Op. cit., p. 189.)
[3] *The Meaning of Meaning*, p. 149. See also pp. 153–9 and 235–6.

effect. Even more, a given grouping of words could be symbolic in one context and emotive in another. S. K. Langer clinches the issue when she says:

Now I maintain that the difference [sc. between poetry and literal discourse] is radical, that poetry is not genuine discourse at all, but is the creating of an illusory 'experience', or a piece of virtual history, by means of discursive language; and that 'poetic language' is language that is particularly useful for this purpose. What words will seem poetic depends on the central idea of the poem in question.[1]

The last sentence is all-important, and will be found to be particularly relevant when Rilke's own handling of language is examined.

Within the broad differentiation made by C. K. Ogden and I. A. Richards, language has many purposes, and according to these different functions, so there is a variation in the relationship between content and medium. The significance of this variation in the task of evolving a valid basis of poetic evaluation is that upon it depends the degree to which it is possible or justifiable to apply objective or discursive methods of interpretation. In its simplest form, language is the means of practical, everyday speech and communication. Here, choice of words and form do not matter greatly so long as the general utilitarian purpose is achieved. In a scientific, philosophical, or logical system, words and form assume a greater importance, but it is still the idea which preponderates, and considerable freedom and flexibility of expression are possible. A scientific or philosophical treatise can be translated without loss. Within the field of art itself, a gradation in this balance between content and medium can be observed. In the novel, the drama, the epic poem, choice of words and form becomes progressively more important, though these are still to a varying extent amenable to manipulation and modification in relation to the 'idea'—in the form of plot, characterization, narrative.

It is in the lyric poem that this gradual process of convergence of medium and content reaches its literary ultimate; here, language attains its quintessential quality. It is the nearest approach literature can make to music, though it is still impossible to circumvent

---

[1] Op. cit., p. 252. This passage is reproduced for its general validity and its applicability to our argument. We may, however, regret such unfortunate terms as 'illusory' and 'virtual'. The experience created, so far from being 'illusory', is very real.

what C. M. Bowra calls the 'obstinate element'[1] of the medium. It
is easy to see how Mallarmé, with his predilection for music and
his unrealizable hope of finding 'la parole sous la figure du silence',
must sink inevitably into creative impotence. It is fortunate for
Rilke's art that temperament and circumstance led him to the other
extreme of the representational arts, and that his most crucial
formative years were spent in contact with Rodin. The literary
medium can never take the final step into the domain of the purely
aesthetic, for in the last resort there can be no escape from the fact
that words have meanings. S. Alexander points out that 'the mere
sound of words is vital to the art. Yet words have meaning and it is
never possible to dissociate the meanings of words from the words
themselves.'[2] S. K. Langer adequately sums up the problem which
faces the critic of poetry:

> Whole libraries of books have been written on the principles of literary
> art, because the intellectual approach which is natural to scholars makes
> those principles at once very intriguing and very confounding. The
> significance of any piece of literature must lie, supposedly, in what
> the author says; yet every critic who is worth his salt knows that *the
> way of saying things* is somehow all-important. This is especially obvious
> in poetry. How, then, is the reader to divide his interest between the
> value of the assertion and the special way it is made? Isn't the wording
> everything? And yet, must not the wording itself be judged by its
> adequacy to state the author's ideas?[3]

The radical importance of realizing the implications of the
problem of language can therefore be clearly seen in the context of
Rilke criticism. It was suggested earlier that the present age, with
its scientific climate and its tendency towards factual and objective
assessment, militated against literary criticism and was in part
responsible for the failure of so many writings on Rilke.[4] Their
shortcomings can now be seen as the failure to perceive the various
levels of language usage. We may summarize by saying that language is not one medium, but several, each, because of similarity
of vocabulary and construction, bearing a superficial resemblance
to the others.

.    .    .    .    .

It is now possible to turn to a consideration of the nature of
Rilke's art, of how he has achieved his effect, and of what is new in

[1] Op. cit., p. 14.    [2] *Beauty and other Forms of Value*, pp. 69–70.
[3] Op. cit., p. 208.    [4] See pp. 7–9.

his poetry. Recognizing the difficulty of defining lyric poetry and the dangers of a rational or systematized approach, is it nevertheless possible to arrive at a critical method which has general validity and acceptance and yet does no violence to the personal and subjective nature of poetic appreciation?

Lyric poetry may be described as the poetry of mood and emotion. In one sense human emotions are capable of infinite variety and shades and are liable to swift change; but in another sense, just as human nature does not change in its essence, they have common and unchanging elements, in the same way as variations on a musical theme have a common thread running through them. It is thus that the recurrent themes of love, joy, hope, fear, compassion, arising out of the eternal facts of life and death and the hazards of existence, are the fabric of lyric poetry, inexhaustible though the ways of expressing and exciting them may be. In this respect the lyrical field is a restricted one, and as the scope for novelty is thereby diminished, the task of the poet is made more exacting. It is therefore pertinent to ask what there is new in Rilke, what, in fact, is the *raison d'être* of any lyric poet since the first. In spite of the many affinities which can be detected between lyric poets throughout literary history, it cannot be pretended that Rilke's poetry is the same as, for example, that of Goethe. Although great poetry transcends time, what is produced in one generation cannot be repeated or imitated in the next. Yet clearly Rilke has succeeded in creating something new.

The answer lies simply in language. If the fundamentals do not change, circumstances and conditions do. Society, its way of life, its customs, its mode of expression, are in a constant state of transition, and the artist must constantly adapt himself to these changing factors. Thus, the function of the lyric poet is to re-express the emotional fundamentals in the light of altered conditions; to reassert those things which are eternal and unchanging in language applicable to the age in which he lives. 'It is language itself', says E. M. Wilkinson, 'which is important in poetry, its sonorous sounds, its suggestiveness, its power of calling up associations.'[1] The lyric poet must deploy fresh symbols, images, rhythms, and combinations of sound. He must, by mastery of language, by word-magic, by the power of evocation, by the manipulation of his medium, fashion the phrase which will strike home. By these means

[1] Op. cit., p. 117.

he must, in fact, *create the illusion that he is creating something new in content as well*. All this is aptly summed up by S. K. Langer:

The initial questions, then, are not: 'What is the poet trying to say, and what does he intend to make us feel about it?' But: 'What has the poet made, and how did he make it?' He has made an illusion, as complete and immediate as the illusion of space created by a few strokes on paper, the time dimension in a melody, the play of powers set up by a dancer's first gesture. He has made an illusion by means of words— words having sound and sense, pronunciations and spellings. . . . But what he creates is not an arrangement of words, for words are only his materials, *out of which* he makes his poetic elements. The elements are what he deploys and balances, spreads out or intensifies or builds up, to make a poem.[1]

Lyric poetry, then, is emotive and evocative. It is compelling or stimulating, but it does not instruct or inform. The content, as compared with that of other literary forms, is slight, the force and the appeal deriving from the wording. It is for this reason, as S. K. Langer also points out, that lyric poetry exploits to the full linguistic, verbal devices and resources, with the emphasis on the emotional quality of language; and while any of these devices may be found in other literary forms, their frequency and importance in lyric poetry are what gives it its special character.[2]

The fruitless examination of Rilke for logical, philosophical, metaphysical, or religious concepts will therefore be renounced. His problem was that of language in the twentieth century, and the manner in which he has achieved a solution is a particularly interesting one. In one sense he was an anachronism, if the postulate is accepted that he wrote for an age which is predominantly scientific and factual in its approach and aspirations, and in which the word is no longer valued as a thing of beauty in its own right. It is an age in which everything is rationalized, when the mechanics of living have become very much more complicated, and when the simple emotions, the indispensable ingredients of the lyric poet's art, have become overlaid with an artificial veneer of false values and over-civilized standards, making it correspondingly difficult to penetrate to realities and command attention and sympathy. It is, moreover, an age of greatly increased means of communication, all of which have had a tremendous impact on language, and each of which has

[1] Op. cit., p. 211.     [2] Ibid., pp. 258–9.

evolved its own specialized verbal technique. Among these may be instanced the telephone, radio, and the great spread of the popular press. 'Ich fühle zu deutlich', writes Rilke, 'die Scheinverwandt-schaft zwischen Literatur und Journalismus, von denen das eine eine Kunst ist und also die Ewigkeit meint und das andere ein Gewerbe mitten in der Zeit. . . .'[1] Many of these developments were established fact at the time when Rilke was writing his greatest poetry, and, however much he might profess aloofness from the world about him and deplore the brash and stereotyped philistin-ism of modern life, he could hardly remain untouched by them. Their implications could not fail to be noticed, neither could they be left out of account, by a poet highly sensitive to the transition which was taking place in language, and who himself had an over-whelming inner compulsion to communicate.

For all these reasons the challenge was perhaps greater than any which lyric poets of the past had had to face. If Rilke was to succeed, he must assimilate and adjust himself to both the mood of his time and contemporary linguistic tendencies. That he has suc-ceeded is evident, and in this sense he is not an anachronism. The trend of the twentieth century has been towards terseness of ex-pression and economy of vocabulary—characteristics which can be clearly seen in Rilke's later poetry and which become progressively more noticeable in the course of his long association with France. The extent to which he comes to terms with his age is powerfully and conclusively demonstrated in the *Duineser Elegien*, the style of which is predominantly ejaculatory, nervous, spasmodic, elliptical. He does, in fact, employ a declamatory, argumentative technique, which is probably yet another reason why critics have applied the methods of logical and discursive thought in evaluating his work. This is what was meant when it was suggested earlier that Rilke has succeeded in resolving the problems posed by the twentieth century for the creative artist, whereas a great part of his com-mentators have failed in the task of adapting themselves.[2]

One of the few critics to perceive the crucial importance of this question of language is H. E. Holthusen, in his essay *Der späte Rilke*, and it is this critic who indicates the lines along which this examination will proceed. He comments significantly:

Man entdeckt einen sprachlichen Fortschritt, der über alles, was bis dahin in der deutschen Lyrik möglich war, George, Dehmel, auch

[1] *G.B.*, Bd. I, p. 336.          [2] p. 4.

Hofmannsthal, auch die bedeutenden Expressionisten nicht ausgenommen, entscheidend hinausgeht. Man steht vor sprachlichen Errungenschaften, die von der literarischen Kritik immer noch nicht befriedigend ergründet und interpretiert worden sind, einer Erweiterung des Empfindungs- und Ausdrucksvermögens ohnegleichen. Die deutsche Sprache erscheint als in einem vor Rilke undenkbaren Grade erweicht, verinnerlicht, verflüssigt und gleichzeitig doch auch präzisiert, gehärtet, intellektualisiert, versachlicht. Was Marcel Proust für die französische Prosa geleistet hat, das tut Rilke für die deutsche Lyrik. . . .[1]

He later stresses the subjectivity of Rilke's thinking and points out that all truth has a relative and an absolute aspect. When a poem succeeds, it acquires a value which transcends all considerations of conceptual thinking, the value of 'concrete beauty'.[2]

This study will have three aspects. First, it is founded on the premiss that the key to an examination of Rilke is language. Words are the raw material of his art, and it is only by going right back to these materials that a valid assessment of the final product can be made. Secondly, the development of his use of language, his verbal technique and resources, will be traced through the successive stages. Thirdly, the investigation will be based on the conviction that France, with its cultural climate, its linguistic discipline, and the various artistic influences which Rilke experienced there, was the most decisive factor in the development of his poetic style.

[1] Op. cit., pp. 12–13.          [2] Ibid., pp. 63–64.

# II

## RUSSIA OR FRANCE?

Nationale Kunst! Und jede aufrichtige Kunst ist national. Die Wurzeln ihres Wesens wärmen sich in dem heimatlichen Grund und empfangen ihren Mut von ihm. Aber schon der Stamm steigt einsam auf, und wo die Krone sich entbreitet, da ist niemandes Reich. Und es kann sein, daß die dumpfe Wurzel nicht weiß, wenn die Zweige in Blüten stehn.[1]

So wrote Rilke in the *Florenzer Tagebuch*. Had these words been written at the end of his life, they would have been accepted as a perspicacious and accurate appraisal informed by experience. Written, however, in 1898, when Rilke could have no foreknow-ledge of his future career, of the number and diversity of his travels, or of the unusual nature of his artistic development, they have an arresting prophetic ring, the force of which is in no way diminished by the fact that the context in which they appear is a general and not a personal one. They do, in fact, epitomize his own growth; for if ever the shift and spread of growth away from the roots, the flowering and fruition far away from the point of origin, were illustrated in any poet, that poet was Rilke. That he could never be severed from his roots is indisputable—his remarkable and constantly increasing sensitivity to his own language is indica-tion enough of the infrangibility of his attachment. But it is para-doxical that, not merely did his control over the German language thrive on foreign soil and under alien cultural influences, but that absence from Germany of a more or less permanent nature even appears to have been an indispensable element in its development. His acute awareness and supreme mastery of German as a poetic instrument seem to have been in inverse proportion to his proximity to the country of its use. Even allowing for their obvious external distractions, the war years were the least productive period in Rilke's life—in spite of the fact that the Fourth Elegy was written in 1915. And when, at the beginning of 1920, so soon after his long and enforced confinement in Germany, he writes: 'In Deutschland

[1] *Tagebücher aus der Frühzeit*, p. 48.

wird sich unsereiner erst recht in der Fremde fühlen —',[1] it is reasonable to see as much the recognition that his artistic destiny must be fulfilled elsewhere as reaction against the war and disillusionment with post-war conditions in Germany.

There is inevitable difficulty and frustration for anyone seeking in Rilke a systematic plan of existence or a continuous thread of development, unless it be his unswerving devotion to the cause of his art. With his restlessness and constant travels, his multifarious experiences, his innumerable friends and acquaintances, and above all his cosmopolitan and eclectic tastes, he presents obvious complexities in the task both of disengaging those factors in his life which have a vital bearing on his art and of giving the various elements their true weight. It is, however, impossible, especially in view of the later examination of the contrasting role played by France, not to make a reference to Russia.[2] It is particularly important, considering his uninhibited enthusiasm for what he himself avowed to be his spiritual home and the significance attached to the Russian experience by some of Rilke's commentators, to emphasize the facts and to put this episode in his life in its proper perspective. That it was a notable experience is undeniable. But exactly what was the quality of the experience, and how far it had any long-term relevance to his art, is another question.

By the end of August 1900, Rilke had had his last physical contact with Russia, and it is not inappropriate to note that he had not yet reached the age of 25. In all he spent less than six months in Russia, and E. M. Butler comments, perhaps a little harshly, that he 'never seriously attempted to return, a fact which arouses some scepticism about the reality of his feelings'.[3] The first, and less eventful, visit lasted seven weeks, from the end of April until June 1899, and was divided between Moscow and St. Petersburg. The most notable occurrence was a meeting with Tolstoy. But Rilke was not as well prepared as he was on the second occasion, and in the year between the two trips he worked feverishly at a concentrated study of everything Russian, acquiring a certain mastery of the language and even attempting original Russian verse. The second visit lasted from 11 May to 23 August 1900

---

[1] *G.B.*, Bd. IV, p. 286.
[2] For a detailed account of Rilke's Russian journeys see E. M. Butler, op. cit., pp. 49–86.
[3] Op. cit., p. 49.

and was much more comprehensive. The crowded and hectic itinerary[1] is indicative of the mood and temper of Rilke's Russian experience. Moreover, the nature of his activities in the great Russian cities is revealing. In St. Petersburg he zealously sought the company of artists, writers, professors, journalists, and visited galleries, museums, libraries, theatres. However great his eagerness and interest—and they were great—there is something factitiously stylized and regimented about his programme.

He certainly embarked on this meteoric adventure with immense enthusiasm and, no doubt, in all sincerity as he understood it. But it was the enthusiasm of youthful romanticism, based on nebulous longings and preformed ideas as to where his artistic destiny lay, and these two journeys savour very much of a strenuous determination to validate his preconceptions. The time spent in Russia may be briefly described as a breathless and forced attempt to see the right places, meet the right people, and do the right things—Butler aptly calls him 'a summer tourist in a rosy dream'.[2] His guide and mentor on both journeys was Lou Andreas-Salomé, a dominating personality, who was herself of Russian birth and who had exerted a powerful stimulus on Rilke's growing interest in Russia and Tolstoy for some time before the first visit was undertaken. Rilke was, therefore, very much the modern traveller abroad, out to assimilate 'culture' by numbers, without departing too long from the beaten track and without too much sacrifice of comfort, and his efforts to capture the spirit of Russian peasant life were artificial to the point of being disingenuous. (Butler gives an amusing and illuminating account of his stay with the peasant-poet Drojin,[3] which shows how remote Rilke was from a genuine immersion in the simple life.)

When one passes to the more specific question of Rilke's inheritance from Russian literature, the results are hardly more impressive. He appears to have read Russian authors with more energy than discretion, and even his two eagerly anticipated meetings with Tolstoy, with whom he was so much preoccupied at the time, bequeathed nothing to him for the road ahead. Of all the Russian writers, the only one who seems to have remained with Rilke in a measure sufficient to be noticed in his work is Dostoevsky, of whom echoes can certainly be found in *Die*

[1] E. M. Butler, op. cit., p. 51.      [2] Ibid., p. 61.
[3] Ibid., pp. 51–54.

*Aufzeichnungen des Malte Laurids Brigge.* In fact, Rilke's approach
to Russian literature, like his approach to the country, was too
much like an abortive attack on an educational syllabus—albeit a
congenial one—and was too much the product of the will to succeed at all costs for any real receptivity to be possible. E. M. Butler
comments that 'Russia did not affect Rilke's art to nearly so great
an extent as one would have expected from the profound impression it made on him',[1] and clearly the explanation of this apparent
contradiction is that the Russian experience was much more
emotional than artistic in its character. A reason why Russia could
not make a profound and lasting contribution to Rilke's artistic
development will be suggested later. For the moment, we may
draw attention to Butler's thorough and useful survey of Rilke's
Russian reading,[2] which reveals the perfunctory nature of his
approach and the limited extent to which any true assimilation
took place.

In terms of Rilke's own production Russia plays a comparatively small part. The first section of *Das Stunden-Buch, Das Buch
vom mönchischen Leben,* and the *Geschichten vom lieben Gott* were
written in the latter part of 1899. They bear obvious traces of the
inspiration of Russia, though the fact that they were written before
the much more thorough second journey is in itself significant,
since it suggests that such influence as did operate was that of the
Russia of Rilke's imagination rather than the result of such brief
cultural association as there was. The list of works with direct
affinities with Russia is completed, if one accepts the aforemen-
tioned traces of Dostoevsky in *Malte Laurids Brigge,* with the
second section of *Das Stunden-Buch, Das Buch von der Pilgerschaft.*
This last, though written in September 1901, in Westerwede, and
though, as its title implies, bearing indications of Rilke's onward
progress, still has its inspiration rooted in Russia.

These early poems of *Das Stunden-Buch* are of a kind Rilke was
never to write again. They are heavily charged emotionally, highly
subjective, personalized, unashamedly sentimental in a Romantic-
religious way. They owe their essence to the poet's own youth and
immaturity, which found brief but eruptive expression under the
largely self-induced excitement of the Russian experience. They
are the uninhibited outpourings of one who has discovered his
strength but has not yet learnt how to discipline it:

[1] Op. cit., p. 58.          [2] Ibid., pp. 64–66.

Ich komme aus meinen Schwingen heim,
mit denen ich mich verlor.
Ich war Gesang, und Gott, der Reim,
rauscht noch in meinem Ohr.[1]

But that the strength is there is unquestionable, and it would therefore be wrong to reject these early writings as unimportant or as having no literary merit. They are not without beauty, and, above all, the reader who looks beyond their declamatory exhibitionism will find an earnest of what is to come. Here, already, in embryo, are the rich imagination, the power of evocation, the word-mastery. If at this stage Rilke has one besetting failing as an artist, it is too great a facility, a tendency to virtuosity, the inability to direct, control, modulate the overpowering urge to express himself and his wealth of talent in a way that was to become possible under the rigorous schooling of France.

*Das Buch vom mönchischen Leben* and *Das Buch von der Pilger-schaft* are, then, the burgeoning of Rilke's art, of which the flowering and the fruit were to come later. C. M. Bowra accurately estimates these early writings when he states that 'Rilke's early poetry belongs to the last wave of Romanticism'. He notes, with examples, Rilke's anti-intellectualism and 'the denial of reason and the emphasis on "Sehnsucht" '—in which he sees 'the old German spirit, the desire for something beyond the frontiers of being'. He concludes: 'This poetry has virtues of its kind. It is melodious in an obvious way, touching, sensitive, true perhaps to the frustrated longings of youth, but too remote from life, too dream-laden and too derivative. It tells of Rilke's longings but not really of himself. He has not found out what he can do or where his true self lies.'[2]

Rilke's Russian experience was, therefore, an adolescent dream, though to dismiss it as such without further comment would be less than just. Everyone has adolescent dreams, and adolescent dreams have their uses. But it must be stressed again that the significance of Russia for Rilke was not progressive. It contributed little or nothing to his later development as a poet, which is our chief concern here, though certainly the powerful effect it had on him in other respects lasted throughout his life (at the time of his

---

[1] *Das Buch vom mönchischen Leben, A.W.*, Bd. I, pp. 38–39.
[2] Op. cit., pp. 57–58.

death he was planning a book on Russia). In 1920[1] and even 1926[2] Russia still figures prominently in Rilke's acknowledgements, though with the addition of France. H. Goertz sums up adequately the relationship between Rilke and Russia: 'Dieses Verhältnis ist mehr landschaftlich gebunden, Landschaft hier gefaßt als Einheit von Raum und Volk. . . . Dieses Erkennen und Erfühlen bedeutete für seine Entwicklung viel, und hier im Osten findet man mit dem "Stundenbuch" den eigentlichen Ansatzpunkt, von dem aus Rilke sein Werk aufwärts führte.'[3]

The first two sections of *Das Stunden-Buch*, with their idealized vision of Russia (the third section, *Das Buch von der Armut und vom Tode*, inspired by Rilke's early impressions of Paris, will be referred to later), represent the first major product of Rilke's creative powers. They do not compare in quality with what was to follow, but they do mark the first step on the poet's path towards self-realization, a path which was to change its direction completely in a very short time. The importance of this early work in an aesthetic and artistic appreciation of Rilke is not in its intrinsic merit, but in the revelation it gives of his consciousness of his poetic calling and of his unequivocal self-dedication to his art. For already he was groping, however falteringly, towards fulfilment of his powers, and, naïve though he may have been, his attitude to Russia is at least intelligible. Rilke was disillusioned with the artificial materialism, the industrialism, the sterile uniformity and urban banality of Western *bourgeois* life. Russia, for him, remained untouched by the erosion of modern civilized life; he saw in her vast spaces, her primitive nearness to 'things' (the word was to take on a different meaning under Rodin) and to God, a magnificent opportunity of dispensing with the stultifying layers of conventionality and stereotyped values with which a machine-minded age was encrusted, and of coming face to face with reality.

Rilke was both wrong and right. In one sense Rilke and Russia were contradictory and irreconcilable; for one side of him was highly civilized, highly organized, and therefore the antithesis of what he conceived Russia to be. This aspect of Rilke's character

---

[1] *G.B.*, Bd. IV, p. 292.

[2] *G.B.*, Bd. V, p. 409. Rilke's reference to Paris is significant: 'Rußland . . . wurde, in gewissem Sinne, die Grundlage meines Erlebens und Empfangens, ebenso wie, vom Jahre 1902 ab, Paris — das unvergleichliche — zur Basis für mein Gestaltenwollen geworden ist.'

[3] *Frankreich und das Erlebnis der Form im Werke Rainer Maria Rilkes*, pp. 1–2.

justifies Butler's judgement: 'A more highly civilised and complex
person than Rilke it would be hard to find; the very strength of his
desire for simplicity and primitive conditions was one of the symp-
toms of decadence seeking its cure. . . .'[1] It is paradoxical that this
excursion into dreamland was made in the disingenuous belief
that he was on the track of 'reality'. But dream it was, vivid and
lingering; and perhaps Rilke's failure ever to return to Russia was
a psychological defence against having his dream shattered.

And yet, in another sense, Rilke's intuitive perception of the
bond between Russia and himself was correct. When, in the letters
already mentioned,[2] to Leopold von Schlözer and to 'Eine junge
Freundin', he speaks of 'alle Heimat meines Instinkts, all mein
innerer Ursprung' and 'die Grundlage meines Erlebens und
Empfangens' in connexion with Russia, he is not being as extravagant as might appear. For Rilke was that strange and seemingly
contradictory combination of the highly civilized and the primitive:
the one by environment and upbringing, the other by temperament. We have already noted that he was predominantly a creature
of impulse and intuition.[3] The most potent elements in his character were emotion and instinct, to which intellect was subordinate;
and these elements found their artistic expression in his fertile
and surging imagination. It is here that we find the reason why
Russia *could not* make a vital contribution to Rilke's development.
For the Russia of Rilke's conception, primitive, instinctual, anti-
intellectual, represented precisely those qualities which Rilke
himself already possessed in rich measure. The only thing which
could help him was something which offered him what he did not
possess, something which would belatedly supply the discipline
he had missed through lack of a formal education, something
which would canalize and give order to his rich imagination.
This is not to suggest that Russia had no influence on his art, for
clearly the first two sections of *Das Stunden-Buch* would not have
been written but for the impact of Russia. But it was an influence
of a very limited kind—and this explains why the Russian experience was so congenial to Rilke—in that it ministered to what was
already in him. It was essentially an emotional release, and had
none of the quality of the slow technical and stylistic advance
which marked the superimposition of the schooling of France.

---

[1] Op. cit., p. 52.                    [2] p. 29, nn. 1 and 2.
[3] p. 15.

And it is significant that France, in its first impact on him, was as unpalatable and antipathetic as Russia had been congenial.

Rilke, in retrospect and at the end of his life, accurately perceived the dichotomy in his life represented by Russia and France. For if, in the letter 'An eine junge Freundin', he refers to Russia as 'die Grundlage meines Erlebens und Empfangens', he is swift to add that Paris was the 'Basis für mein Gestaltenwollen'.[1] To his credit, it is evident that he quickly realized that Russia had nothing to give him in the stern task to which he was committed of forging his artist's tools. He soon perceived that reality, however stark and repellent, was for him in his own world of the West, with its noise and congestion, its factories, its commerce, its teeming cities with their squalor and poverty. This was the soil in which his art must be rooted. Somehow, if his poetic fulfilment was to be accomplished, he must come to terms with this world and learn to express it.

It is fitting to conclude this consideration of Russia with Rilke's own words, which, though written many years after his Russian journeys, and though belonging to a different context, nevertheless provide a very pertinent commentary both on his early poetry of *Das Stunden-Buch* and on the nature and measure of the task which lay ahead of him. In a letter 'An N.N.', dated 26 December, 1911, he writes:

Was man mit einundzwanzig Jahren schreibt, ist ein Schrei, — denkt man bei einem Schrei daran, ob er hätte anders geschrieen sein müssen? Die Sprache ist noch so dünn um einen in diesen Jahren, der Schrei dringt durch und nimmt eben nur mit, was an ihm hängen bleibt. Die Entwicklung wird immer die sein, daß man die Sprache voller, dichter, fester macht (schwerer), und dies hat dann freilich nur Sinn für einen, der sicher ist, daß auch der Schrei in ihm unablässig, unaufhaltsam zunimmt, so daß er später, unter dem Druck unzähliger Atmosphären, aus allen Poren des fast undurchdringlichen Mediums gleichmäßig austritt.'[2]

In 1900 Rilke, if physically of age, had done no more than barely reach his majority as an artist.

.    .    .    .    .    .

One of the remarkable things about Rilke's life is that, eclectic, impulsive, and unpredictable though he was by nature, the critical and decisive periods of his career were resolved in a manner

[1] See p. 29, n. 2.          [2] *G.B.*, Bd. III, pp. 154-5.

which had all the appearances of a foreordained plan. It was as though a divinity shaped his ends, rough-hew them how he would. The years 1900 to 1902 were such a period.[1] As far as his poetry was concerned, they were a kind of creative pause, for, with the exception of *Das Buch von der Pilgerschaft* and a few of the poems which were eventually to be included in *Das Buch der Bilder*, little of note was written. And yet, in the light of later developments, Worpswede and Westerwede were of great significance; in fact, but for them it is difficult to see how Rilke could have emerged as the fully fledged and complete poet he was to become. These years were, geographically and artistically, a staging-post, intervening between Russia and Paris. He had already briefly visited Worpswede in 1898, when it had made a considerable impression on him. Now, his longer stay brought Rilke for the first time into intimate contact with the representational arts, which were to play such an important part in his evolution in the coming years. Here, among the artist community, he was able to watch with his own eyes the act of artistic creation, the making of 'things', thereby giving a new twist to his interests and to his conception of the creative act. This was the preparatory school, preparing him for Rodin and laying the foundation of what was to follow.[2] Worpswede supplemented and consolidated the process begun in Italy, where his enthusiasm for the plastic arts had had its vivid awakening. There, his imagination had been fired by the glory of the finished works; here, he was able to study their genesis.

His closest associations were with the sculptress Clara Westhoff, who was to become his wife in 1901, and the painter Paula Becker: the early and lesser counterparts of Rodin and Cézanne. Thus, as if by predestination, events far ahead—the Cézanne experience was still seven years away—and of which at the outset of his stay in north Germany Rilke could have no knowledge, were being anticipated, and he was being made ready for them. Here was the true nursery of his nascent genius. But if the formative influence of the artist community was the most direct and important gain from this generally quiescent period, Worpswede performed another salutary service. The flat, expansive solitude of the landscape,

---

[1] For a detailed account of these years, see E. M. Butler, op. cit., pp. 86–116 (Worpswede) and pp. 116–35 (Westerwede).

[2] Cf. E. M. Butler, op. cit., p. 90 and F. W. van Heerikhuizen, op. cit., p. 127.

reminiscent of Russia, helped to soften the severity of his departure from that country, with which he was still very much
preoccupied, and, in creating the illusion of a Russian home-
from-home, served to bridge the interval before the plunge into
the turmoil of Paris. Worpswede at once reached backward and
forward, weaning Rilke from the past and giving him direction for
the future. The final, and more specific, link between the present
and the future was that Clara Westhoff herself had been a pupil
of Rodin. E. Buddeberg summarizes, if a little ponderously, the
significance of Worpswede and, after underlining the preparation
for Rodin, concludes with Rilke's own words, written during the
Cézanne experience:

Aber erst noch über Rodin hinaus, wiederum in der Erschütterung
auch seiner an Rodin geschulten Kunstauffassung, wird er erst vor den
Bildern Cézannes im Herbst 1907 erkennen, daß ihm in Worpswede
'die Natur noch ein allgemeiner Anlaß (war), eine Evokation, ein
Instrument, in dessen Saiten sich meine Hände wiederfanden; ich saß
noch nicht vor ihr; ich ließ mich hinreißen von der Seele, welche von
ihr ausging.' (13. Okt. 1907; Br. 06/07, p. 377.)[1]

Nearby Westerwede, to which, during May 1901, Rilke and
Clara moved after their marriage earlier in the year, continued the
process of guiding Rilke steadily but relentlessly towards France,
though in the narrower and more personal domestic environment.
For the fourteen months spent in Westerwede were the only
period in which he ever lived with Clara and led what was the
nearest he could approach to normal married life. Russia receded
more and more.

Westerwede, with its suggestion of an uneventful withdrawal
into a narrow private existence, may not appear so significant as
Worpswede in Rilke's evolution. But one thing can be inferred with
certainty. In the intimate contact with Clara, Rodin must have
loomed ever larger. This point is noted by J. F. Angelloz, the
percipient French critic of Rilke, who writes:

Ainsi, le poète qui, en Allemagne, s'était ouvert à l'influence de
Jacobsen et de Maeterlinck, qui était parti d'Allemagne pour annexer
à son espace spirituel l'Italie et la Russie, voyait venir vers lui, en
Allemagne même, Paris et Rodin. Claire Westhoff l'orientait vers le

---

[1] *Rainer Maria Rilke. Eine innere Biographie*, pp. 59–60.

monde français; il était intérieurement prêt lorsqu'on lui demanda d'écrire un livre sur Rodin.[1]

Angelloz places this commentary in the context of Worpswede (cf. the use of Clara's maiden name); but it is evident that the process of orientation towards Rodin and Paris must have become progressively more pronounced at Westerwede, especially when account is taken of the fact that Rilke spent less than two months at Worpswede against the fourteen at Westerwede.

The double decision to write the book on Rodin and to go to Paris was made at least two months before the departure for France, and there is a letter to Rodin on the subject, dated 28 June 1902.[2] After the conditioning resulting from Rilke's association with the Worpswede artists and from Clara's close connexion with the French sculptor, it is probable that, soon or late, the appointment with Rodin and Paris was inevitable. The immediate, and more ignoble, reason for the departure from Westerwede was, however, economic: Rilke's inability to maintain his wife, child, and cottage, and the consequent need to undertake some kind of work to support them.

It is fitting to list and stress, once again, the remarkable conjuncture of circumstances which played their part in this crucial period of Rilke's career. It was like the pieces of a complicated jigsaw coming together. First, there was an environment which, while creating the physical illusion of a continuation of the Russian experience, unobtrusively drew him away from Russia, on the homoeopathic principle that *similia similibus curantur*. Secondly, community with the Worpswede artists completed what had begun in Italy, and firmly established the studious interest in the representational arts which was to be such a significant element in his artistic development. Thirdly, Clara's professional admiration for, and personal acquaintance with, Rodin led directly to Rilke's next move. A fourth factor may also be mentioned which, if it is hardly likely to raise Rilke's credit in the eyes of the world, cannot be overlooked in any discussion of his evolution as a poet: his final realization of the impossibility, in his own case, of submitting to the conventional ties and duties of a husband. This inability to reconcile the responsibilities and demands of the restraining routine implicit in membership of a household with the unfettered

---

[1] *Rainer Maria Rilke — l'Évolution spirituelle du poète*, p. 164.
[2] *G.B.*, Bd. I, pp. 227–9.

freedom consonant with genius was to last all his life. Rilke was unfitted for marriage, however loosely its obligations be construed. He was equally unfitted to pursue the corollary to marriage— an ordered, salaried occupation. Confinement in an office with regular hours of work would almost certainly have stifled the creative spark. Rilke's domestic conduct may be condemned, but if the fact of his incapacity had to be accepted, it was better, for the sake of his poetry, that he should accept it early and not late. And if this side of Rilke's career is distasteful, there is the compensating thought that had he been more normal as a man, it is improbable that he would have been as great an artist.

# III

## PARIS AND RODIN

RILKE arrived in Paris on 28 August 1902. It was to be his home—if the term can be used in respect of a man of Rilke's nomadic proclivities—until the First World War, though in the years 1910 to 1914 the total time he spent there can be counted in months. But in all his journeyings, Paris remained the magnet which always drew him back. The contrast between the initial impression made on him by the French capital with that made by Russia renders this attachment, at first sight, all the more remarkable. Here was none of the taking by storm, none of the unbridled rapture which marked the Russian travels. On the contrary, it was a harsh and sobering experience: *Die Aufzeichnungen des Malte Laurids Brigge* and *Das Buch von der Armut und vom Tode* provide a vivid record of the bitterness and despair of the poet's early acquaintance with his adopted home. But in its severity it was salutary; in terrifying and oppressing him it started the cure. Paris, with all the manifestations of the modern age—crowds, machinery, materialism, regimentation, mass poverty and mass disease—which so horrified Rilke, administered, and at the right moment, just the shock treatment necessary to rescue him from his cloud-cuckoo-land. If there is one physical fact above all others to be adduced in support of the contention that the outcome of Rilke's artistic career was inseparably linked with the effects of French environment and influence, it is that, against all rational expectations and against his own frequent consciousness of anti-pathy, Paris and France remained the one enduring element in the life of a man who was egregiously unstable and rootless. Even in his last years at Muzot, when his greatest work was accomplished, it is possible to see the continuation of this association. For not only was he, in the Canton of Valais, in French-speaking territory, but his reading was predominantly of French literature, his links with his friends in France were diligently maintained, and he even turned to writing original French poems.

Rilke's references to Paris over the years are interesting and instructive, revealing his conflict of emotions. For the most part these varied with location: when he was away from Paris he wanted to be back; when he was there he was disillusioned. This is a common enough human reaction. What is important is that, of all the places he knew, for Rilke it was France alone, whether attracting or repelling, which held him in thrall for the rest of his life. Only four months after his arrival, on New Year's Eve, 1902, he wrote from Paris to Otto Modersohn:

Lieber Otto Modersohn, halten Sie an Ihrem Lande! Paris (wir sagen es uns täglich) ist eine schwere, schwere, bange Stadt. . . . Paris hat für mein geängstigtes Gefühl etwas unsäglich Banges. Es hat sich ganz verloren, es rast wie ein bahnverirrter Stern auf irgendeinen schrecklichen Zusammenstoß zu. So müssen die Städte gewesen sein, von denen die Bibel erzählt, daß der Zorn Gottes hinter ihnen emporstieg, um sie zu überschütten und zu erschüttern.[1]

From Viareggio, on the other hand, he wrote to Clara on 8 April 1903: 'So viel ist sicher, daß ich zunächst wieder nach Paris kommen werde, vielleicht um das Carrière-Buch zu schreiben; es ist mir immer, als ob Paris mir noch eine Arbeit schenken müßte . . .'[2] On 9 February 1907, he wrote to Paula Modersohn-Becker from Capri: 'Aber fast noch mehr bin ich mit meinen Gedanken in Paris, das im Sommer verlassen zu haben ich noch immer nicht verschmerzen kann. Mir ist, als ob alles, d.h. meine Arbeit vor allem, davon abhinge, wie bald ich wieder hin zurückkomme.'[3] To the same person and from the same place he wrote, on 17 March of the same year: 'Dazu ist meine Bewunderung für Paris zu groß und meine Überzeugung, daß man dort alles werden kann, zu aufrichtig.'[4]

But again from Paris, on 21 October 1913, he wrote to Lou Andreas-Salomé: 'Paris war diesmal genau, wie ich mirs versprach; schwer. Und ich komme mir vor wie eine photographische Platte, die zu lange belichtet wird, indem ich immer noch dem hier, diesem heftigen Einfluß, ausgesetzt bleibe.'[5] Two months later, on 27 December 1913, in a letter to Fürstin Marie von Thurn und Taxis-Hohenlohe, the words of condemnation are even stronger: 'Ich habe von Paris über und über genug, es ist ein Ort der

[1] *G.B.*, Bd. I, p. 294.    [2] Ibid., p. 343.
[3] *G.B.*, Bd. II, p. 257.   [4] Ibid., p. 290.
[5] *G.B.*, Bd. III, p. 315.

Verdammnis, das hab ich immer gewußt, aber damals wurden mir
die Peinen der Verdammten von einem Engel auseinandergesetzt
. . .'¹ It may be recalled that these last two quotations belong
to the period of greatest personal crisis in Rilke's life.²

The war years gave him a long opportunity of contemplating
the unattainable and of assessing his relationship to Paris *in
absentia protracta*. On 20 July 1919, in a letter from Zürich to
Hauptmann Otto Braun, his tone is very different, and he speaks
of Paris, 'wo mir Unstätem ein kleiner Ansatz zur Ansiedlung
entstanden war . . .'³ On 16 August 1920, from Geneva, he wrote
to Helene Burckhardt-Schatzmann of his departure from Switzerland: 'Und von hier fortgehen, heißt es nun auch, von alledem
Abschied nehmen, was geeignet war, mir hier Paris heraufzurufen!
Auch diesen beglückenden Anklang subtiler und unsagbarer
Ähnlichkeiten empfind ich diesmal noch stärker, als vor einem
Jahr — . . .'⁴

At last came the brief return to Paris, lasting only six days.
'Aber sehen Sie nur, sehen Sie nur!: was soll ich sagen, es ist
vollkommen, vollkommen gut; ich empfinde, zum ersten Mal seit
den entsetzlichen Jahren, wieder die Kontinuität meines Daseins
. . . la même plénitude de vie, la même intensité . . .'⁵ ('An Gräfin
M.', Paris, 27 October 1920). On 19 November, less than a month
later, he wrote of the visit in the same strain to Fürstin Marie von
Thurn und Taxis '. . . *mein* Paris, das ehemalige, ich möchte
sagen: ewige'.⁶ And to Hans Reinhart, on the same day, he spoke
of his journey to Paris, 'deren Ergebnis es ist, daß ich nun wieder
ein vollständiges Bewußtsein meines ganzen Lebens verwalten
kann'.⁷ There was one more stay in Paris, from January to August
1925. But by this time Rilke's fatal illness was far advanced and he
was physically beyond responding strongly to any environmental
stimulus: Paris was no more than a last, and foredoomed, attempt
to escape his sickness, as yet undiagnosed.

When all allowance is made for Rilke's susceptibility to sentiment—which may sometimes lead to an extravagantly rhapsodical
description of mood, but seldom to the invention of feelings which
are not there—the tenor of these passages is unmistakable. When

---

¹ *G.B.*, Bd. III, pp. 335–6.     ² See p. 10.
³ *G.B.*, Bd. IV, p. 243.          ⁴ Ibid., pp. 312–13.
⁵ Ibid., p. 323.                   ⁶ Ibid., pp. 325–6.
⁷ Ibid., p. 328.

to them is added the tribute to Paris, already quoted,[1] in the letter
'An eine junge Freundin' of 17 March 1926, we have a record
spanning all the years from the time of his arrival in France: a
record covering nearly half his life. There can be no doubt of the
tenacity and durability of the hold France had over him. In this,
as in many other things, Rilke was the antithesis of Stefan George,
who was in a very real sense a 'national' poet, though he, too, had
stayed in Paris in his youth and had been an ardent admirer of
Mallarmé.[2]

It is important to note at this point that there are two factors
which need to be considered in Rilke's attachment to France: his
relationship to the various figures in French art and letters who
played an important part in his development, and his more general
relationship to France as a whole, as a cultural and artistic environment. Up to a point, of course, these two factors cannot be
separated, since inevitably Rilke's attitude to France was conditioned to a certain extent by his sense of community with
individuals whom he regarded as having something to contribute
to his evolution as a poet, and particularly by personal friendships.
Nevertheless, some distinction is both possible and necessary. It lies
in the noticeable contrast between the persistence and permanence
of his ties with France as a whole and the much more transient
nature of his relationship to individuals. Rilke's eclecticism has
been mentioned before;[3] it will emerge even more notably when
his attitude to French literature comes under discussion. In general,
his contacts with artistic figures have the character of a series of
separate, and sometimes apparently unrelated, episodes. As soon
as their purpose was fulfilled, they ceased. When Rilke had exhausted their possibilities and assimilated all he could from them,
they were discarded. Rilke's progress, in fact, resembles a series of
distinct scaling operations, after each of which the ladder was
kicked away. This is not to say that he forgot these associations,
and certainly he never lost what he had gained from them; but
they were never allowed to outstay their usefulness. Nowhere
is the curious and apparently contradictory make-up of Rilke's
personality better illustrated than in the ruthless competence in all

---

[1] p. 29 n. 2.
[2] Cf. C. M. Bowra, op. cit., pp. 98–99. It is interesting that two such contrasting poets as Rilke and George may be ranked as 'inheritors' of Symbolism.
[3] p. 31.

matters relating to his artistic development; he, who was so demonstrably feckless and disorientated in the ordinary mechanics of living, was—though perhaps, a creature of instinct ever, involuntarily—a model of practicality and efficiency where his art was concerned.

The nature of the parts played by the succession of French artists and literary figures who impinged on Rilke's poetic career, and the extent of his debt to them, will be considered, as far as is possible, in chronological order. But for the moment, a little more needs to be said on the subject of his relationship to France as a whole. This question has rarely been discussed by Rilke's critics (J. F. Angelloz, in the work already quoted, is an exception). Admittedly, its implications are more imponderable and less easy to determine than the respective influences of individuals, but they are probably no less important and far-reaching. An attempt to assess the reasons for the one sustained attachment in Rilke's life, and why France and no other country was the object of this attachment, will be left until a later point in the examination, when it will be possible to survey the whole of the French experience in retrospect. Then, it will also be easier to form a balanced estimate of the effects on his art. But, bearing in mind that we are concerned with Rilke's poetic development, with particular emphasis on his progressive mastery and consciousness of language, some preliminary remarks at this stage may help to direct attention to some of the essentials and indicate points deserving special investigation.

It is, therefore, pertinent to recapitulate and underline certain facts. Rilke left Germany in 1902 and, with the exception of the war years, never lived there again. Stress has also been laid on the paradoxical fact that, so far from suffering from this prolonged and deliberate absence from the life-source, Rilke's power over the German language as a poetic medium steadily increased.[1] It is surprising that the magnitude of this apparent contradiction has either been overlooked or has been regarded as of insufficient importance to merit comment by Rilke's critics. We may therefore profitably examine some of the implications of his voluntary exile in the context of language. Rilke did, of course, continue to read his own language extensively; he also wrote in it copiously, though quantitatively his prose writing, particularly in the form of letters,

[1] See p. 24.

far exceeded his poetry. There were, too, his frequent contacts with his German-speaking friends, as well as his occasional visits to Germany, though these last, excluding the enforced stay of the war years, were on the whole brief and rare enough to be of little use as infusions. But even when the maximum weight is given to the various means by which Rilke maintained his touch on the German instrument, these do not compare with the constant usage and immersion of the poet who lives in his own country all his life. In short, for the greater part of the second half of his life, and above all during the periods of his greatest poetic achievement, Rilke was surrounded by, and for the purposes of his day-to-day living compelled to use, a language which was not his own. Thus, in view of the earlier suggestion that lyric poetry represents the supreme distillation of language sensitivity and manipulation,[1] the question of Rilke's separation from his native land can be seen to be one of no little importance.

Clearly, therefore, there is a problem here which should be borne in mind as the discussion advances. If France, rather than Germany, was vital to his poetic development, how did Rilke contrive to perfect his mastery of language when, to use his own metaphor of the *Florenzer Tagebuch*,[2] he was to a large extent cut off from his roots, and the supply of sap was, at best, a mere trickle? The compensating gains from the individual influences under which he came in France do not provide the whole answer, important though they are. It will be necessary to probe more deeply into the question of language itself. Since anything which affected in any way or helped to mould his capacity to express himself is significant, Rilke's knowledge of French cannot be left out of account. Here, again, is to be found an interesting contrast with the Russian experience. Here was none of the violent frontal assault, which gained a few positions but did not win the battle. Rather it was the slow and painstaking technique of infiltration, which was as unspectacular as it was successful. That Rilke had a useful working knowledge of French before he went to Paris is indicated by the fact that his letter to Rodin of 28 June 1902,[3] was written in that language. His command over it naturally increased in Paris, not only from practical necessity, but even more, no doubt, from his intimate contact with Rodin, who in any case

[1] p 18.      [2] See p. 24.
[3] *G.B.*, Bd. I, pp. 227–9.

knew no German. Nevertheless, even in 1905, when he became Rodin's secretary, Rilke was still having difficulty with the written language.[1] But by the end of his life his knowledge of French was more than competent, and it is probably true to say that, for prose purposes, it came almost as naturally to him as German (in the letters written during the last few years of his life he frequently switches spontaneously into French). His *Poèmes français*, if not without technical faults, and however modest their literary merit, are final evidence that his command of French was considerable.

The extent and nature of the effect of the French language on Rilke's development will be examined in greater detail when reference is made to his translations, and particularly when Paul Valéry's impact comes under discussion. For the present, it is sufficient to draw attention to a factor in Rilke's evolution which deserves consideration and which has been neglected, and one, moreover, which has puzzling and apparently contradictory features. It is a truism that the more he used French and thought in it, the less he practised German, and it would not be unreasonable to expect this to constitute a deprivation in respect of the literary genre which, from the point of view of language, is the most exacting of all. It is impossible to disregard the fact that, for all the reading and writing in his own language, Rilke's staple nourishment from 1902 onwards was very different from that which Germany would have given him. Thus, throughout the examination of the more specific influences exerted on Rilke by individual artists and men of letters, it should be remembered, in estimating his poetry, that his development took place against the background of an ever-growing familiarity with and affection for an alien linguistic medium. And, so far from resulting in a diminution of his powers in his own medium, the curve, or perhaps it would be more correct to say the successive stages of Rilke's ascent correspond closely to his increasing knowledge and practice of French. (Later discussion may be briefly anticipated here by mentioning that the creation of his greatest poetry, the *Duineser Elegien* and the *Sonette an Orpheus*, occurred in the midst of the most concentrated, prolonged, and the most demanding exercise concerned with the French language which Rilke ever undertook: the Valéry translations.) Not to attempt to establish a link between the two would be to ignore a most intriguing problem. We may

[1] Cf. Butler, op. cit., p. 160.

therefore temporarily leave this subject with the most interesting question of all: whether, in fact, there is not some quality *in the French language itself* which, however paradoxically, was able to make a direct and indispensable contribution to Rilke's progressive mastery over the *German* poetic instrument; whether the completely different discipline of French did not provide just the strengthening for the weaker or incomplete parts of his artistic equipment which could not have been supplied by Germany alone.

.    .    .    .    .

In passing to Rilke's contact with Rodin, it is appropriate to consider how far his association with the representational arts could have any significant effect on his poetry, and particularly on the evolution of his language-consciousness. It did, in fact, have a perceptible effect, if only because the Rodin and Cézanne experiences were instrumental in bringing about what was probably the most profound modification in his artistic and aesthetic concept that ever took place; and anything which modifies a poet's approach to his work is inevitably reflected in the means by which he expresses himself. It is, nevertheless, right that these two experiences, crucial though they were, should be introduced with a note of caution, especially as much that has been written about them appears to ignore the fundamental problems which arise when assessing the impact on each other of artists using different media.

The first important point to note is that Rilke's preoccupation with the representational arts belonged to the most formative period of his life, to those years when his poetry was passing through its most tentative, experimental, and uncertain phases. This preoccupation began effectively in Italy, with his enthusiasm for Renaissance art; it continued in Worpswede and Westerwede; it reached its grand climax in Paris. After Cézanne, in 1907, Rilke was never again concerned to any notable degree with other than literary artists. (Despite the inspiration of the Fifth Elegy, there is no evidence that Picasso had any general impact on Rilke comparable to that of Cézanne.) At a time when his own artistic approach was in such a state of transition and indecision, it would not have been unreasonable to suppose that Rilke would automatically turn to his fellow-poets for sustenance and help. In the event, whether by good fortune or whether by the operation of that instinctive taste and astuteness which so often stood him in good stead in times of crisis, the fact that Rilke resorted to art forms completely different from his own was of decisive importance in the resolution of his early problems and in his ultimate development as a poet.

Rilke's years with Rodin have probably been discussed more than any other episode in the poet's life; so much so that qualities and results have come to be unquestioningly attributed to the Rilke–Rodin relationship in such a way as almost to make Rodin appear as the creator of Rilke. That the Rodin experience had a profound effect on Rilke is not in doubt. It is, however, important to keep an open and clear mind in distinguishing the two aspects of this relationship—the artistic and the emotional; in assessing in what way and to what extent this experience marked a genuine stage in Rilke's *artistic* progress, and how far it acted merely as a psychological stimulus—always remembering that Rilke's temperament was highly sensitive and emotional, and that Rodin was a dominating personality. Moreover, in the broader context of Rodin and Cézanne there is a further and basic problem which is seldom considered, namely, to what degree a creator in a mobile, 'living' medium can draw artistic sustenance from those whose medium is inanimate; how far there can be cross-fertilization between language, which is dynamic and organic, and stone and colour, the values of which are static. It is another facet of Lessing's distinction between 'Nacheinander' and 'Nebeneinander' or, in Herder's more descriptive phraseology, between the arts on the one hand which produce 'Energie' and those on the other which produce 'Wirkung'.

The relationship between Rodin and Rilke in the years 1902 to 1906 may be said to have been close, considering the disparity in years and, more especially, in reputation, and allowing for the fact that the initiative not unnaturally came from Rilke. It is well known that Rodin showed his youthful admirer great kindness and was without doubt instrumental in enabling Rilke to survive the early anguish of Paris and to stay there. It is evident that, in his prevailing mood of uncertainty, the young Rilke had a deep hunger for the society of one—anyone—who had already achieved greatness as an artist, the established 'success'. In his own bewilderment and feeling of insecurity, Rilke could enjoy, in the accomplishment and universal repute of Rodin, a vicarious sense of stability. This was the second attempt to hitch his wagon to a star: Rodin assumed the role that Rilke had once hoped might be played by Tolstoy. Like

Goethe's Tasso, Rilke needed a rock to which to cling, and it had to
be a rock of impressive dimensions, a rock which was at once an
anchor and a challenge; for not only did it give him stability, but it
confronted him as something immeasurably greater than himself
on which he could fix his sights in his own long and painful climb
to the summit.

Rilke's association with Rodin was founded in the first instance
upon hero-worship, and this attitude is reflected in the tone of
sycophantic humility which runs through all the letters which
he wrote to Rodin. The motif of adulation also recurs in Rilke's
other letters of the period—the long description to Clara, dated
2 September 1902, of his first meeting with Rodin may be cited
as a particular example.[1] This aspect of the relationship is well
summarized by Buddeberg, who emphasizes the 'aura of the divine'
woven round Rodin in the letters.[2] It is interesting to note how the
tone of subservient devotion diminished when the association was
broken, even though Rilke continued to labour for a while on
Rodin's behalf. This point and the reason for it are well expressed
by Angelloz: 'Le Dieu est devenu voisin, non seulement parce que
le créateur des *Nouveaux Poèmes* et des *Cahiers de Malte Laurids
Brigge*, a pris conscience de sa valeur, mais aussi, croyons-nous,
parce que le modèle vivant avait brisé sa propre statue.'[3] For,
although the occasion of the rupture was unpleasant and painful,[4]
the real reason for the parting was that the relationship had fulfilled its purpose. Rilke had reached the point where he no longer
needed Rodin, and separation was inevitable.

There was, therefore, a strong emotional content in Rilke's
approach to Rodin. But if he raised Rodin 'au rang d'un mythe
ou d'un Dieu',[5] he also acquired in the process an intelligent interest
in the sculptor's art and his methods of working. There is ample
evidence that his knowledge of Rodin and of the technicalities of
sculpture became quite authoritative.[6] It is here that we pass to
the much more important question of Rodin's contribution to
Rilke's art: a question which is not to be easily resolved in terms
of a balance-sheet, the more so as it is bound up with the psychological effects of Rodin's imposing personality. Much that has been

[1] *G.B.*, Bd. I, pp. 249–56.          [2] Op. cit., p. 62.
[3] Op. cit., p. 187.                    [4] See *G.B.*, Bd. II, pp. 134–7.
[5] J. F. Angelloz, op. cit., p. 189.
[6] Cf. *G.B.*, Bd. I, pp. 257 f. and pp. 375 f.; also the essay *Auguste Rodin*,
*G.W.*, Bd. IV, pp. 299–418.

written on the interrelationship between different arts is glib and unsatisfying. There has been, moreover, a growing tendency among modern critics of the arts to employ a common definitive vocabulary for different media—such expressions as 'texture' and 'tone colour', for example, are now frequently to be found in musical criticism. Even where this practice is pursued thoughtfully and with care, it has its dangers. At best it is liable to be confusing, at worst the terms themselves can soon become debased and devitalized; and in the hands of the less capable or the less scrupulous they quickly degenerate into mere jargon. These dangers have not been entirely avoided in Rilke criticism. It is not difficult to bandy about meaninglessly such expressions as 'form' and 'architecture'; from which it is but a short step to the simple argument that since Rodin, as a sculptor of genius, was a master of form, he could somehow impart this mastery to Rilke. Two concessions only may be made. First, the word 'form' has a legitimate application to all arts, though it is obvious that its meaning is different in each case and that, in particular, there is a widely divergent significance between its application to the representational or static arts and to those which are dynamic, mobile. Secondly, Rilke, straight from the plethoric effusion of the first two parts of *Das Stunden-Buch*, certainly needed the element of restraint and control which may be paraphrased by the word 'form'.

It is important to note in this connexion that not least among Rilke's deficiencies at this time was his general immaturity, which in turn had its origin in his lack of formal education referred to earlier.[1] For all his 26 years, it was as a callow and untutored youth that he came to Rodin. Commenting on the lessons learnt from the sculptor, Angelloz pertinently notes that Rilke was deeply aware of the need of a more complete culture and that, with Rodin's example before him, he considered himself as an eternal student.[2] He goes on to cite the proposed academic tasks listed by Rilke in the letter to Lou Andreas-Salomé of 12 May 1904[3]—a list which, in the light of actual achievement and in the knowledge of his constitutional antipathy to being tied down by any discipline or system, now appears rather pathetic.

It is possible to consider the artistic and aesthetic significance

[1] p. 30.          [2] Op. cit., p. 192.
[3] *G.B.*, Bd. I, pp. 471–2.

of the Rilke–Rodin relationship only from the starting-point that they worked in two absolutely different art media. A moment's thought on this question is sufficient to show that there must be strict limits to what Rodin could give Rilke *directly*. The character of the creative act—a character which is, after all, largely imposed on it by the nature of the medium—in the two arts is completely different, involving not only a radical contrast in technique, but even a basic difference in the quality of the inspiration. Not only is there the contrast between the static and the mobile, but also between the tangible and the intangible. The question of inspiration will occur again. For the moment, it is enough to point out that in sculpture, however momentaneous the original conception of the work, the inspiration is wedded to the manner of execution and is spread over the period of performance in a way that does not happen in the writing of poetry. The work evolves under physical contact; inspiration is inseparable from the element of manual skill, of craftsmanship, and to that extent its operation is much more prolonged and controlled than the sudden vision, or series of visions, by which the composition of poetry proceeds.[1] F. W. van Heerikhuizen aptly expresses the gulf between the two arts when, after noting the manual nature of the plastic arts and the tangibility of the material, he says that the literary artist 'is almost entirely dependent on intuition; the relation between words and reality cannot be sensorily realised'.[2] As well as setting the limits to what Rilke could receive from Rodin, the fundamental difference between their arts, coupled with the degree to which Rilke enthusiastically staked his future on and placed his hopes in the outcome of his association with the great French sculptor, ultimately and inevitably produced in Rilke, as we shall see, inner conflict and a sense of failure—which, nevertheless, were all to the good.

We must, therefore, regard Rodin's importance as being primarily concerned with the broader lessons of life. The contribution he could make to Rilke's evolution as a poet was necessarily

---

[1] This is not intended to imply that there is no element of 'craftsmanship' in the writing of poetry; nor that its operation does not 'prolong' the creative act. But the 'prolongation' is not dictated *physically* by the medium. The crucial point is that in poetic creation each poetic thought—even if it is subsequently modified (when, of course, it becomes a different thought)—can be *instantly* transferred to paper.

[2] Op. cit., p. 164.

*indirect*, but, given this qualification, the latter clearly drew a rich dividend. Rodin came into Rilke's life at a moment when the latter himself was acutely aware that his artistic education, rooted, as it was, in his general development, was only just beginning, when he was deeply conscious of his own uncertainty and lack of direction; in short, at a moment when he was particularly receptive to the impact of a man of Rodin's stature and authority. Rodin as it were guided Rilke through the labyrinth of his own personality, channelled his creative energies by giving them order and purpose. Above all, he taught Rilke the great lesson which transcends all art forms and which should inform all human endeavour: that nothing worth while is achieved easily.

J. F. Angelloz, in the work already quoted, undertakes a long and careful analysis of the Rilke–Rodin relationship.[1] He points out that Rodin was Rilke's one happiness in the overall suffering of the Parisian experience. And if we should think it strange for a poet to place himself under the tutelage of a sculptor, we may remember that they both lived on the same spiritual plane, on which their meeting-point was their common pursuit of beauty. Rilke, moreover, was conscious that a completely new phase in his poetic development was taking place, which not only prevented him from being content with the poetic prescriptions of his predecessors, but even caused him to fear that contact with them would cost him his individuality. On the other hand, he was aware of his own powerlessness to create the figures great enough to express his inner world, and, as Angelloz puts it,

l'œuvre de Rodin qu'il admirait, la personnalité de Rodin. . . . lui offrait le spectacle d'un homme qui, se réalisant par un effort de sa volonté, dressa autour de lui les créations de son génie. Et c'est précisément de cela qu'il avait besoin. Le problème qui s'imposait à lui était beaucoup plus vaste et plus angoissant qu'un simple problème poétique; il cherchait le secret de la vie, la forme qu'il devait donner à son existence, afin de réaliser une œuvre, qui serait l'épanouissement dans l'espace de sa vision intérieure du monde; il ne cherchait pas un maître de poésie mais un maître de vie.

Rodin confronted Rilke with the example of a man who had known the suffering of the lonely and uncomprehended artist, who had developed along his own personal path by a constant effort of will, and who had dedicated his life to his work. To Rilke's anxiety and

[1] Op. cit., pp. 184–95.

feeling of impotence he offered confidence and infinite patience. Rilke, the dreamer, came face to face with reality.

It is interesting to note, in passing, that although Rilke appeared to be as preoccupied as ever with 'things', the term underwent a subtle transformation during the Rodin period;[1] and this change was in itself symbolic of the transition from the primitive and the elemental represented by Russia to the civilization of the West. The 'Dinge' of *Das Buch vom mönchischen Leben* and *Das Buch von der Pilgerschaft* were simply inanimate objects, near to God because they had not become corrupted by human society. Now the word came to mean the products of men's hands: the creations of the artist, who was himself *in statu Dei*.

Angelloz specifies some of the important lessons Rilke received from Rodin and quotes Rilke's own list of acquisitions given in a letter to Holitscher, dated 13 December 1905: ' "Vivre, avoir de la patience, travailler et ne laisser échapper aucune occasion de joie" . . . Vivre', comments Angelloz, 'avec l'assurance paisible des animaux, des plantes, des choses. . . . Vivre avec la sérénité de ce vieillard, de ce sage. . . .'[2] This critic further remarks that 'Rilke apprend à voir pour la première fois "la vie ouverte"'—the antithesis of 'la vie bourgeoise qui est la vie fermée, l'absence de vie. . . . La vie ouverte est une vie dans la joie.'[3]

It is less easy to agree with Angelloz when, seeking to demonstrate that Rilke achieved this 'vie dans la joie', he says: 'Vivre dans la joie, telle était donc la condition première d'une création poétique.'[3] It would be impossible to pretend that Rilke ever conquered this secret. This lesson of joy was one which he might learn; but he was temperamentally and occupationally prevented from practising it with any enduring success. No one can read *Die Aufzeichnungen des Malte Laurids Brigge* itself or Rilke's correspondence over the years and remain in any doubt of the louring cloud of depression and neurosis under which the greater part of his adult life was spent. He was to know little joy or serenity in his life, and none in sustained measure until after his greatest work was completed in 1922. It is another facet of the contrast between the two media. For the plastic artist, tranquillity is inherent in, even enforced by, the slow and painful process of manual work; for the poet, the creative act is punctuated by stresses and tensions,

---

[1] Cf. p. 29.   [2] Op. cit., pp. 189–90.
[3] Ibid, p. 190.

it is movement, restlessness, systole and diastole.[1] It may be conceded that Rodin was the one factor which mitigated the nightmare of the early period in Paris—a circumstance which may have led Angelloz to over-estimate the efficiency of Rodin's lesson—and it is probable that under the influence of Rodin's immediate presence Rilke was as near as possible to being untroubled; but these moments were intermittent, they were very different from 'vivre dans la joie', which connotes a permanent state. And, above all, such serenity and joy as he knew were borrowed, and therefore not immanent. They were experienced because he was watching and sharing in Rodin's work, because, at the times of experiencing them, *he was not himself working in his own medium* but was, so to speak, a sculptor by delegation.

Angelloz goes on to list the second lesson. He reminds us that up to that time Rilke had relied solely on inspiration. Rodin, on the other hand, is scornful of inspiration, considering it incapable of producing anything other than 'une fausse originalité'. Rilke 'ne retouchait pas ses poèmes' or, Rodin 'n'a cessé de remanier ses œuvres et parfois, notamment pour la "Porte de l'enfer", il les détruisait afin de les refaire plus conformes à sa vision'.[2] Rilke, he points out, could create only if certain favourable conditions were fulfilled; Rodin, on the other hand, went to his studio with invariable regularity and, according to Rilke, for years never went to bed without having realized what he had set out to do during the day. 'Rilke qui, pendant des mois, vit Rodin au travail, s'efforcera de l'imiter.'[2] If the foregoing discussion partially qualifies our agreement as to what conditions had to be fulfilled before Rilke could create, notably in the matter of the 'calme' and 'sérénité intérieure' mentioned by Angelloz, the general statement is true: Rodin could create at will, Rilke could not. It is also true that Rilke sought to imitate Rodin's method of work and to subject himself to the same discipline, which in the long run served only to augment his doubts and consciousness of incapacity. It is possible to understand why Rodin, as a sculptor, and with the extreme emphasis he placed on hard work, ridiculed inspiration, though it

[1] This is not to suggest that plastic artists are never neurotic or never suffer from restlessness or tension. What is meant is that where, because of the nature of the medium, the creative act of the plastic artist has an evening and tranquillizing effect, poetic composition normally proceeds in a series of creative spurts, and therefore contains in itself the elements of stress.

[2] Op. cit., pp. 190–1.

is probable that it was the more restricted, emotional conception
of it of which he was sceptical. The subject of inspiration is a
controversial one. One thing, however, can be said with certainty:
whether inspiration be regarded as the activity of an external agent,
a divine *inflatus*, or whether merely as the operation of a highly
developed and sensitized system of reflexes and nerve cells, the
act of artistic creation remains a mystery. The reason why a work
of art is conceived and executed in a particular way, at a particular
time, by a particular man, is unexplained and, to all appearances,
inexplicable.

But, whatever definition one gives to inspiration, Rodin could
never convince us of its absence in his own work. If the rigorous
principles upon which he based his creative activity, and the resistant and retarding medium in which he worked, led him to scorn
anything which savoured of the easy way out, it is, nevertheless,
evident that hard work alone is not a sufficient explanation of his
genius: otherwise, he could have trained many more to be as great
as himself. It is equally clear that the instantaneous, intuitive flash
of the imagination must always figure more prominently, or at
least operate more unrestrainedly, in the writing of poetry and
music, where there is no hard material to impose its arresting and
spreading effect. Rodin's view of inspiration serves to bring us
back firmly to the gulf which separates the two art forms, and
which, therefore, at bottom, separated Rilke and Rodin.

No better illustration of this gulf may be offered than the contrast between Rodin's approach to his great conception of the
*Porte de l'enfer* and the nature of Rilke's creative climax in February
1922, when the *Duineser Elegien* were completed and the *Sonette an
Orpheus* were written in entirety. In the first we see the prolonged
and painstaking process, which was inherent in the work and the
medium, of fashioning and refashioning, touching and retouching,
destruction and re-creation; in the second we have the astonishing
and breathtaking spectacle of a sudden and tempestuous act of
creation, perhaps unsurpassed in its intensity in all literary history.
We may recall in fairness that Rilke had been at work on the
Elegies at intervals for ten years, and that to this extent, therefore,
the element of trial and error and alteration was present. But this
was not a condition of the material, in the sense that it was with
Rodin, and there is no escaping the fact that in February 1922
Rilke underwent a creative experience the rapidity and immediacy

of which are impossible in a work of sculpture. After years of
waiting until hope had almost gone, and at a moment when he was
preoccupied with other things, he wrote all the Sonnets and the
great remaining part of the Elegies in a little more than a fortnight.
Moreover—and this is of particular interest in the context of the
present examination of Rilke's conscientious pursuit of Rodin's
principles—he recorded in a letter to Xaver von Moos, dated
20 April 1923, that the first part of the Sonnets was written
between 2 and 5 February 1922, 'in einem atemlosen Gehorchen
. . . ohne daß ein Wort in Zweifel oder zu ändern war'.[1] Straight
from the completion of the last Elegy, on the evening of 11
February 1922, in the excitement of success, and with no thought
of the metaphysics of inspiration, Rilke wrote to the Fürstin von
Thurn und Taxis-Hohenlohe, at whose castle at Duino the cycle
had been started ten years earlier: 'Alles in ein paar Tagen, es
war ein namenloser Sturm, ein Orkan im Geist (wie damals auf
Duino), alles, was Faser in mir ist und Geweb, hat gekracht, — am
Essen war nie zu denken, Gott weiß, wer mich genährt hat.'[2] And
in the letter to Xaver von Moos already quoted—which, be it
noted, was written over a year later, when his judgement was not
influenced by the emotional heat of the moment of achievement—
he said of the Sonnets: 'Sie sind vielleicht das geheimste, mir
selber, in ihrem Aufkommen und sich-mir-Auftragen, rätsel-
hafteste Diktat, das ich je ausgehalten und geleistet habe . . .'[1]

These are significant revelations of the way in which Rilke's
creative powers worked when they were at their peak, and it is
appropriate that they should be brought into relief in this examination of the Rodin experience, which was the opposite pole of
Rilke's artistic existence in respect of the conception of the nature
of inspiration. But the lines of longitude pass through both poles,
and, strangely, perhaps, but pertinently, it was of Rodin that Rilke
thought little more than a month after the completion of the
Sonnets and the Elegies. In a letter 'An E. de W.', dated 20 March
1922, we find one of Rilke's most penetrating passages. In its acute
exposition of the doubts and problems of the earlier years, of his
debt to Rodin, and of the nature of the latter's inspiration, it
crystallizes admirably the discussion so far:

Mich vor solchen Schwankungen im zu leichten Kahn einigermaßen
zu bewahren, tat ich alles mögliche, einen verläßlichen immer zu

_____

[1] G.B., Bd. V, p. 205.          [2] Ibid., p. 114.

fassenden Ballast für derart entledigte Momente bereitzuhalten, — aber
sei es, daß meine Kraft nicht groß genug war, um so teilbar zu sein, sei
es, daß ich zu spät und wider zu viel Schwierigkeiten in Kindheit und
Jugend zu meinen eigensten Beschäftigungen vorgedrungen war, oder
daß überhaupt die Zeit, in der ich diese aufnahm, eine solche Einseitig-
keit und Einschränkung auf *Eines* befürwortete: es gelang mir nicht,
trotz mancher angefangener Studien, mir ein eigentlich ständiges
Gegengewicht auszubilden. Später tröstete ich mich, tant bien que mal,
damit, daß die Kunst — ohnehin eine zu lange Aufgabe selbst für das
längste Leben — unter solcher Teilung würde gelitten haben, und die
ungeheuere Bestärkung Rodins zum métier kam mir da völlig zurecht,
um mir den Willen, in *Einem ganz* zu sein, in die innerste Mitte einzusetzen und ihm dort, bis ans Ende, recht zu geben. Aber ich hatte
nicht das in diesem Sinn so hilfreiche métier Rodins, keines, das mir
mit solcher täglichen Greifbarkeit und Sicherheit im Sichtbaren, als
fortwährend vorhanden, beizustehen fähig gewesen wäre, — auch
fehlte mir jene Vitalität des großen Meisters, die ihn, nach und nach,
instand gesetzt hatte, seiner Inspiration unaufhörlich mit so viel Ar-
beits-Vorschlägen entgegenzutreten, daß sie nicht umhin konnte, auf
*einen* der angebotenen, fast ohne daß eine Pause entstand, einzugehen.
Dieser mit Überlegenheit und nicht ohne List herbeigeführte 'accord'
machte den gewaltigen Künstler seiner Inspiration so sicher, daß er
ihre Existenz und ihren Eingriff geradezu leugnen durfte: ihre ihm
immer erreichbare Schwingung unterschied sich in nichts mehr von
seiner eigenen Kraft, er verfügte über sie wie über sich selbst. . . .[1]

This Rilke could write in the wisdom of retrospect, with his
development completed and his greatest work accomplished. But
in the Rodin years Rilke was only at the beginning of the road, the
completed Elegies and the Sonnets were nearly twenty years away,
and his immediate programme was a diligent—if, at least in the
early stages, and by comparison with the above passage, largely
uncritical—application to Rodin's artistic principles and method of
work. For the moment, Rodin was to be the answer to all his
difficulties. Angelloz enumerates the third lesson as 'avoir de
la patience'.[2] This lesson is a corollary to the other two, and
can again be seen as proceeding naturally from the nature of
the sculptor's medium. In one sense it had a particular relevance
for Rilke, who was to wait so long for the consummation of his
task. But, once more, we may detect the essential difference
between its application to the two men. For Rodin, patience

[1] Ibid., pp. 135–6.        [2] Ibid., p. 191.

evolved *from* and *with* the pursuit of his work, it was produced by his work; for Rilke, it could be associated *only with his periods of non-work*, it was the antidote to frustration, the quality which alone could make his long spells of inactivity bearable.

These, then, are the three primary lessons which Angelloz notes as being inculcated by Rodin: 'vivre'; 'travailler'; 'avoir de la patience'. The last two are not without ambiguity in the context of the contrast between the two art forms. But Rilke's association with Rodin lasted nearly four years, and in its early stages the poet was not so conscious of the doubts, the underlying conflict in the relationship, and the frustration, the feeling of impotence, which were to become manifest to him later. It is interesting to note that, in the first flush of his new enthusiasm, Rilke himself also fastened on to Rodin's cardinal principle of 'travailler' and accepted it as a major contribution to his own evolution. We may recall the well-known words of the famous letter to Rodin of 11 September 1902:

> Ce n'est pas seulement pour faire une étude, que je suis venu chez vous, — c'était pour vous demander: comment faut-il vivre? Et vous m'avez répondu: en travaillant. Et je le comprends bien. Je sens que travailler c'est vivre sans mourir. Je suis plein de reconnaissance et de joie. Car depuis ma première jeunesse, je ne voulais que cela. Et je l'ai essayé. Mais mon travail, *parce que je l'aimais tant*, est devenu pendant ces années une chose solennelle, une fête, attachée à des inspirations rares. . . Mais en tout ce qui était raisonnable sans doute, je n'ai pas eu le courage de remporter les inspirations lointaines en travaillant. Maintenant je sais que c'est le seul moyen de les garder.[1]

Leaving aside for the present the incomplete validity of the injunction, as from a plastic artist to a poet, there is another noteworthy aspect of this question. Stripped of its origin, of the magical aura with which the name of Rodin surrounded it, the counsel of hard work is seen as a very simple recipe, one which could have been given him by a hundred people—by people, even, outside the world of art. But for Rilke, only a man admired almost to the point of worship, a man whose majestic prestige invested even his simplest words with oracular properties, could administer the lesson; a man, above all, whom Rilke could watch putting the grand concept into practice, who proved precept by example.

More important than Rodin's precepts were the indirect and

---

[1] *G.B.*, Bd. I, pp. 266-7.

incidental effects of the association, and it is in this connexion that we may pass to the vital question of the radical change which came over Rilke's poetry during this period. It was in practical matters that the sculptor could most help the dreaming, excessively subjective, and self-centred poet. Rilke's early weaknesses stemmed from the fact that he was, in some respects, too liberally endowed with poetic gifts. His failing, of possessing too great a facility without compensating discipline, has already been mentioned.[1] The very richness of his talents could easily have caused him, like Lamartine and Byron, to fall short of the best, had he not, at this critical stage of his development, been directed by Rodin to pursuits which drew his thoughts away from himself, enhanced the effectiveness of his natural ability by introducing the wholesome element of conscious effort, and thereby taught him restraint, control, and selection. The weakness and the corrective are well noted by Angelloz:

. . . son talent s'épanchait en un flot de vers qui lui paraissaient nés d'une nécessité intérieure; jamais il n'appliquait à ses créations la critique de sa raison, jamais il ne retouchait ce qui lui semblait dicté par l'inspiration souveraine. Rodin, qui niait l'inspiration, remettait son ouvrage sur le métier jusqu'à ce qu'il eût obtenu l'effet qu'il avait conçu.[2]

The first advantageous result, therefore, of seeing Rodin at work, and above all of being able to experience the finished product in visible and tangible form, was to wean Rilke away from his hyper-sensitivity and force him to concentrate his attention on things outside himself. This process of occupying himself with external objects and of increasing his powers of observation was further promoted in various ways under Rodin's guidance. On the latter's advice, Rilke spent many hours in the Jardin des Plantes, and, as Angelloz points out, he was not merely concerned with the superficial observation of the external appearance of the animals, but studiously attempted to probe their character and consciousness. In the words of this critic, 'c'est peut-être au conseil bourru et bizarre en apparence de Rodin que la poésie allemande doit *La Panthère*, dans laquelle nous verrons une des créations les plus achevées de Rilke'.[3] And, of course, Rilke saw Paris in a way that he had never seen any other city, certainly not Moscow and St. Petersburg. In addition, Rodin took him to the great cathedrals

[1] p. 28.    [2] Op. cit., p. 194.
[3] Ibid., p. 195.

and instructed him in a knowledgeable appreciation of Gothic architecture. As well as diverting his attention away from himself and sharpening his sensory perception—especially training him in the art of seeing—these pursuits had the further immeasurably valuable result of vastly enriching the poet's store of general experience. A final—and not the least significant—item may be noted in the list of Rilke's acquisitions: Rodin piloted him through the task of improving his knowledge of the language and stimulated his reading of French literature. This stimulus will come under discussion again when the influence of Baudelaire is examined.

The collection of poems most closely related to the Rodin years and in which the effects of the association are most clearly and most consistently demonstrated is the *Neue Gedichte*. Written between 1903 and 1907, they do, in fact, enclose the greater part of the Rodin years. In the light of Rodin's influence, we may expect to find indeed something 'new' in the poetry; we may expect a swing away from the personal, emotional outpouring of Rilke's earlier work, more objectivity, and a marked emphasis on the visual element. One of the most helpful of Rilke's expositors, C. M. Bowra, noting this change to a 'more sincere, less personal and in some senses less intimate' kind of poetry, comments: 'But in it he found the real range of his gifts. His earlier books seem to have been a preparation for it. They taught him his craft and showed him what he could do and could not do. At last he wrote poetry that no one else could have written.'[1] We may perhaps qualify the statement that Rilke's earlier books taught him his craft by adding that he was very much exercised in learning his craft in Paris, and that he was, in fact, to go on learning it all through his life. The Rodin experience was itself responsible for a radical modification in his artistic concept, and therefore in his craftsmanship.[2] But that the early works were a necessary preparation is unquestionable, if only because they represented a tradition and a conception of poetry for Rilke to react against. The swing, during the Rodin years, away from the former exaggerated emotionalism and subjectivity was for Rilke the widest travel of the pendulum. Ultimately, in the years to come, when the corrective process and his own development were complete, Rilke was to find the balance between the two extremes. After noting the impact of France and Rodin, Bowra further comments that, instead of among dreams,

[1] Op. cit., p. 58.                    [2] Cf. p. 43.

Rilke lived among works of visual art until he wished to make his own poems self-sufficient and perfectly wrought like them. He essayed 'the patient, passive, absorbing state of the aesthete', though he demanded more than the mere collection of impressions and sensations. They must be reduced to order and turned into art, just as the medieval stonemason transformed his feelings into the permanence of a cathedral. The poet's experiences must be transmuted into something independent of himself, something existing in its own right.[1]

An interesting question arises here, one to which Bowra also refers, and one which will present itself even more prominently in the context of the Cézanne experience. Bowra justifiably places Rilke among the inheritors of Symbolism. We know, moreover, that, in so far as Rilke was drawn to any one particular group of poets, his tastes were strongly disposed towards the French Symbolists, including their precursor, Baudelaire, and their successor, Valéry. With the exception of Rimbaud, all the notable names associated with the movement figure among Rilke's translations. This is historical fact, even without any supporting literary evidence we may find as we examine his poetry. The intriguing thought is whether, in view of the effects of Rodin's influence, we should not logically expect something rather different, at least during the Rodin years. Do not these effects—the move away from preoccupation with self, the conscious effort towards greater objectivity, the attention to the visual element—look very like the blueprint of the poetic principles of the Parnassians? In the event, as we shall see by placing a poem by Rilke against one by Leconte de Lisle, the likeness did not materialize in practice, even though Rilke might aim for, and achieve, a technical perfection comparable with that of Le Parnasse. To illustrate the contrast, we may profitably take, on the one hand, *Der Panther*:

> Sein Blick ist vom Vorübergehn der Stäbe
> so müd geworden, daß er nichts mehr hält.
> Ihm ist, als ob es tausend Stäbe gäbe
> und hinter tausend Stäben keine Welt.
>
> Der weiche Gang geschmeidig starker Schritte,
> der sich im allerkleinsten Kreise dreht,

---

[1] Op. cit., pp. 59–60. Rilke was even more than the 'passive aesthete'. Under Rodin, he actively sought impressions.

ist wie ein Tanz von Kraft um eine Mitte,
in der betäubt ein großer Wille steht.

Nur manchmal schiebt der Vorhang der Pupille
sich lautlos auf —. Dann geht ein Bild hinein,
geht durch der Glieder angespannte Stille —
und hört im Herzen auf zu sein.[1]

The illustration may be brought into greater relief by selecting
from Leconte de Lisle a poem which also treats an animal subject,
*Le Colibri*:

Le vert colibri, le roi des collines,
Voyant la rosée et le soleil clair
Luire dans son nid tissé d'herbes fines,
Comme un frais rayon s'échappe dans l'air.

Il se hâte et vole aux sources voisines,
Où les bambous font le bruit de la mer;
Où l'açoka rouge, aux odeurs divines,
S'ouvre, et porte au cœur un humide éclair.

Vers la fleur dorée il descend, se pose,
Et boit tant d'amour dans la coupe rose,
Qu'il meurt, ne sachant s'il l'a pu tarir.

Sur ta lèvre pure, ô ma bien-aimée,
Telle aussi mon âme eût voulu mourir
Du premier baiser qui l'a parfumée!
(*Poèmes et Poésies*)

There is no mistaking the different conception behind these two
poems. On the surface, *Der Panther* is just a description of a caged
beast; the poet himself does not intrude, the first person does not
occur, the personality of the observer is carefully withheld, no
judgement is expressed. And yet the poem is charged with power
and feeling. Not merely are the visible happenings inside the cage
described, but the whole character of the animal is penetrated;
Rilke, without protesting, completely identifies himself with the
emotions and the nature of the panther. His sympathy with its
plight and his tender compassion are transmitted all the more
impressively for being left unsaid. After the unrestrained torrent
of 'stated' emotion of the early works, Rilke has begun to learn the

[1] *A.W.*, Bd. I, pp. 189–90.

lesson that feelings can often be more eloquently and powerfully expressed by what is left unspoken.[1] But that this poem is redolent of feeling there can be no doubt.

*Le Colibri* is very different. Here one can see, not the controlled abstention practised by Rilke, which serves only to intensify what Bowra calls the 'assault on the emotions',[2] but the studied and deliberate effort on the part of the poet to withdraw completely from the object. There is no bond between him and the bird, he remains detached; he does not identify himself with his subject in any way, but seeks merely to produce a visual effect by means of words. Even the transition to the first person in the closing lines does not modify this judgement, for this ostensible sentiment is nothing more than a conventional device which could never be confused with genuine experience. *Le Colibri* is, in fact, a cameo, highly polished, beautifully turned and balanced, a faultless example of its kind, but standing in the same relationship to *Der Panther* as a perfectly finished, machine-made article does to the sympathetically conceived and fashioned handiwork of the craftsman.

The cold, marmoreal quality of the poetry of the Parnassians was not for Rilke. In a passage in which he comments on Leconte de Lisle's *Les Éléphants*, which, he says, appeals to the 'inner eye', Bowra confirms this assessment of the two styles: 'His [sc. Rilke's] poems were much more than pictures in words; much more went into their making than what he had seen. However independent he wished his poetry to be, its independence would not be of the impersonal, pictorial, Parnassian kind.'[3]

The root of the difference between the two styles is that Rilke would and could never eliminate his feelings and personality from his art in the calculated and uncompromising way which characterizes the Parnassian conception of poetry; for him, objectivity was comparative, not absolute. But, in drawing this line between them, it is important to note, keeping in mind Rilke's affinity with the French Symbolists, that, just as Le Parnasse was a reaction against the excesses of Romanticism and was therefore a consequence of the latter, so Symbolism had followed and grown out of Le Parnasse, and to that extent had assimilated and retained those elements of the Parnassian concept which were in harmony with its own poetic ideals. These elements were scrupulous attention to

---

[1] This lesson is taken to its conclusion under Cézanne.
[2] Op. cit., p. 67.     [3] Ibid., p. 60.

form and meticulous use of language, both of which were corner-
stones on which Rilke was building his new poetry. Thus can be
seen the points of contact and divergence between Rilke, the
Romantics, the Parnassians, and the Symbolists, though more
remains to be said later of Rilke's links with the Symbolists. It is
too often forgotten that the so-called artistic schools and movements—which are sometimes ill-defined and frequently owe their
denomination to historical convenience—cannot be isolated into
separate and independent compartments. The changes in the
conception and practice of art in different historical periods
represent a continuous process of evolution, and each movement
owes its existence to what has gone before and, in particular,
emerges from its immediate predecessor. Rilke's own development
offers interesting food for thought in this connexion. In a matter
of only a few years he had passed from Romanticism to something
which approximated to Symbolism. In this short space of time,
and in the life and experience of one man, was therefore compressed
an evolutionary process which in the history of French poetry as a
whole had taken place over a period of something like half a century.
Even if Rilke is seen as catching up with his own retarded development, the transition is still remarkable; and he still had a lot
further to go. This capacity for continual and rapid change and
self-adjustment is one of the significant features of Rilke's career,
and effectively insulated him against membership of any school or
group. An individualist, Rilke brushed against several literary
movements, but belonged to none.

   *Der Panther* may, for several reasons, be suitably examined
in greater detail as a basis for appraising the effects of Rodin's
influence on Rilke's poetry. Written in 1903, it was a first-fruit
of the Rodin experience; it demonstrates admirably how the
lessons which have been noted as being inculcated by the sculptor
were translated into practice; and it is, moreover, one of the most
accomplished short poems Rilke ever wrote. Above all, Rilke had
a special regard for this poem and looked upon it as a milestone
in his artistic progress—a fact which he acknowledges in a letter
to the Gräfin Manon zu Solms-Laubach, dated 16 September
1907.[1] And nearly twenty years later, in the last months of his life,
his memory of the genesis of this poem remained undimmed and
his estimate of its significance unchanged. On 17 March 1926, in

[1] *G.B.*, Bd. II, p. 374.

the revealing letter 'An eine junge Freundin' referred to in the previous chapter, he wrote:

Unter dem großen Einfluß Rodins, der mir eine lyrische Oberflächlichkeit und ein billiges (aus lebhaft bewegtem, aber unentwickeltem
Gefühl stammendes) À peu près überwinden half, durch die Ver-
pflichtung, bis auf Weiteres, wie ein Maler oder Bildhauer, *vor der*
Natur zu arbeiten, unerbittlich begreifend and nachbildend. Das erste
Ergebnis dieser strengen guten Schulung war das Gedicht Der Panther
— im Jardin des Plantes in Paris —, dem man diese Herkunft ansehen
mag.[1]

In the detachment of this long backward look, Rilke was able to see very clearly not only the decisive operation 'dieser strengen guten Schulung', but the artistic weaknesses, the immaturity, the lack of discipline, the 'à peu près' with which he came to Rodin.

The first impression gained from *Der Panther* is of the minute observation which has gone into its making. Each movement and feature relevant to the effect to be created is carefully recorded; not a detail is missed which will heighten the emotive force of the picture. Not the least impressive aspect of the thoroughness of the poet's observation is the strict pruning of everything which is not essential, such as the size and colour of the animal. He could easily have over-elaborated, but by careful selection the impression is immeasurably enhanced. The physical features described are few, but they are vital: the look passing back and forth behind the bars of the cage; the soft, padded walk, the supple, powerful steps which are forced into small circles by the confinement of the prison; the movement of the eyelid; the flexed, poised tranquillity of the limbs—these are the frame on which the poem is built. The next stage is the imaginative expansion of each of these physical details: the look betrays a tiredness which renders it no longer capable of holding visual impressions, it has become an exhausted, empty stare; the repetitive circular progress suggests a dance of power around a central point; and finally, the continuity of the unseeing gaze is suddenly broken by the silent, scarcely per-ceptible, but dramatic upward motion of the eyelid, letting in a picture which percolates through the limbs and which ceases to exist only when it can go no further, when it has reached the hidden heart.

[1] *G.B.*, Bd. V, pp. 409–10.

Rilke's concern, learnt from Rodin, to go beneath the surface, to penetrate the nature of his subject, has already been mentioned;[1] and enough has been said of *Der Panther* to show that it is no mere superficial recital of externals. But there is a third, and still more important, phase in the construction of the poem which grows out of the other two. Rilke starts with the physical attributes, which in turn are seen as revealing the mood and mental state of the animal. Lastly, the progress from the particular to the general is taken a stage further: the endless march of the animal multiplies the bars of the cage into a thousand,

> und hinter tausend Stäben keine Welt.

With a few terse strokes, and with powerful and arresting imagery, Rilke has broadened immensely the scope of his picture. However many times the prison is magnified, the efforts, the living motions of the animal, are wasted; the end is still disillusion and despair, the prison remains, and beyond the bars there is no world. There is a wealth of suggestiveness in this line, closing, as it does, with sombre emphasis with the words 'keine Welt'. For all the relentless and undiminished strength of the beast, for all the nobility of its struggle and its courageous refusal to yield, it cannot destroy its prison; this is not life, but the nihilism of a mere existence, terrible in its mechanical repetition and for its revelation of the infinite capacity for life, if the bars were not there. The mighty will is stupefied; each successive visual picture enjoys a brief life as it courses through the limbs, which themselves create the illusion of life, but fades into oblivion when it reaches the heart, which is the seat of life, but which, when it is empty and dead with hopelessness, must annihilate everything which comes to it. As the poem develops, as its ambit widens and its evocativeness is intensified, so the vision of the reader expands until he is no longer conscious of the particular. The subject is no longer just a panther in the Jardin des Plantes; it has become the symbol, the representative of all strong beasts in captivity everywhere. The application of the poem is universal.

This, then, was the influence of Rodin at work: the patient, accurate observation, the sympathetic attention to and identification with something outside the poet himself, and withal the studied effort to penetrate beneath the surface. Here was no

[1] p. 55.

'lyrische Oberflächlichkeit', no 'billiges à peu près'. The same technique can be seen in *Die Flamingos*,[1] also a product of the visits to the Jardin des Plantes. It does not have the emotive power and the tension of *Der Panther*, though Bowra is perhaps too severe in calling it a failure.[2] It is less successful because of the nature of the subject, which, as Bowra points out, is not really suited to Rilke's gifts.[2] The nature of the subject, with the dominant effects of immobility, or at most only occasional and leisurely movement, and the vivid interplay of colours, is essentially visual, giving little opportunity to exploit the emotions. *Die Flamingos* is, nevertheless, a polished and finely balanced poem which is worth noticing as an illustration of Rilke's approach to a subject to which, in contrast to the panther, he was not perfectly attuned. Other poems on 'natural' subjects occur in the *Neue Gedichte*, such as *Persisches Heliotrop* (to which Bowra applies the same criticisms as he does to *Die Flamingos*), *Die Gazelle*, *Schwarze Katze*, *Der Apfelgarten*. To all of them—some less, some more successful, though none of the quality of *Der Panther*—the same critical criteria apply, and in all the same poetic method has been used.

It is not difficult to see why Rilke set such store—and rightly— by *Der Panther*. Written so early in his association with Rodin, he could fairly look back on it as an important landmark; and at the time, he could hopefully regard it as a favourable augury for the future. It is interesting to consider how, in this poem, Rilke resolved the central problem of reconciling the diligent and zealous pursuit of the sculptor's approach to the subject, to which he had committed himself, with the very different nature and demands of his own medium. (It is reasonable to assume that, at this stage of his relationship with Rodin, he had not yet begun to think of the problem theoretically, and to this extent we may conclude that his solution was empirical.) Put in another way, the problem was how to extract the maximum gain from Rodin's advice and example without limiting or jeopardizing the scope and flexibility of his own medium and, above all, without sacrificing his own individuality and rich intuition. The answer has been partly supplied in the above evaluation of the poem. The poet certainly keeps himself in the background, he points no moral and makes no direct judgement; but he does *suggest*. Had Leconte de Lisle

---

[1] *A.W.*, Bd. I, p. 189.     [2] Op. cit., p. 67.

written on this subject,[1] the result would have been no more than
an enumeration, aesthetically pleasing and technically perfect, of
physical features and visible manifestations. But Rilke could not
withdraw that far; he could not stifle his feeling without denying
himself, and, in poetry as in life, he was always ill at ease with the
purely factual. The way in which emotion is introduced is subtle
and controlled, but it is there. He does not know that the fixed gaze
of the panther betokens frustration; he infers it. There are not
really a thousand bars to the cage; it is only by projecting himself
into the existence and movements of the animal, by the operation
of the creative vision, that the image is expanded into something
greater than the object actually seen by the eye. Leconte de Lisle
would have been content to record the animal walking in circles;
but Rilke sees the repeated, monotonous movement as a dance,
at the centre of which is a great will. And Rilke does not know that
the beast takes in a visual picture every time the eyelid moves; nor
that this visual impression proceeds through the muscular limbs
to the heart. It is this constant working of the poet's inner vision,
the unobtrusive, scarcely perceptible commentary of the imagination, raising and transmuting the physical into the stuff of mind
and the emotions, which gives the poem its distinctive character
and prevents it from becoming a mere statuesque portrayal. In this
way, Rilke retains his poetic individuality and integrity even while
obeying Rodin's counsel and honouring his methods.

A few final remarks on this poem are needed, which are of
particular relevance in the context of our study of the development
of Rilke's use of language. Such is the wealth of impressions packed
into *Der Panther*, and so complex and compelling are the feelings
aroused, that it comes as something of a surprise to the reader to
find that all this has been achieved in a matter of only twelve lines.
This concision and economy of words—a notable feat by any
standards—is a marked step forward from the prolixity and diffuseness of the earlier works. *Der Panther* is complete; short as it is,
not one word could be added. Thus, even at this early date,
the impact of France can be seen. Already Rilke is learning the

[1] It is true that Leconte de Lisle wrote such poems as *Le Rêve du jaguar* and
*La Panthère noire*. But he purports to portray the animal in its natural state;
he does not treat it in captivity. And even in these poems, although the reader
may find sections where the emotional participation of the poet appears a little
greater, the general comments on Leconte de Lisle's handling of animal subjects
and on the contrast between him and Rilke remain valid.

disciplined and critically informed handling of language; he is developing the mastery by which, through careful selection and skilful placing, the utmost emotive value is extracted from every word.

The *Neue Gedichte* range widely, from things which Rilke saw about him with the new capacity for seeing learnt from Rodin to legendary and biblical subjects—although some of the latter are evidently inspired by paintings rather than by the episodes themselves. Inevitably the quality of these poems varies considerably. As has been indicated in the reference to *Die Flamingos*, the success of a poem during this phase of Rilke's career was in proportion to the sympathy which he instinctively felt with his subject —a limitation which will be discussed later when a final assessment is made of the Rodin experience. As is to be expected, some of these poems are inspired by works of sculpture. An example is *Die Fensterrose*:

> Da drin: das träge Treten ihrer Tatzen
> macht eine Stille, die sich fast verwirrt;
> und wie dann plötzlich eine von den Katzen
> den Blick an ihr, der hin und wieder irrt,
>
> gewaltsam in ihr großes Auge nimmt, —
> den Blick, der, wie von eines Wirbels Kreis
> ergriffen, eine kleine Weile schwimmt
> und dann versinkt und nichts mehr von sich weiß,
>
> wenn dieses Auge, welches scheinbar ruht,
> sich auftut und zusammenschlägt mit Tosen
> und ihn hineinreißt bis ins rote Blut —:
>
> So griffen einstmals aus dem Dunkelsein
> der Kathedralen große Fensterrosen
> ein Herz und rissen es in Gott hinein.[1]

The treatment of the inanimate may well be thought to present the greatest difficulty of all to a poet of Rilke's temper; and it is true that such subjects could not produce a poem quite of the calibre of *Der Panther*; but even when he was dealing with the inanimate, Rilke never lapsed into the purely descriptive. In *Die Fensterrose*, even though the poet is treating a subject with ostensibly a purely visual appeal, the subtle way in which he weaves in a powerful emotive thread invests the poem with an unmistakable

---

[1] *G.W.*, Bd. III, p. 38.

compulsion. It has a dynamism which could hardly be anticipated from the title. The poetic imagination and creative vision which see the rose-window as a living organism possessing the irresistible power of attraction of a whirlpool give the subject a motive force which makes the poem pulsate with feeling. The fundamental truth is that, however conscientiously he practised the method of observation taught by Rodin, however strongly he reacted to visual impressions, and however careful he was to be accurate in detail, for Rilke the eye was always an auxiliary member. Its function was, if not subordinate to, at most coequal with that of feeling. This view is supported by Bowra, who also points out that Rilke could escape from the deep pity which certain sights aroused only by translating it into poetry; and he further reminds us that these things were not always the accepted objects of pity.[1]

The *Neue Gedichte* can, therefore, be said to be successful on the whole, certainly a notable advance on anything Rilke had written previously. If there were failures among them, it can be argued that no poet can write masterpieces all the time. But the final weighing up of this collection and of the Rodin experience must go deeper than this. One basic fact must not be forgotten: for the first time in his life Rilke was attempting to conform to a definite artistic concept; he was writing largely according to a calculated formula, a formula, moreover, which was not evolved by himself, but prescribed for him by someone else—and that an artist in a different medium. It was a mode of approach which was well suited to the inspiration and technique of the sculptor, but which, although it could, as we have seen, be fruitful to the poet in certain circumstances, had patent limitations when transplanted into the realm of literature. This is not to say that Rilke was wrong in his enthusiastic pursuit of Rodin's ideals, for the latter provided a very necessary corrective, and that at a time when Rilke needed it most; and it is inconceivable that he could have become the poet he did eventually become without these richly rewarding years. But it will explain why Rodin could not supply the final answer to the poet's problems, why there had to be a term to the association, and why before the end of the association and for some time after it Rilke was beset with doubts and disillusionment and a sense of incapacity.

First, we return briefly to the primary problem of the different

[1] Op. cit., p. 67.

media in which the two artists worked.[1] In the last analysis, there could be no compromise between the two arts, demanding, as they do, a completely different creative approach. Rilke was, in fact, doing no more than go through the outward motions of the sculptor's approach. Between the hard, inanimate stone and the mobile, intangible, elusive material of the poet there is a gulf which cannot be bridged. The two men could confront each other across this gulf, they could communicate with each other; but they could not meet. In the last resort, Rilke had to turn back and rely upon his own resources; his whole thought-process and imagination had to be geared to the exigencies of a material which was dynamic and organic.

This fundamental distinction is underlined by an interesting incident recorded by Angelloz,[2] in which Rodin undertook to demonstrate movement in a piece of his sculpture—a demonstration which, as the critic stresses, was bound to lure Rilke, who had the advantage over the sculptor or the painter of inscribing his work in time and not in space. Well might this question of movement engage Rilke's attention, and the very fact that it did so is symptomatic of his incipient awareness of the barrier which divided him from Rodin. For movement was the one thing the sculptor could never create; he could create only its illusion. We are thus confronted with the interesting contradiction of two men trying to reach out in opposite directions, beyond the circumscribing limits of their media: Rodin, on the one hand, was striving for movement, for the impossible; on the other, Rilke, under the influence of Rodin and seeking to imitate him, was aiming to produce the stability and solidity and self-contained completeness of a work of sculpture.

Beside this juxtaposition of irreconcilables—stone and language —Mallarmé's preoccupation with music is much more intelligible, even though it was unsatisfactory for other reasons and led him into a state of advanced abstraction which reduced him to silence. At least language and music both belong on the same side of the general division between the arts; they both represent Herder's 'Energie' and Lessing's 'Nacheinander'; they can even coexist in a single work of art. This is to not say that we should wish Rilke's predilections to have been otherwise, for, as we have observed, it was fortunate that he had recourse to the other extreme of the

[1] See pp. 46 f.                    [2] Op. cit., p. 194.

representational arts.[1] For in this tempting correspondence between language and music lay a deception upon which Mallarmé
came to grief; Rilke, who in the end was bound to accept the
incompatibility of sculpture and poetry as regards their power
to fertilize each other, was in no such danger. One of the greatest
benefits of Rilke's sojourn with sculpture was that it had to come
to an end. Mallarmé's tragedy was that, because of the tantalizing
and illusory similitude between poetry and music, his preoccupation with the latter never came to an end.

To the antithetical qualities of tangibility and intangibility, and
immobility and movement, which effectively separate the media of
the sculptor and the poet, must be added the most significant and
distinctive feature of all. It is that, alone among artists, the writer
uses words, which have meanings. This point was emphasized in
a different context in the first chapter,[2] where the broader implications of language were discussed at some length. Its importance
in the present context of the Rodin experience lies in the consequent recognition that, whereas sculpture (painting and music
as well) is sensorily perceived, poetry, even when it is appealing
to the emotions, is absorbed and interpreted by the intelligence;
though not an intellectual exercise, it does belong to the realm
of ideas, however swift or spontaneous the emotional or sensory
response to the words. Where in the other arts the effect produced
by the work proceeds through the senses and feelings to the intelligence (in some cases it may not reach the intelligence at all), in
literature the process is reversed. This vital distinction in the
nature of the artists' materials needs no amplification in its application to the Rilke–Rodin relationship. For it can be seen that
its significance reaches right back to the act of creation itself—and
even beyond, to the preparation for the creative act.

While we must, therefore, recognize the ultimate irreconcilability of the two media, it may be stressed again that such
recognition does not mean that Rilke's studious interest in sculpture
was valueless; neither can we forget that he reaped a rich incidental
harvest which he was able to put to fruitful use in the practice of
his own art. There can be no regret for these years. What it is
necessary to realize is that, in more senses than one, Rilke did
not go to Rodin with his eyes open; and his initial blindness to
the problems posed by the different natures of the media, and

[1] p. 19.                    [2] pp. 16–17 and 19.

the consequent extravagant hopes and reliance he placed on the association, while having the advantageous result of prolonging a relationship which was profitable in other ways and which above all anchored him firmly to France, inevitably made his final frustration all the greater, and perhaps even prolonged the years of comparative impotence which followed.

If the contrast between the media constituted the most obvious and insurmountable barrier between Rilke and Rodin, there was another disturbing aspect to Rilke's attempt to emulate the sculptor, though this, too, had its origin in the nature of the materials in which they worked. It will be recalled that Rodin's cardinal principle, and the one upon which Rilke seized so avidly, was that of hard work.[1] The manner in which Rodin worked has already been indicated;[2] and reference has been made to the fact that physical contact and manual skill play a large part as conditioning factors in the sculptor's creative process.[3] It is thus quite clear that, in accepting Rodin's principle while lacking the sculptor's means of putting that principle into effect, Rilke was laying the foundation of a deep inner conflict. As early as 1903, less than a year after his arrival in Paris, he had become conscious of the existence of a problem, though it is apparent that his incomplete knowledge of himself and of the requirements of his art prevented him from understanding all its implications and how closely it was linked to his uncritical acceptance of Rodin's prescription. On 10 August of that year he wrote to Lou Andreas-Salomé:

Du hast so wunderbar recht, liebe Lou: ich litt an dem übergroßen Beispiel, dem unmittelbar zu folgen meine Kunst keine Mittel bot; die Unmöglichkeit, körperlich zu bilden, ward Schmerz an meinem eigenen Leib, und auch jenes Angsthaben (dessen stofflicher Inhalt die enge Nähe von etwas zu Hartem, zu Steinernem, zu Großem war) entsprang aus der Unvereinbarkeit zweier Kunstwelten. . . .[4]

Discussing this question of work, Angelloz finds further evidence, eight months later, of the struggle building up within the poet. In another letter to Lou, dated 15 April 1904, Rilke, who had earlier prided himself on having written the *Geschichten vom lieben Gott* in a few days and *Die Weise von Liebe und Tod des Cornets Christoph Rilke* in one night, says that he will probably never again manage to write a book in ten days (or nights). He sees in this need

[1] p. 54.                      [2] pp. 50 and 51.
[3] p. 47.                      [4] *G.B.*, Bd. I, p. 384.

for more time a step towards the goal of continuous work. (His words make interesting reading in the light of what was to happen in the short space of a fortnight in February 1922.) But, Angelloz notes, Rilke is already admitting that he cannot escape all the troubles of a prolonged period of gestation, and this critic sees the coming conflict within the poet between, on the one hand, the will to work and, on the other, the impulse to give himself up to long-awaited inspiration. He aptly concludes: 'Il aura contre lui son extrême sensibilité et la matière même de son œuvre, le verbe, qui n'attend pas, comme le marbre, le ciseau du sculpteur et ses mains, créatrices de formes.'[1]

Rilke's longing to be able to produce his best all the time, to order, is understandable. It is the ambition of every poet. But it was not to be expected that the eager and perplexed young Rilke should see that, in a sense, time did not matter; that the process of trial and error, of alteration and modification, of destruction and re-creation, which characterized Rodin's chiselling, corresponded to the poet's own comparative failures, and even to his periods of gestation and silence as well; that the fact that a poem could be *physically* written in a few minutes was the poet's compensation both for the periods of creative impotence and for being spared the arduous and protracted physical effort demanded of the sculptor; and that, because of this, the poet could afford a certain measure of failure and silence, since, from the resistant and retarding quality of his medium and the prolonged nature of his task, the sculptor's expectation of completed works would normally be far smaller than the number accomplished by the poet. In short, the nature of Rodin's medium and work was such that the 'failure content' was disguised so that it was not apparent to Rilke as was his own.

From all this emerges the fact that Rilke's conflict was the direct outcome of the strength of his desire to succeed and the intensity with which he applied himself to Rodin's precepts and example. His aspirations during this period and the frustration implicit in them have been noted by other critics. Buddeberg, in a passage[2] which lends strong support to the present discussion, quotes an important extract from one of the poet's letters of these years: 'Das ist die Hauptsache, daß man nicht beim Träumen, beim Vornehmen, beim In-Stimmung-Sein bleibt, sondern immer mit

Gewalt alles in Dinge umsetzt' (Br. 02/06, p. 37). This critic appropriately uses the one word which best describes Rilke's uncritical approach to Rodin: exaggeration.

Van Heerikhuizen also places his finger on the aim which motivated Rilke during this period, and makes an interesting analysis of the reason for it.[1] He sees Rilke converted to the belief that the world had to be controllable, with art becoming a craft capable of being plied daily throughout the artist's life. In a later passage the same critic, surveying more generally the years 1902 to 1908, comments on the poet's inner conflicts in broader terms. He suggests that Rilke, under the influence of the French spirit, envisaged a distant classical ideal which clashed with his own 'romantic-intuitive' nature.[2]

One can see the dual nature of Rilke's inner conflict: first, there was a large intellectual content in Rodin's discipline, and for this reason it was bound to place a heavy strain on a man whose personality was predominantly emotional and intuitive, and who, in any case, was less equipped for it than most as a result of the lack of formal training in his youth (in going some way to making good this loss, however, Rodin conferred an immeasurable long-term benefit on his pupil). Secondly, in aspiring to a state of perpetual and uninterrupted artistic creation on the Rodin pattern, while remaining unpossessed of the quality of the sculptor's material and of the manual nature of his work, Rilke presented himself with an insoluble problem. For the crux of the matter is that the poet cannot create at the behest of his will. It is possible to command the body and secure obedience; it was possible for Rodin to go to his studio each day and take up his tools, even if only to destroy, or to put the finishing touches to something on which he had been at work for months. This was what continuous work meant for Rodin: each day achieving probably no more than an infinitesimal portion of a complete work of art, and sometimes undoing what he had done the day before. It is curious that Rilke failed to see that he could not prevail over his art 'mit Gewalt' for the simple reason that physical attributes play no part in the poet's creative process.

Finally, to the problem of medium and method of work must be added a third factor present in Rilke's poetry of this period, which, inasmuch as it imposed general aesthetic and artistic limitations

[1] Op. cit., p. 169.                    [2] Ibid., p. 218.

on him, contributed to the eventual decline in the impetus which
actuated this phase in his career. It is of particular importance
in evaluating the development of Rilke's poetic style, since it
touches his successful as well as his less successful poems. And it
is further significant in that it stemmed from an aspect of Rodin's
influence which was, in itself, salutary to the poet coming from the
first two parts of *Das Stunden-Buch*. Rilke's extreme swing away
from the subjectivity of his earlier work, achieved only by doing
considerable violence to his nature and his conception of the
making of poetry, which were essentially instinctive and 'inspirational', was characterized by his deliberate concentration on things
outside himself. He went out, as it were, and looked for his art
instead of waiting for it to germinate and come to fruition from
within. Valuable though this was, intrinsically, as a discipline, it
did mean, as we have seen, that he was disproportionately dependent on the harmony existing between himself and his subject;[1] he
was in a large measure at the mercy of his subject. The calculated
reliance on external impressions meant that, however happy the
result, the control over the success of the poem was vested, at least
in part, in the subject instead of belonging wholly to the poet.
Such a situation could not last indefinitely when the poet possessed
Rilke's strong individuality and fertile creative imagination. It
could be only a matter of time before his natural propensities,
never far below the surface, reasserted themselves as a counter-
corrective.[2]

The *Neue Gedichte* [says Bowra] were Rilke's first completely mature
poetry. But they pointed to something else. The strange imaginative
ideas which occasionally inform them were capable of development;
the symbols suggested might well be used for poetry more self-revealing.
And no poet can write in this way for ever. The most receptive of minds
may be dulled and cease to absorb any more. The most aesthetic of
poets may wish sooner or later to assert fully his private ideas. This
happened to Rilke.[3]

It is thus paradoxical that Rilke's concentration on objectivity
was both a limitation and a source of strength. It involved subduing
his natural talents, it meant a denial of himself; but it was instrumental in immeasurably increasing his mastery over his medium.
There can be no doubt that Rilke was an infinitely better craftsman

---

[1] p. 65.                    [2] Cf. p. 56.                    [3] Op. cit., p. 71.

after the Rodin years, that he gained something which he never lost: a greatly increased power over language. The end of what may be called Rilke's aesthetic period did not come immediately, although the parting from Rodin did mark the beginning of Rilke's retreat towards a middle road. The Cézanne experience was, ostensibly, a continuation of his preoccupation with visual impressions; but, in fact, as we shall see, it was an important landmark in his process of self-adjustment, in his progress towards achieving the ideal balance between the natural endowment of his richly imaginative and creative intuition and the discipline implicit in detached observation and selection. Rilke could never become the poet of the Elegies and Sonnets without effecting a marriage between instinct and some sort of intellectually imposed control. The one he possessed already; the other had to be won by long and hard schooling.

We can agree unreservedly with Angelloz when, commenting on Rilke's ill-judged equation of Rodin with Jacobsen, he says that Rilke's development would conceivably have been the same if, when he was twenty, his enthusiasm had been for someone other than the Danish writer; but that it is impossible to imagine him becoming what he did without Rodin's contribution and that of Paris.[1] In these years was laid the foundation upon which Rilke was able to build a more complete conception of his art than would ever have been possible otherwise. It was, in many ways, a strange partnership: the old and the young; the man at the height of his powers and achievements and the youthful and groping beginner; the artist in stone and the artist in language. Not all that Rilke hoped for from it could be realized, for the obstinate and insurmountable barrier of their respective media lay between them. Rodin's counsel and example, governed as they were by the nature of his material, could have only restricted validity for the poet, and in the years which followed, Rilke was assailed by greater doubts and problems than ever. But it was a healthy crisis, the crisis of self-examination. For Rodin had belatedly subjected Rilke to a planned and systematized training. We may value the *Neue Gedichte* for their own sake, based though they were upon an incomplete artistic concept; but of far greater importance is their promise for the future, their revelation of a new and maturer Rilke—a Rilke who had at last come to manhood. Here was a poet who not only

[1] Op. cit., p. 196.

felt, but who had learnt to think as well; a poet whose touch on his instrument was far more sure.

The aspects of the Rodin experience, coming, as it did, at such a crucial and opportune time in Rilke's life, are so complex and interrelated that it is difficult to isolate any one as being more important than the rest. To the deepening of the poet's knowledge of himself may be added the broadening of his horizon, the increased consciousness of life and the world around him, and especially of the great artistic heritage of France; in these years Rilke's lifelong association with France was ensured. Lastly, there was the profound impression made on Rilke by Rodin's indomitable will and unshakable determination, which rode imperiously over setbacks and disappointments. Rilke leaves us in no doubt of his reaction to the sculptor's apparent capacity to fashion his own destiny by an act of will:

> ... Und kamen Zweifel, kamen Ungewißheiten, kam die große Unge-
> duld der Werdenden zu ihm, die Furcht eines frühen Todes oder die
> Drohung der täglichen Not, so fand das alles in ihm schon einen stillen,
> aufrechten Widerstand, einen Trotz, eine Stärke und Zuversicht, alle
> die noch nicht entfalteten Fahnen eines großen Sieges.[1]

And again:

> Man wird einmal erkennen, was diesen großen Künstler so groß
> gemacht hat: daß er ein Arbeiter war, der nichts ersehnte, als ganz, mit
> allen seinen Kräften, in das niedrige und harte Dasein seines Werkzeuges
> einzugehen. Darin lag eine Art von Verzicht auf das Leben; aber
> gerade mit dieser Geduld gewann er es: denn zu seinem Werkzeug kam
> die Welt.[2]

To the young Rilke, who needed encouragement and assurance as much as he needed instruction, such an example provided the justification he sought for his chosen course; it reinforced his own faith in himself, and strengthened his resolve to carry on in the face of difficulties and disappointments—'die ungeheuere Bestärkung Rodins zum métier kam mir da völlig zurecht, um mir den Willen, in *Einem ganz* zu sein, in die innerste Mitte einzusetzen und ihm dort, bis ans Ende, recht zu geben.'[3]

Rilke's sense of indebtedness to Rodin and his awareness of the decisive importance of these years remained with him—we may

---

[1] *Auguste Rodin, G.W.*, Bd. IV, p. 312.        [2] Ibid., p. 372.
[3] See p. 53.

refer to the letter to Witold von Hulewicz, dated 14 December 1922.[1] And in the well-known letter to Hermann Pongs of 21 October 1924, we find perhaps the most percipient judgement of his association with Rodin that Rilke ever wrote:

Hier will ich, nochmals, (aus Ihrem Fragebogen entnehmend, wie sehr Sie sich weiter nach 'Einflüssen' umsehen) verweilen und betonen, wie weit dieser unmittelbare und vielfältige Einfluß des großen Bildhauers jeglichen, aus der Literatur stammenden, überwog und gewissermaßen überflüssig machte. Ich hatte das Glück, Rodin in jenen Jahren zu begegnen, da ich reif war für meine innere Entscheidung und da andererseits, für ihn, der Moment eingetreten war, die Erfahrung seiner Kunst in eigentümlicher Freiheit auf alles Erlebbare anzuwenden. Das Gegenteil von dem bei Tolstoj Beobachteten fand hier statt: Einer, der dem inneren Auftrag seiner gestaltenden Genialität, das unendliche göttliche Spiel, völlig und tätig bejaht hatte, nahm, mittels der dort erworbenen Einsicht, mehr als nur seine Kunst in Besitz . . .[2]

We may leave the Rodin years by drawing attention to the penetrating summary by Angelloz[3] of their place in Rilke's development and achievement, which he concludes with the significant judgement that 'avec *La Panthère; Orphée, Eurydice, Herm* èset d'autres œuvres semblables, la poésie allemande atteint un sommet comparable aux cimes goethéennes'.

[1] *G.B.*, Bd. V, p. 170.   [2] Ibid., pp. 328–9.
[3] Op. cit., pp. 219–20. We would qualify the parallel he draws in this passage between Rilke's work and Hugo's *La Légende des siècles* with the reminder that Rilke's poetry was essentially lyrical, whereas Hugo's great cycle was epic.

# IV

## CÉZANNE

ILKE'S discovery of the art of Cézanne was made in the autumn of 1907, and thus followed closely, by little more than a year, the parting from Rodin. (If one takes account of the fact that Rilke's preoccupation with Rodin continued after the separation,[1] the two experiences are brought even more closely together historically.) We may again wonder at the way in which the successive chapters in Rilke's life were linked in strict correlation, for, in retrospect, it is possible to see how vitally important Cézanne was as a sequel to Rodin. Not only was the Parisian counterpart to the double association of Worpswede with sculpture and painting brought to completion, but Cézanne can now be seen as making an indispensable contribution to Rilke's poetic evolution, a contribution the absence of which would have been an incalculable loss. And the particular value of this contribution lay in the fact that Rilke's acquaintance with Cézanne's paintings immediately followed his association with Rodin: before Rodin, Cézanne would have been meaningless; later in life, when other experiences had intervened, Rilke would have gained far less from contact with Cézanne's art, and might even not have noticed it at all. But the most remarkable feature of this episode in Rilke's career is the accidental manner in which it came about, on a Sunday morning walk. It was only because of Rodin that Rilke was ready for this encounter with Cézanne, whom Angelloz appropriately calls 'son deuxième Rodin'.[2]

The Cézanne experience has not generally received extensive treatment at the hands of Rilke's critics. The probable reasons for this are various: the episode was less spectacular than the association with Rodin, and its duration was much shorter; coming immediately after the much more publicized Rodin years, it has to a certain extent been dwarfed by the earlier event; the fact that there was no personal relationship (Cézanne had died in the

---

[1] The second part of *Auguste Rodin* appeared in 1907.
[2] Op. cit., p. 204.

previous year) has perhaps made this contact less attractive and interesting, superficially, than that with Rodin, and has also made it necessary to probe more deeply for its significance; and finally, it is more difficult to trace the effect that Cézanne had on Rilke's art, there being no collection of poetry comparable to the *Neue Gedichte*, by which the results of Rodin's influence can be so readily perceived. The most notable exception is again Angelloz, who has made a careful and shrewd examination of Cézanne's importance in Rilke's development. I believe that detailed consideration of the available evidence will demonstrate that those critics who have ignored the Cézanne experience completely, or who have given it only passing attention, have underestimated its significance in Rilke's evolution; that by doing so, moreover, they have left the Rodin experience itself incomplete.

Rilke's acquaintance with Cézanne was, in fact, a confirmation of the training and approach initiated by Rodin, though at the same time going beyond the latter. In the words of Angelloz: 'Rodin lui a ouvert la voie, Cézanne lui a montré le but.'[1] One significant difference between the influences of Rodin and Cézanne is that Rilke's relationship to the latter was a 'purer' experience for not being founded on personal contact; there was no distortion of artistic values or obscuring of real issues by the physical presence of a powerful personality. At the same time, he found much in Cézanne, too, which he had venerated in Rodin, and his letters leave no doubt that Cézanne's approach to his work and his mode of life fired the poet's imagination almost as much as the paintings themselves. For Cézanne pursued his art to the exclusion of all else. He was a man of iron self-discipline, a man of complete dedication, relentlessly carrying on with his work in the face of discomfort, ill health, the world's failure to understand him, and even local ridicule and persecution. (Angelloz makes an interesting allusion to the similarity between Cézanne's and Rodin's approach to their work.[2]) Again we may detect the self-consciousness, the sense of inferiority, which played such a prominent part in Rilke's psychological motivation. Uncertain of his capacity to succeed, and uneasy about the denial of domestic obligations and social responsibilities implicit in the solitary and self-centred way of life he had chosen, he was only too ready to grasp at anything which could justify him to himself. His attitude to Cézanne is indicative of the

[1] Op. cit., p. 206.　　　　[2] Op. cit., p. 205.

eager attempt to draw strength from someone who could give
him the assurance he needed. Cézanne provided at once a salve
for Rilke's conscience and the promise of final fulfilment, which
would vindicate any means he adopted to achieve the end. If there
is more than a hint of casuistry and selfishness in the way in which
Rilke placated his qualms, we may remind ourselves that he did
succeed in the end, and that he might well not have done so had he
lived his life differently and made a more conventional division
of his allegiance to his art and his family.[1]

But Cézanne held more for Rilke than mere dogged, unswerving
pursuit of the artistic ideal of perfection, important though this
was in itself. The poet's attention, still preoccupied with the
problems created by, and left unsolved at the end of, the association
with Rodin, was still concentrated on the representational arts, and
it is against this background that we must estimate the events of
1907. Angelloz stresses the vital nature of this stage in Rilke's
evolution.[2] It is, however, first necessary to remember the problems
arising from the nature of the artists' media which recurred constantly in the examination of Rodin's influence on Rilke.[3] The
remarks made then apply, in a large measure, in the present
context; if there are differences, they are, with one exception, of
degree rather than of kind, although in a process of maturing as
gradual as Rilke's even differences of degree are not without significance. But in the broad distinction between arts that are static
and those that are mobile, dynamic, Rilke was in the same relation
to Cézanne as he had been to Rodin. It is true that, because his
material has not the hardness and resistance of the sculptor's,
and because he is working in two dimensions instead of the sculptor's three, the duration of the creative act is frequently shorter
for the painter, and this may in some degree modify the nature of
the painter's inspiration so as to bring it, in the temporal sense, a
little closer to that of the poet; but the painting of a picture is still,
physically, a more prolonged operation, and its inspiration and
execution are distributed more evenly than is the case with a piece
of lyric writing. There is, moreover, present in painting, as in
sculpture, the element of physical dexterity: visual judgement of
form and proportion, and manual skill. (The close affinity between
the two art forms is exemplified by the fact that most sculptors are

[1] Cf. p. 35.                              [2] Op. cit., p. 204.
[3] See particularly pp. 46–47 and 66–68.

also competent draughtsmen and many painters model in three dimensions as well.) And there yet remains the factor which separates the writer from all other artists: the meaning of words.[1]

There is, however, one notable difference between painting and sculpture which is of particular relevance in the present discussion: the painter's use of and reliance on the effect of colour—a factor which has an importance for him comparable to that of form, and which at once establishes some measure of common ground between him and the poet. It will, in fact, be seen that colour plays a big part in Rilke's reaction to Cézanne. It may perhaps be unwise to press this point too far—this question will be referred to again later—but we may, nevertheless, see in this qualitative difference between the two arts, and in the cumulative, if lesser, significance of the differences of degree, the symbol of Rilke's progressive movement. The nature and magnitude of Rilke's preoccupation with the representational arts during these early, formative years, the character of his, a poet's, relationship to Rodin, and the manner in which the Rodin and Cézanne experiences followed each other as self-contained but inseparable episodes, are in themselves unusual. Since Rilke's development was to embrace major contacts with both sculpture and painting, it was important, if he was to gain the most from them, that they should come in the right order. The nature of Rilke's aim as an artist during this period and the appropriateness of the order in which events overtook him are well indicated by Angelloz:

Or, Rilke a été un impressioniste; mais, depuis son séjour à Worpswede et surtout depuis 1902, il aspire lui aussi à une synthèse plastique. Il la découvre, réalisée, dans la peinture, c'est-à-dire dans un art moins éloigné de la poésie que la sculpture. Non seulement l'exemple de l'artiste mais son œuvre elle-même devient un appui.[2]

A further factor which helps to make up the background against which the Cézanne experience should be judged is the fact that Rilke had painted before he turned to writing, from which we may perhaps infer a closer artistic bond with Cézanne than with Rodin. An interesting incidental point is that Rilke, although, as he confessed, untrained, revealed considerable perception and sympathy

---

[1] An interesting comparative discussion of poetry and painting occurs in Schiller's essay *Über Matthissons Gedichte*. See Schiller's *Sämtliche Werke* (Säkular-Ausgabe, Stuttgart and Berlin, c. 1904–5), Bd. XVI, pp. 250–70.

[2] Op. cit., p. 206.

as a critic of painting. But our principal concern is not with Rilke's knowledge of painting as such, nor even with whether his estimate of Cézanne is generally acceptable. The important fact is that Cézanne did make a tremendous impact on him. The essential questions to be considered are why Cézanne engaged Rilke's attention, and in what way the latter's artistic development was affected and furthered by the experience. Whether because of his early predisposition towards painting, whether because, for the reasons already adduced, especially the additional element of colour, Cézanne's medium was a stage nearer his own than that of the sculptor, or whether from causes more spontaneous, intuitive, and incalculable, Rilke was at once attracted by Cézanne's painting without any of the preliminary planning or the personal link (through his wife) which had contributed to the association with Rodin. And, in the resultant close study he made of the great French painter, Rilke believed, as will be seen, that he had found in Cézanne's art something immediate and personal which he could requisition for his own use. In fact, as with Rodin's doctrine of hard work, his most vital discovery was in the nature of a general principle, and need not have come from a painter (though again he reaped an incidental harvest).[1]

The chief source of reference on this subject is the series of letters, written between 6 October and 4 November 1907, which are known as the 'Cézanne-Briefe'.[2] The method of approach to this important evidence will be to examine the letters in chronological order. In this way it will be possible to trace the genesis and growth of Rilke's interest and study; by following the progressive revelation of the experience, the successive stages of assimilation, and the increasing force of the impact upon Rilke of Cézanne's art, we shall be able to estimate the extent and manner in which the latter was incorporated in, and modified, Rilke's own artistic concept.

The first letter, of 6 October, indicates the chance nature of the

[1] Cf. p. 54.
[2] These letters, all to Clara Rilke, are contained in the series which ends Bd. II and begins Bd. III of the *Gesammelte Briefe*. They run, though not consecutively, from no. 181 of Bd. II to no. 3 of Bd. III. They are eighteen in number, although in the selection published in 1954 entitled *Briefe über Cézanne* they are preceded by extracts from ten earlier letters written between 3 June and 4 October 1907. In this last selection the 'Cézanne-Briefe' themselves are edited to eliminate portions of the correspondence not relevant to Cézanne.

discovery: the conventional, contemplative Sunday morning walk
through the Faubourg Saint-Germain, the musings upon the old
aristocratic residences, the sight, at an upper window, of an old
lady, the rich, imagined interior of the apartment with the bright-
ness of the family silver drawing the light to itself—a picture of
a bygone age. He finds it hardly believable that this was the way
leading him into the Salon d'Automne.[1] The reference to Cézanne
is brief, but indicative of the force of the initial impression; it
reveals the transition from the mood conjured up by the effete
world of the past, which has no relevance for Rilke, to something
which at once fires his creative vision, something which belongs
to the present and the future, something which merely awaits
appropriation by the poet and invites the transmuting application
of his imagination. The old lady and her ornamental, stylized
setting are an anachronism: 'Cézanne ist für die alte Dame nicht
mehr möglich; aber für uns gilt er und ist rührend und wichtig.'[2]
The bond is sensed immediately and instinctively.

A letter on the following day, 7 October, records a further visit
to the Salon d'Automne, and it is noticeable that Rilke's impressions
are already crystallizing with greater precision and critical awareness. The powerful attraction of the Cézanne room is again evident,
and Rilke comments:

Da ist alle Wirklichkeit auf seiner Seite; bei diesem dichten wattierten
Blau, das er hat, bei seinem Rot und seinem schattenlosen Grün und
dem rötlichen Schwarz seiner Weinflaschen. Von welcher Dürftigkeit
sind auch bei ihm alle Gegenstände: die Äpfel sind alle Kochäpfel, und
die Weinflaschen gehören in rund ausgeweitete alte Rocktaschen.[3]

It is significant that in these first detailed remarks on Cézanne's art
the dominant theme is that of colour—the main point at which
poet and painter can meet. It is as though at the outset Rilke
perceived, if instinctively, that here was something which had
been lacking in the Rodin experience, and which—whether in
itself it had any aesthetic importance for himself or not—emblema-
tically represented a step onward. Such a reaction is fully in
keeping with one of Rilke's temperament, concerned, as he was,
to realize a synthesis between the representational arts and his own.
For in sculpture, because it lacks colour, more weight is thrown on
dimensions and 'measurability', and therefore on the intellectual

[1] *G.B.*, Bd. II, pp. 400–1.                    [2] Ibid., p. 402.
[3] Ibid., pp. 403–4.

content of the appraisal of the beholder. We may, therefore, infer that even more important to Rilke than the fact that the poet can also reproduce the effect of colour was the fact that, because no two people see a colour in the same way, the presence of this element in painting helped to restore the balance on the side of subjectivity in artistic appraisal. Nevertheless, in spite of this, colour still belongs to the realm of visual effect, and its significance to the poet is in general related to a conscious effort to objectivize. Rilke was thus still preoccupied with visual emphasis; the more subtle— and for him more vital—aspects of Cézanne's art were yet to come.

On 8 October Rilke interrupted his attendance at the Salon d'Automne by a visit to the Louvre, and it is clear that even the brief contact he has had with Cézanne's painting has already conditioned and sharpened his whole vision of pictorial art; his eye has become more discriminating. In the letter of this date he begins characteristically with a cautionary stricture on conventional, borrowed judgements, which can soon become mere vocal repetitions and which, in any case, because they emerge from and appeal to the intellect, destroy the all-important empirical nature of artistic appreciation. Again it is colour which dominates Rilke's attention: 'Als ob diese Meister im Louvre nicht gewußt hätten, daß es die Farbe ist, die die Malerei ausmacht.'[1] He notes the Venetians, who are 'von einer unbeschreiblich konsequenten Farbigkeit'.[1] He finally fastens on the quality of the blue of the eighteenth century, from which he traces the lineage through to Cézanne:

Denn Cézannes sehr eigenes Blau hat diese Abstammung, kommt von dem Blau des 18. Jahrhunderts her, das Chardin seiner Prätention entkleidet hat und das nun bei Cézanne keine Nebendeutung mitbringt. Chardin ist da überhaupt der Vermittler gewesen; schon seine Früchte denken nicht mehr an die Tafel, liegen auf Küchentischen herum und geben nichts darauf, schön gegessen zu sein. Bei Cézanne hört ihre Eßbarkeit überhaupt auf, so sehr dinghaft wirklich werden sie, so einfach unvertilgbar in ihrer eigensinnigen Vorhandenheit.[2]

It is interesting to note that, as with Rodin, Rilke is preoccupied with the artist's capacity to convey the true character, the reality, the 'dinghafte Wirklichkeit', the indestructible essence of an object, free from all 'Prätention'; it is art he wants, not artificiality, and in Cézanne he finds the consummate artist who can penetrate to the

---

[1] Op. cit., p. 404.    [2] Ibid., pp. 405–6.

very being of things, as did Rodin in sculpture.[1] The letter ends with a brief biographical reference to Cézanne's last years—a picture of the lonely, misunderstood, but successful artist which could not fail to commend itself to Rilke.[2]

The letter of 9 October is a long one, in which Rilke makes a comprehensive biographical survey of Cézanne. It is a notable and distinguished piece of writing, and not least remarkable is the careful and penetrating thought that Rilke gives to the technique of the great French painter. It is apparent that Rilke draws comfort and hope from the example of a man who did not begin to work seriously until he was nearly forty, but whose last thirty years consisted only of work:

Ohne Freude eigentlich, wie es scheint, in fortwährender Wut, im Zwiespalt mit jeder einzelnen seiner Arbeiten, deren keine ihm das zu erreichen schien, was er für das Unentbehrlichste hielt. La réalisation nannte er es, und er fand es bei den Venezianern, die er früher im Louvre gesehen und unbedingt anerkannt hatte. Das Überzeugende, die Dingwerdung, die durch sein eigenes Erlebnis an dem Gegenstand bis ins Unzerstörbare hineingesteigerte Wirklichkeit, das war es, was ihm die Absicht seiner innersten Arbeit schien.[3]

Inevitably Cézanne's perfectionism awakened an immediate response in Rilke. It was a quality which he had admired in Rodin, and which he possessed himself. Cézanne attained the heights by reaching for the impossible, and, in one of the most interesting passages in the correspondence, Rilke comments on Cézanne's deliberate choice of a technique which created difficulties for himself. In spite of age, sickness, exhaustion, ill-humour, ridicule, and maltreatment, Cézanne forced himself to paint, hoping for success in his work which he had, by this technique,

auf das eigensinnigste erschwert. Bei Landschaftlichem oder Nature morte gewissenhaft vor dem Gegenstand aushaltend, übernahm er ihn doch nur auf äußerst komplizierten Umwegen. Bei der dunkelsten Farbigkeit, deckte er ihre Tiefe mit einer Farbenlage, die er ein wenig über sie hinausführte und immer so weiter, Farbe über Farbe hinaus erweiternd, kam er allmählich an ein anderes kontrastierendes Bildelement, bei dem er, von einem neuen Zentrum aus, dann ähnlich

---

[1] It is appropriate to recall that Cézanne had died only in 1906. His reputation was thus to a considerable extent still *sub judice*, and Rilke's estimate of his art was therefore very much in the nature of pioneer criticism. It is a tribute to his taste and acumen that posterity has so fully endorsed his judgement.

[2] Op. cit., p. 406.  [3] Ibid., p. 407.

verfuhr. Ich denke mir, daß die beiden Vorgänge, des schauenden und sicheren Übernehmens und des Sichaneignens und persönlichen Gebrauchens des Übernommenen, sich bei ihm, vielleicht infolge einer Bewußtwerdung, gegeneinander stemmten, daß sie sozusagen zugleich zu sprechen anfingen, einander fortwährend ins Wort fielen, sich beständig entzweiten. Und der Alte ertrug ihren Unfrieden . . .[1]

The accuracy or otherwise of this record is less important than the revelation it gives of Rilke's own ideas of the creative act. It can be seen how much he is still drawn, as he had been with Rodin, to the conception of creation by an act of will, 'mit Gewalt'.[2] Difficulties are seen as being desirable in themselves, in so far as they present the artist with a challenge. Even the deliberate creation of difficulties for himself by the artist, inherent in Cézanne's technique, appears to be tacitly approved by Rilke as a virtue.

Rilke is clearly deeply impressed by the ruthless dedication of a man who would not forsake his work even to attend the funeral of his mother, of whom he was fond. And he further describes the incident of Cézanne's recognition of himself in Balzac's character, the painter Frenhofer—

den Balzac, in unglaublicher Voraussicht kommender Entwicklungen, in seiner Novelle des Chef d'Œuvre inconnu . . . erfunden hat und den er durch die Entdeckung, daß es eigentlich keinen Kontur gibt, sondern lauter schwingende Übergänge — an einer unmöglichen Aufgabe zugrunde gehen läßt, — dies vernehmend steht der Alte bei Tische auf . . . und, vor Erregung ohne Stimme, kommt er mit seinem Finger immer wieder deutlich auf sich zu und zeigt sich, sich, sich, so schmerzhaft das auch gewesen sein mag. Nicht Zola hatte es begriffen, um was es sich handelte; Balzac hatte vorausgeahnt, daß es beim Malen plötzlich zu so etwas Übergroßem kommen kann, mit dem keiner fertig wird.[3]

Rilke finds in many of Cézanne's opinions reminiscences of Rodin. His pen-portrait of Cézanne closes with the picture of the artist painting his poses from drawings made in Paris forty years earlier— 'wissend, daß Aix ihm kein Modell erlauben würde'[4]—and surrounded by his apples and wine-bottles: 'Und macht (wie van Gogh) seine "Heiligen" aus solchen Dingen; und zwingt sie, *zwingt sie*, schön zu sein, die ganze Welt zu bedeuten und alles Glück und

<hr>

[1] Op. cit., pp. 407–8.                                    [2] See pp. 70–71.
[3] Op. cit., p. 410. Cézanne and Zola, it will be recalled, were compatriots, and friends from early years.
[4] Ibid., p. 411.

alle Herrlichkeit, und weiß nicht, ob er sie dazu gebracht hat, es für ihn zu tun.'[1] Again it is the idea of success being achieved by compulsion, of the artist ruling his art by an act of force, which allures Rilke. He ends on a note which is expressive of his sense of community with Cézanne and of his growing consciousness that he was going through an experience which was contributing to his own development: 'Das wollte ich Dir alles erzählen; es hängt ja mit vielem um uns und mit uns selbst an hundert Stellen zusammen.'[1]

In the letter of 10 October Rilke returns to the pictures in the Salon d'Automne and describes the 'Déjeuner sur l'Herbe', in which he sees, in the pose of the women, Manet 'an jeder Stelle'.[2] The tone of this letter is more studious and less emotional; the first surprise of Cézanne's impact on him is over, and his approach is now more thoughtful. He concentrates his experience by narrowing his front and spending a long time with one or two paintings.[3] A mood of contemplative examination is being generated in which whatever lessons Cézanne has to offer can be assimilated.

The letter of 11 October contains no reference to Cézanne, although Rilke did visit the exhibition on this date. This visit, which is described in the following letter, dated 12 October, was made in the company of Mathilde Vollmoeller—'ganz malerisch geschult'[4]—whose judgement he had requested, 'um meinen Eindruck neben einem zu sehen, den ich für ruhig und nicht literarisch abgelenkt halte'.[5] Rilke is 'astonished' to find his opinion confirmed with exactly the same simile he had used in his letter of 9 October, when Fräulein Vollmoeller comments: ' "Wie ein Hund hat er davorgesessen und einfach geschaut, ohne alle Nervösität und Nebenansicht." '[6] Once more the link with Rodin, whose example and counsel had so notably enhanced Rilke's own powers of observation, is clearly visible. The letter continues with an interesting discussion on colour, with particular reference to the comparison between the works executed in Paris, when Cézanne was in the company of others, and those painted when he was alone:

In den ersten war die Farbe etwas für sich; später nimmt er sie irgendwie, persönlich, wie kein Mensch noch Farbe genommen hat,

[1] Op. cit., p. 412.
[2] Ibid., p. 414.
[3] Ibid., pp. 413–14.
[4] Ibid., p. 418.
[5] Ibid., p. 417.
[6] Ibid., p. 418; cf. ibid., p. 412.

nur um das Ding damit zu machen. Die Farbe geht völlig auf in dessen Verwirklichung; es bleibt kein Rest. Und Fräulein V. sagte sehr bezeichnend: 'Es ist wie auf eine Waage gelegt; das Ding hier, und dort die Farbe; nie mehr, nie weniger, als das Gleichgewicht erfordert. Das kann viel oder wenig sein: je nachdem, aber es ist genau, was dem Gegenstand entspricht.' . . . Auch fiel mir gestern sehr auf, wie manierlos verschieden sie [sc. die Bilder] sind, wie sehr ohne Sorge um Originalität, sicher, in jeder Annäherung an die tausendartige Natur sich nicht zu verlieren, vielmehr an der Mannigfaltigkeit die innere Unerschöpflichkeit ernst und gewissenhaft zu entdecken.[1]

There is, here, a marked advance in Rilke's perception of Cézanne's use of colour. It is no longer something which merely has a superficial appeal to the eye. It is an integral part of the object itself, something which may be neither over- nor under-rendered. This may seem a truism, but it may be asked how many people look at a painting in this way? And how many artists do not exaggerate their use of colour in order to intensify the purely visual *éclat*, thereby violating the sanctity of the object and departing from the truth? Cézanne is seen as achieving a perfect balance between object and colour; he acknowledges his duty to the object as being paramount, not to be compromised by the abuse of the immense— and tempting—resources of the medium at his command.

Despite the difference of medium, there does appear to be something here which can be reduced to a general artistic principle, and which Rilke could therefore himself adopt and apply to his own work. This principle may perhaps be expressed as artistic integrity. The stress laid by Rilke on Cézanne's scrupulous devotion to the inviolate nature of the object is not to be interpreted as an advocacy of slavish imitation—if, in the realm of the visual, strict, factual reproduction is desired, it can, after all, be best accomplished by such mechanical means as photography— nor as a denial of the legitimacy of the function of the imagination. Neither does the imagination attain its complete fulfilment by being lavished on the object unreservedly and without ulterior considerations. (Rilke's realization of this aspect of Cézanne's art, and the theme of his commentary in this letter, are, in fact, leading up to the central revelation of the Cézanne experience, which emerges in the following letter.) Artistic integrity is thus unswerving loyalty to the subject, not adulterated or debased by secondary

[1] Op. cit., pp. 418–19.

motives. It means the abjuration of virtuosity and ostentatious effect; there must be no colour for colour's sake, or skill for skill's sake, no affectation. The resources of colour, of skill, of artistry, can be fully exploited by being 'manierlos' and 'ohne Sorge um Originalität'. There is in the 'Mannigfaltigkeit draußen' abundant scope for the 'innere Unerschöpflichkeit' of the creative imagination. In short, originality is enhanced in proportion to the absence of any studied, self-conscious attempt to achieve it. The relevance of this recognition to Rilke's own evolution is readily apparent, especially in the light of the affectation, virtuosity, and exaggeration of his earlier poetry. This is an extension of the discipline instituted by Rodin and exemplified in its earliest form in *Der Panther*. For—and this must again be emphasized—it was discipline and control which the young Rilke needed most, to curb the overwhelming torrent of his natural talents and to restrain him from lapsing into mere technical *tours de force*. If we substitute the poet's medium of language for the painter's medium of colour, the burden of this letter becomes even more clear in its application to Rilke. For the young Cézanne in Paris, colour had been 'etwas für sich', just as language had been for the poet of the first two parts of *Das Stunden-Buch*: for both, their medium had been, *not a means, but an end in itself*, a brilliant toy to be played with and shown off. But for the mature Cézanne, 'die Farbe geht völlig auf in dessen [sc. des Dinges] Verwirklichung'; and Mathilde Vollmoeller uses the striking simile of colour and object being perfectly balanced on each side of a pair of scales. This is an ideal which Rilke can perceive and for which he can strive, something which applies to all art and is not restricted to any one material. It is, translated into his own field of poetry, the optimum use of language, the extraction of the maximum value from every word, which in turn imposes the obligation of avoidance of both under- and overstatement. Language must be 'fully used up' in the realization of the subject; but at the same time there must be no gratuitous adornment, the subject must not be outweighed by the language used to render it; there must be 'nie mehr, nie weniger, als das Gleichgewicht erfordert'.

The next letter, dated 13 October, is, as has been indicated, the most important in the series, containing as it does the most vital revelation of the Cézanne experience—a revelation which provoked in Rilke a degree of studious and detached thought rare in one who by temperament and training was not well equipped to linger over knotty problems of art theory. A letter which he has just received from Clara conjures up in his mind the picture of Worpswede in the autumn, which in turn inspires him, against the background of his present preoccupation with Cézanne, to project his thoughts back to his own Worpswede days, eight years previously, and to his own immaturity at that time. It is significant, in view of the remarks in the preceding paragraph, that, in a passage to which reference has already been made,[1] Rilke also recalls *Das Stunden-Buch*.[2] His return to the present demonstrates his consciousness of how far he has travelled since then:

Wie wenig hätte ich damals vor Cézanne, vor van Gogh zu lernen gewußt. Daran, wieviel Cézanne mir jetzt zu tun gibt, merk ich, wie sehr ich anders geworden bin. Ich bin auf dem Wege, ein Arbeiter zu werden, auf einem weiten Wege vielleicht und wahrscheinlich erst bei dem ersten Meilenstein; aber trotzdem, ich kann schon den Alten begreifen, der irgendwo weit vorne gegangen ist . . . Ich war heute wieder bei seinen Bildern . . . Ohne ein einzelnes zu betrachten, . . . fühlt man ihre Gegenwart sich zusammentun zu einer kolossalen Wirklichkeit. Als ob diese Farben einem die Unentschlossenheit abnähmen ein für allemal. Das gute Gewissen dieser Rots, dieser Blaus, ihre einfache Wahrhaftigkeit erzieht einen . . .[3]

The Cézanne experience is becoming condensed; the various threads of the initial impressions are being drawn together; attention is being focused on the central truth from which all other aspects of Cézanne's art emanate. Rilke, it is true, still speaks of becoming 'ein Arbeiter', but it is possible to detect a difference in his conception of the term from that connoted by Rodin's doctrine of 'travailler'. It now suggests not so much the goal of continuous creation as a conscientious and incorruptible respect for and pride in his medium. It is, in fact, the awareness of the need for artistic integrity mentioned in connexion with the previous letter, which was seen as leading up to the present commentary. 'Das gute Gewissen' which underlies Cézanne's use of his colours must also inform the poet's use of words, so that they, too, can 'sich zusammentun zu einer kolossalen Wirklichkeit'.

Rilke continues with the most significant passage of all:

Man merkt auch, von Mal zu Mal besser, wie notwendig es war, auch noch über die Liebe hinauszukommen; es ist ja natürlich, daß man

---

[1] See p. 33.          [2] Op. cit., p. 420.          [3] Ibid., pp. 420–1.

jedes dieser Dinge liebt, wenn man es macht; zeigt man das aber, so
macht man es weniger gut; man *beurteilt* es, statt es zu *sagen*. Man
hört auf, unparteiisch zu sein; und das Beste, die Liebe, bleibt außerhalb
der Arbeit, geht nicht in sie ein, restiert unumsetzt neben ihr: so entstand die Stimmungsmalerei (die um nichts besser ist als die stoffliche).
Man malte: ich liebe dieses hier; statt zu malen: hier ist es. Wobei denn
jeder selbst gut zusehen muß, ob ich es geliebt habe. Das ist durchaus
nicht gezeigt, und manche werden sogar behaupten, da wäre von keiner
Liebe die Rede. So ohne Rückstand ist sie aufgebraucht in der Aktion
des Machens. Dieses Aufbrauchen der Liebe in anonymer Arbeit,
woraus so reine Dinge entstehen, ist vielleicht noch keinem so völlig
gelungen wie dem Alten; seine mißtrauisch und mürrisch gewordene
innere Natur unterstützte ihn darin. Er hätte gewiß keinem Menschen
mehr seine Liebe gezeigt, so er eine hätte fassen müssen; aber mit dieser
Anlage, die durch seine abgesonderte Wunderlichkeit ganz ausentwickelt
worden war, wandte er sich nun auch an die Natur und wußte seine
Liebe zu jedem Apfel zu verbeißen und in dem gemalten Apfel unter-
zubringen für immer.[1]

There is, here, a fundamental problem of technique at issue,
and one, moreover, which was bound to exercise more severely
one whose nature was predominantly 'romantic-intuitive'[2] and
whose early poetry had paraded his emotion uninhibitedly. It is
the question which was posed, and partially answered, in the
previous letter. In this letter Rilke faces it squarely; it is the
problem of 'stated' emotion. It is interesting to note, since Rilke
discovered the existence and nature of this problem through
Cézanne's painting, how much more applicable it is to his own
art, where the medium is language, which has meaning, and where
it is possible, literally, to express feeling in a way which can be
unequivocally assimilated by the intelligence. It was for this reason
that it was earlier remarked that the lesson learnt from Cézanne
need not have come from a painter.[3] We may even be surprised
that it did come from a painter, since, in the absence of a medium
capable of communicating literally to the intelligence, the recognition of this quality in Cézanne's painting involved a large element
of conjecture and subjective criticism on Rilke's part. It is, therefore, justifiable to infer, especially in the light of the history of the
Rodin experience, that Rilke's own artistic evolution had, unknown
to himself, reached a turning-point; and that the perception of this

[1] Op. cit., pp. 421-2.        [2] See p. 71.        [3] p. 80.

aspect of Cézanne's painting (it matters little whether it was real or imagined) was merely the outward manifestation of a change which had already taken place in his own approach to his art.

But whatever the psychological process at work, it does not lessen the importance of Rilke's discovery. It is a discovery which clearly opens up an interesting field of discussion when considered in the context of lyric poetry. It implies a revolutionary approach to a poetic form the tradition of which had been nothing if not subjectively 'partial'. It means objectivity with a difference: not the cold, marmoreal objectivity of Le Parnasse, in which self and emotion are deliberately subdued, but the projection of self into the object so that they can coexist as a unified and separate entity. In the traditional conception of lyric poetry the object was subordinated to, and therefore modified by, self; it was merely the vehicle or symbol through which the poet exhibited a facet of himself, depending for its artistic existence on the poet's indulgence. Rilke now saw this act of 'judging' as an act of violence against the object, and therefore as a diminution of artistic effect. He now sought to bridge the gap between creator and object in such a way as to lose nothing of either; by stating love one dissipates it instead of pouring it all into the act of creation itself, into the object. This is, after all, the poetic counterpart to the more commonplace human foible of 'protesting too much', with its lack of conviction and taint of insincerity (again we are brought back to the idea of integrity, with the corollary of good taste). Rilke's argument is perfectly reasonable: there is no need to say that one loves the object; the very fact that the artist chooses it is proof of his feeling for it, and the best way for him to show this feeling is not to waste the resources of his medium on gratuitous sentimentality, but to expend all his creative energy and ability in such a way that the object will be shown forth as what it is.

This, Rilke's dream of a perfect merger between creator and object, was thus an ingenious attempt to gain the best of both worlds: to be subjective and objective at the same time. It was not difficult to give unchecked rein to the emotions in the traditional Romantic manner, as Rilke had found in his own early poetry. Neither was it difficult to eliminate self completely, or almost so, as the Parnassians had done. But to combine the properties of these two apparently contradictory styles was a major problem of artistic technique. It was one thing to subscribe to the ideal of the

'Aufbrauchen der Liebe in anonymer Arbeit' so that it is 'ohne Rückstand . . . aufgebraucht in der Aktion des Machens'; it was another thing to put it into practice. How was he, on the one hand, with the much more explicit medium of words at his disposal, to avoid intruding himself too much without, on the other, running the danger of withdrawing too far and lapsing into purely descriptive writing? It can be seen that it was essentially a problem of language, of a particularly delicate nature. It will be recalled that Rilke had, four years earlier, made a beginning in this direction in *Der Panther*,[1] though at that time he was not aware of the problem in definitive form and to that extent his approach was empirical.[2] Indeed, the close correlation of this revelation which came through Cézanne's painting with the Rodin experience is clearly visible. The great difference lies, first, in the fact that this ideal, in the form in which it is expressed in this letter, postulates a poetic treatment far more difficult and exacting than anything attempted during the Rodin years—so much so that the possibility of complete attainment of the ideal was questionable, to say the least. The second, and more important, difference is that Rilke was now aware of the existence of the problem as such; he had at last formulated it and was able to consider it objectively.

The significance of this letter and of Cézanne's contribution to Rilke's artistic development, in fact, lies not so much in that it presages a kind of poetry he had not tried to write before—since many of the *Neue Gedichte* written under Rodin's influence exemplify, inchoately, the approach set out in this letter—as in the fact that Rilke was now rationally conscious of the underlying principle involved; he could now grasp it and examine it with his intelligence; it had become solidified, and in this perceptible form could more easily be incorporated permanently into his artistic concept. The immediate implication of Rilke's enlightenment is that it indicates the need for a renewed and relentless assault on the task of making himself the complete master of his medium. For it is obvious that a technique which aims at making the subject of a poem a thing of such passing beauty and perfection as to demonstrate, by its own existence alone, the poet's feelings without his having to state them implies a use of language in its quintessential form. Whether Rilke, in the extreme and uncompromising formula expounded in this letter, was confronting himself with the

[1] See pp. 58–59.                    [2] See p. 63.

near-impossible is less important than the fact that he was being
driven further into the salutary discipline of self-examination and
of the quest for greater control over the material of his art. He
was being fortified in his resolve to wrestle with his medium until
it was completely obedient to his touch, to be satisfied with nothing
less than the best. How far the conclusions reached during this
period and expressed in their most categorical form in this letter
remained with Rilke through the years must be estimated against
his later poetry. It is, however, interesting to note that a year
later—a year, incidentally, of almost continuous travel and of
varied experiences, at the end of which the vividness of the first
impact of Cézanne must have passed—in November 1908, he
wrote these lines in the *Requiem für Wolf Graf von Kalckreuth*:

> ... O alter Fluch der Dichter,
> die sich beklagen, wo sie sagen sollten,
> die immer urteiln über ihr Gefühl,
> statt es zu bilden; die noch immer meinen,
> was traurig ist in ihnen oder froh,
> das wüßten sie und dürftens im Gedicht
> bedauern oder rühmen. Wie die Kranken
> gebrauchen sie die Sprache voller Wehleid,
> um zu beschreiben, wo es ihnen wehtut,
> statt hart sich in die Worte zu verwandeln,
> wie sich der Steinmetz einer Kathedrale
> verbissen umsetzt in des Steines Gleichmut.[1]

This is an exact poetic paraphrase, even to the point of using the
same words, of the present letter. And, as if to emphasize the
sequent logic of his development, Rilke takes us right back to
the Rodin years with the imagery of the last two lines.

The next letter in the series follows two days later, on 15 October.
It adds an interesting rider to the preceding remarks indicating that
Rilke had progressed beyond the Rodin experience, since Rilke
describes a visit to an exhibition of Rodin's drawings, among
which are many he had helped to frame. Rilke's comments on
these familiar works are illuminating[2] in that there is no longer the
unqualified acceptance of his old master's handiwork. The things
which were once artistically sufficient for Rilke and which were
approved without question no longer exercise the same effect; he
is developing more critical reserve. He asks whether Cézanne or

[1] *A.W.*, Bd. I, pp. 224–5.                [2] Op. cit., p. 423.

time has brought about the change—to which one can only answer that both have done so.

The theme of the following letter, dated 16 October, is the incomprehension of the public, and Rilke describes the people who visit the exhibition for reasons quite divorced from artistic appreciation. But the letter closes with the recognition that what is more important is the artist's own disinterested opinion of his work, and the onus which rests upon him not to compromise his ideals by being attracted by easy popularity:

Und dem Alten in Aix erzählte einer, er wäre 'berühmt'. Der aber wußte es besser in sich und ließ reden. Aber vor seinen Sachen kommt man wieder auf die Idee, wie sehr jede Anerkennung (mit ganz vereinzelten, unverkennbaren Ausnahmen) einen mißtrauisch machen muß gegen die eigene Arbeit. Im Grunde, wenn sie gut ist, kann man gar nicht erleben, daß sie erkannt wird: oder ist sie eben doch nur halb gut und nicht rücksichtslos genug. . . .[1]

There is, however, the obverse side of the coin. The counsel of indifference to general opinion can soon lead to the artist's own peculiar vanity, in which lack of recognition is claimed as the assurance of merit.

The letter of 17 October brings a variation in the form of a discussion of van Gogh, which further shows Rilke's growing sensitivity to painting. The next letter, of 18 October, returns to Cézanne, and it is again an important document in evaluating the progress of the Cézanne experience and, in particular, Rilke's own development. He writes to Clara:

Was Du nun sagst und herzlich feststellst, das vermute ich irgendwie, wenngleich ich nicht hätte angeben können, wie weit in mir jene Entwicklung schon verwirklicht ist, die dem immensen Fortschritt in den Cézanneschen Malereien entspricht . . . Es ist gar nicht die Malerei, die ich studiere (denn ich bleibe trotz allem Bildern gegenüber ungewiß und lerne nur schlecht, gute von weniger guten unterscheiden, und verwechsle beständig frühe mit spät gemalten). Es ist die Wendung dieser Malerei, die ich erkannte, weil ich sie selbst eben in meiner Arbeit erreicht hatte oder doch irgendwie nahe an sie herangekommen war, seit lange wahrscheinlich auf dieses eine vorbereitet, von dem so vieles abhängt.[2]

The first significant feature of this passage is that Rilke himself

[1] Op. cit., pp. 426–7.
[2] Ibid., p. 430.

now seems to realize that the fact that the revelation of the past days has come to him through the medium of painting is only incidental. He now sees his relationship with Cézanne as the crystallization of a stage already, if unconsciously, reached in his own evolution.[1]

We may also, in passing, read into these words a note of warning against the careless use of the term 'influence'—so often regarded as a force acting blindly and imperiously. There can be no 'influence' except where receptivity and potential response already exist, and in the broader context of this study as a whole, Rilke's association with and experiences in France may be seen, even more than as the *cause* of certain changes in him, as the *fruition* of something the germ of which was already there. In other words, for the artist 'influence' involves going where he can acquire something, frequenting places and people which have something to impart to him. This subject will be referred to again in the final chapter.

Rilke thus acknowledges that it is not painting that he is studying. It is its application to himself. Cézanne's art is grist to his own private mill, something which can help to promote the flowering of his own genius. This theme of the personal nature of his acquisition is amplified in the remainder of the letter.[2] It summarizes in the clearest and most persuasive manner the salient features of the Cézanne experience; and it shows Rilke at the peak of this experience, at the point where he is appropriating for his own use all that Cézanne has to offer. Again there is the emphasis on the paramountcy of the artist's work, into which no partiality, no idiosyncrasy, no fastidious indulgence may be admitted ('judging' was the word Rilke had used five days earlier); the artist's mind must be open and incorruptible, the smallest ingredient of his work must be weighed in the balance of his conscience, the sanctity of his medium must never be violated or compromised. Again there is the reference to a boundless and unadulterated 'Sachlichkeit' which 'mit der bloßen Farbe' can give life even to common things; and implicit in these words is Rilke's resolution to make himself master of his own medium in like manner.

The letter of 19 October has a particular interest in that it furnishes a link with the next chapter, in which Baudelaire will come under discussion, and in that it provides further evidence of

[1] Cf. pp. 89–90.          [2] Op. cit., pp. 430–2.

the remarkable integration of the artistic influences which operated on Rilke during his early years in Paris. He recalls, in this letter, a reference to Baudelaire in *Malte Laurids Brigge* (as yet unfinished):

Du erinnerst sicher . . . aus den Aufzeichnungen des Malte Laurids, die Stelle, die von Baudelaire handelt und von seinem Gedichte: 'Das Aas'. Ich mußte daran denken, daß ohne dieses Gedicht die ganze Entwicklung zum sachlichen Sagen, die wir jetzt in Cézanne zu erkennen glauben, nicht hätte anheben können; erst mußte das künstlerische Anschauen sich so weit überwunden haben, auch im Schrecklichen und scheinbar nur Widerwärtigen das Seiende zu sehen, das, mit allem anderen Seienden, *gilt*. Sowenig eine Auswahl zugelassen ist, ebensowenig ist eine Abwendung von irgendwelcher Existenz dem Schaffenden erlaubt: ein einziges Ablehnen irgendwann drängt ihn aus dem Zustande der Gnade, macht ihn ganz und gar sündig.[1]

A more detailed commentary on this passage, and on its continuation, will be made in the following chapter, where the appropriate extract from *Malte* will be adduced and the two pieces of evidence considered as a whole.

For the moment, it is sufficient to add a note on the integration of influences mentioned above. Here, Rilke suggests that 'die ganze Entwicklung zum sachlichen Sagen', which has been the focal point of the Cézanne experience, would have been impossible without the foreknowledge of Baudelaire's *Une Charogne*. If this is perhaps too extreme a supposition, we must nevertheless accept Rilke's consciousness of the link as implying the presence of some measure of cause and effect in the process of maturing through which his artistic concept was passing. Secondly, the close correlation and indivisibility of the Rodin and Cézanne experiences has repeatedly been noticed. Thirdly, we may note that Rodin was a devoted reader of Baudelaire, and that Rilke's interest in this poet was established during the Rodin years. Thus, these three men, each a representative of a different art and each supremely individualistic, converge at this moment in Rilke's evolution: and their meeting-point is 'Sachlichkeit'. And, if this conjuncture is not remarkable enough, there is a further coincidence recorded in this letter: 'Du kannst Dir denken, wie es mich berührt, zu lesen, daß Cézanne eben dieses Gedicht — Baudelaires Charogne — noch in seinen letzten Jahren ganz auswendig wußte und es Wort für Wort hersagte.'[2]

---

[1] Op. cit., pp. 432-3.          [2] Ibid., p. 433.

The 20th of October was a Sunday, and, as in the letter which opened the series, Rilke again describes his customary walk through the Faubourg Saint-Germain, with its rich monuments of the past. Cézanne's name is not mentioned; there is only an oblique reference to him, in the closing lines. What he has seen on his walk induces again the theme of poverty upon which he had touched three days earlier, with the further thought of the need to be close to the earth, like the first man.[1]

In the letter of 21 October, Rilke has more to say on the subject of colour:

... Ich wollte aber eigentlich noch von Cézanne sagen: daß es niemals noch so aufgezeigt worden ist, wie sehr das Malen unter den Farben vor sich geht, wie man sie ganz allein lassen muß, damit sie sich gegenseitig auseinandersetzen. Ihr Verkehr untereinander: das ist die ganze Malerei. Wer dazwischenspricht, wer anordnet, wer seine menschliche Überlegung, seinen Witz, seine Anwaltschaft, seine geistige Gelenkigkeit irgend mit agieren läßt, der stört und trübt schon ihre Handlung. Der Maler dürfte nicht zum Bewußtsein seiner Einsichten kommen (wie der Künstler überhaupt): ohne den Umweg durch seine Reflexion zu nehmen, müssen seine Fortschritte, ihm selber rätselhaft, so rasch in die Arbeit eintreten, daß er sie in dem Moment ihres Übertritts nicht zu erkennen vermag. Ach, wer sie dort belauert, beobachtet, aufhält, dem verwandeln sie sich wie das schöne Gold im Märchen, das nicht Gold bleiben kann, weil irgendeine Kleinigkeit nicht in Ordnung war. Daß man van Goghs Briefe so gut lesen kann, daß sie so viel enthalten, spricht im Grunde gegen ihn, wie es ja auch gegen den Maler spricht (Cézanne danebengehalten), daß er das und das wollte, wußte, erfuhr; daß das Blau Orange aufrief und das Grün Rot: daß er solches, heimlich an dem Inneren seines Auges horchend, hatte drinnen sagen hören, der Neugierige. So malte er Bilder auf einen einzigen Widerspruch hin, dabei auch noch an die japanische Vereinfachung der Farbe denkend, die eine Fläche auf den nächsthöheren oder nächsttieferen Ton setzt, unter einen Gesamtwert summiert; welches wieder zu dem gezogenen und ausgesprochenen (d.h. erfundenen) Kontur der Japaner führt als Einfassung der gleichgesetzten Flächen: zu lauter Absicht, zu lauter Eigenmächtigkeit, mit einem Wort zur Dekoration.[2]

Rilke goes on to contrast the clumsiness and inarticulateness of Cézanne's letters when it came to discussing his painting.

Again, the acceptability or otherwise of Rilke's views is less important than the insight they give into the process which was

---

[1] Op. cit., pp. 437–8.      [2] Ibid., pp. 442–4.

taking place within him. It is noteworthy that his emphasis here is all on the virtue of a mode of creation which is empirical and inspirational; the less the artist 'understands' what he is doing, the better. His work should proceed by the operation of an instinctive taste, without any detour 'durch seine Reflexion'. Not only can the mystery of the moment of creation not be understood, but if the artist 'belauert, beobachtet, aufhält' the process, the gold is thereby transmuted into baser metal. We may remember the suggestion made in the first chapter that the function of the intellect in Rilke's poetry was not to initiate.[1] And it is also appropriate to recall the earlier remarks on inspiration, particularly with regard to the nature of the creative event which occurred more than fourteen years later at Muzot.[2] In this letter we can see Rilke's 'romantic-intuitive' nature reasserting itself. If, artistically speaking, the Rodin experience can be termed Rilke's 'intellectual' period (the use of this term in this context will be amplified later in the chapter), we are now witnessing the process of adjustment in the form of a reversion to the instinctive, intuitive approach which was natural to him. The pendulum was beginning to swing back, though it was never again to swing to the extreme of the Russian days.[3] Rilke was thus already seeking out, if unconsciously, the compromise between his innate propensities and endowments and the external discipline which must be imposed on them; between the flood of his creative energies and the control over them which alone could make them fully effective. The evidence of his advance, under the influence of Cézanne, since his association with Rodin, is becoming more and more conclusive. But perhaps the most thought-provoking aspect of this letter is that this panegyric of the inspirational nature of the creative act should have been touched off by the work of a man who, like Rodin, was an artist in a 'static' medium. It is, however, significant that Rilke's whole argument is linked to, and develops from, Cézanne's use of colour: for the creation of a colour effect is the

[1] pp. 15–16.
[3] pp. 50–52. In order to avoid misunderstanding, it may be repeated that, in recalling the nature of Rilke's creative activity at Muzot, there is no intention to ignore the fact that he had been at work on the Elegies for ten years. Neither is it forgotten that his notebooks reveal alterations and corrections. It does, however, seem clear, at least as far as the events of February 1922 were concerned, and particularly when one thinks of the composition of the Sonnets, that the moment of creation approximated to the spontaneous and unreflecting process outlined in this letter.                              [3] Cf. p. 56.

one element (unlike the more protracted and laborious process of drawing) in painting which can be instinctive and momentaneous— which, in short, most nearly corresponds to the immediacy of poetic composition (and to which, of course, there was no counter- part in Rodin's art).

The letter of 22 October records Rilke's last visit to the Salon, which has closed on this date. He devotes the letter to a description of the picture of the 'Frau im roten Fauteuil'. Once more, it is the balance and integration of colour and subject achieved by the painter which occupy Rilke's attention.[1]

The letter of 23 October begins with an interesting echo of an earlier theme in the correspondence which is of particular applica- tion to the problem of translating the Cézanne experience into the context of the poet's medium:

. . . Ich mußte denken, gestern abend, ob mein Versuch, die Frau im roten Polstersessel anzudeuten, Dich zu irgendeiner Vorstellung bestim- men könnte? Ich bin nicht sicher, auch nur das Verhältnis ihrer Valeurs getroffen zu haben; mehr als je schienen mir Worte aus- geschlossen, und doch müßte die Möglichkeit, sich ihrer zwingend zu bedienen, dasein, vermöchte man nur, ein solches Bild wie Natur anzuschauen: dann müßte es als ein Seiendes auch irgendwie aus- gesagt werden können.[2]

It is true that Rilke is here concerned only with the lesser problem of transmitting the effect of a particular picture in the prose of a letter. But since he is concerned with Cézanne's painting primarily as a means of furthering his own artistic development, since, moreover, the principal advance which he claims to have made as a result of the Cézanne experience is the 'Entwicklung zum sach- lichen Sagen',[3] and since, above all, language-consciousness and the use of words—whether in poetry or prose, the same problem is involved in this instance—are the central issue in Rilke's evolution, this passage does serve to underline the fact that, however much more closely he could approach Cézanne than Rodin, a gulf still exists between the two media. The letter continues with what Rilke conceives to be the easier task of describing Cézanne's self- portrait, again returning, in the closing lines, to the theme of objectivity.

The first part of the letter of 24 October resumes the subject of

[1] Op. cit., pp. 447-8.          [2] Ibid., pp. 448-9.
[3] See p. 95.

the self-portrait, with some corrective second thoughts on Rilke's colour impressions. We find yet another reference to 'das innere Gleichgewicht von Cézannes Farben, die nirgends herausstehen und vordrängen'.[1] The remainder of the letter discusses generally Cézanne's colour predilections in his still-life paintings, and once more we find how impressed Rilke is with Cézanne's ability to 'realize' an object. Rilke closes on this note, and with a condemnatory comment on the brash intrusion of modernity: the Salon is shortly to be followed by an automobile exhibition.[2]

An interval of eleven days elapses before the next letter, dated 4 November. This is the final letter in the series and is written after Rilke's visit to Prague, in the train taking him to Breslau. It is noteworthy for two coincidences which it records: '. . . wirst Du es glauben, daß ich nach Prag kam, um Cézannes zu sehen? Daß neben Deinem Brief ein Brief Rodins in meiner Tasche war, als ich in den Vortrag fuhr? (Gestern abend um fünf.) So kommt alles und kommt, und man hat nur mit ganzem Herzen dazusein.'[3] The letter from Rodin is, in this, the last of the 'Cézanne-Briefe', a fitting reminder, if one were needed, of the close interrelation of the two experiences. Some final remarks on this subject will be made shortly.

Und Cézanne. Draußen im Manes-Pavillon, wo seinerzeit Rodins Ausstellung war, gab es (wie ich zum Glück noch rechtzeitig erfuhr) eine Exposition moderner Bilder. Am besten und merkwürdigsten: Monticelli, Monet gut, Pissarro einigermaßen vertreten; drei Sachen von Daumier. Und vier Cézannes. (Auch van Gogh, Gauguin, Emile Bernard: jeder mit mehrerem.) Aber Cézanne . . .[4]

And Rilke goes on to describe the four pictures. His delight at this unexpected discovery is obvious. The coincidence of finding Cézanne in Prague is yet another of the curious incidents which occurred so regularly in Rilke's life and which gave his artistic development the appearance of working to an externally ordained plan. It is almost as though the lesson of the Salon d'Automne were being driven home with double force, as though Rilke himself were being reminded that the experience was not expendable, that it was an inalienable and permanent part of himself as an artist.

·        ·        ·

[1] Op. cit., p. 452.                    [2] Ibid., p. 453.
[3] G.B., Bd. III, p. 9.                 [4] Ibid., p. 10.

As has already been noted, there is no collection of poems written during this period, comparable to the *Neue Gedichte* which encompassed the Rodin experience, by which an immediate translation of the Cézanne experience into practice may be observed.[1] Less than a year later, on 8 September 1908, Rilke adds an interesting comment on Cézanne. Discussing Malte, he writes:

. . . nach den Cézanne-Briefen, die so nah und hart mit ihm sich berührten, war ich an den Grenzen seiner Gestalt angekommen: denn Cézanne ist nichts anderes als das erste primitive Gelingen dessen, was in M.L. noch nicht gelang. Der Tod Brigges: das war Cézannes Leben, das Leben seiner dreißig letzten Jahre.[2]

The exploration of this statement and an examination of *Malte Laurids Brigge* are not of primary concern in the present study, though references to Rilke's novel will occur. It is, however, important to note that the writing of *Malte*, with its strong autobiographical strain, is closely related to Rilke's poetic development. It was written between 1904 and 1910, during which years so much that was vital to his evolution occurred; and the long and laborious nature of its composition was itself symbolical of the hard struggle towards fulfilment through which Rilke was passing. Even more, it was one of the means by which Rilke's art was purified and sensitized and by which ultimate consummation was achieved.

But the absence of a convenient yardstick for estimating the transformation of the Cézanne experience into poetry does not relieve us of the obligation to look for its effect on Rilke's art, neither should it persuade us into minimizing its importance. Rather should the impact of Cézanne's painting on Rilke, like all the formative experiences in his evolution, be borne in mind when his later poetry comes under consideration. Rilke, many years later, offers some pertinent comments on this subject, and on the controversial question of the poet's relation to the representational arts. In a letter to Joachim von Winterfeldt-Menkin, dated 2 February 1921, he writes:

Der Fall Rodin ist für mich völlig unvergleichlich. Rodin ist, wie ich wohl sagen darf, mein Lehrer gewesen, das Beispiel seines gewaltigen Werkes war mir, während vieler Lehrjahre, maßgebend, und aus dem freundschaftlichen Umgang so vieler Zeiten konnte sich schließlich eine Reihe von Aufzeichnungen niederschlagen. Schon im nächsten

[1] See p. 77.          [2] *G.B.*, Bd. III, p. 50.

Falle, da ein Werk der Malerei mir vom größten Einfluß war, vor dem Oeuvre Cézannes, hab ich mir jede schriftliche Feststellung meines Erlebnisses versagt, — da mir nichts unzuverlässiger scheint, als die literarische Auslegung malerischer oder plastischer Produktion. Der gegenwärtige Stand der Künste auf der einen Seite, auf der anderen die ungemeine Beweglichkeit und Bereitschaft des Schriftlichen verpflichtet zu der größten Sparsamkeit und Vorsicht der Äußerung; auch der verantwortlichste Schriftsteller ist heut mehr denn je in Gefahr, ihn irgendwie angehende Gestaltungen der bildenden Kunst zu übertreiben oder mindestens voreilig einzuschätzen, da sich die Einteilung der Maßskala nicht so ausführlich hat verändern und einrichten lassen, wie das der Abwandlung und Vielfalt des bildnerischen Gedränges entspräche.[1]

The use of this quotation needs to be qualified by the explanatory admission that Rilke was declining a request to write a critique on a representational artist. His reasons for not writing a Cézanne counterpart to *Auguste Rodin* do not therefore necessarily have any bearing on the absence of a collection of poems resulting from the Cézanne experience, although there could be a connexion. There are at least good grounds for thinking, on the evidence of the 'Cézanne-Briefe', that the impact on him of Cézanne's art coincided with—or even was responsible for—a period of thoughtfulness and assimilation, during which he was at pains to digest and apply the experience rather than produce.

The chief interest of the passage, however, is that it reveals the attitude to the plastic arts of the mature Rilke, looking back over a long period of years; its chief use, here, is that it provides a convenient basis for summing up the Cézanne experience, and the results in general of Rilke's contact with sculpture and painting. First, there is the fundamental and inescapable fact that there is a point beyond which the 'mobile' artist cannot go in any attempt to effect a synthesis between his art and the 'static' arts. Even in the restricted application of this letter, Rilke's comment on the 'unreliability' of 'die literarische Auslegung malerischer oder plastischer Produktion' is not without relevance in the broader context of considering how a poet is to translate such experiences as Rilke's into terms of poetry. For the object of Rilke's long and diligent immersion in the representational arts was to equip himself better, to adopt what he could from the artists' technique; which

[1] *G.B.*, Bd. IV, pp. 374-5.

in turn meant trying to see with their eyes and project himself as far as possible into their creative process—a creative process totally different from his own. It is sufficient to recall the earlier comment that, in a large measure, the remarks made in this connexion in the chapter on Rodin apply in the Cézanne context as well.[1]

But just as the irreconcilability of the media did not invalidate the Rodin experience, neither does it do so in the case of Cézanne. It is merely that awareness of the unproductive or negative side of Rilke's relation to sculpture and painting helps to concentrate attention on the positive aspects. The examination of the Cézanne correspondence has justified the view that Rilke's preoccupation with sculpture and painting must be regarded as an entity. Cézanne completed what Rodin had begun—he confirmed and consolidated the Rodin experience, while at the same time taking Rilke a stage further. Rilke found in both the justification he sought for the solitary, dedicated existence he had chosen; he found in both the absolute and uncompromising devotion to the ideal of artistic perfection which spurned all extraneous considerations such as popularity and relaxation; he found in both, because they were his elders and because their achievement was complete, the hope that he, too, could succeed. On the other hand, the signs of inner conflict and tension which marked the end of the Rodin period are much less in evidence under Cézanne's influence; in fact, Rilke at this time seems much less troubled by his own creative problems. Even the preoccupation with the idea of 'continuous work' seems to find its proper level. Whilst he admires Cézanne's ruthless application to his work, Rilke now appears to regard it less as a physical manifestation which he can emulate than as a symbol of the artist's constant struggle to improve on what he has done—the Faustian principle of never being able to rest satisfied.

The one concrete element in the Cézanne experience which took Rilke beyond Rodin was the presence of colour in painting. A caution was earlier expressed against over-stressing this factor.[2] This reservation was made because too great an emphasis on this element might concentrate attention on purely visual considerations, and therefore throw us back into the problems of medium from which we have been trying to escape. It would be a mistake

[1] See p. 78.                    [2] p. 79.

to regard colour, though it is present in both literature and painting, as meaning the same thing to the poet and the pictorial artist. Nevertheless, it does establish a point of contact between Rilke and Cézanne which did not exist with Rodin. It is significant that the theme of colour, and not Cézanne's draughtsmanship, dominates the 'Cézanne-Briefe'.[1] It is, in fact, through colour that Rilke arrives at the central revelation of the Cézanne experience—objectivity: though not the objectivity which suppresses feeling, but which, by incorporating it, by 'using it up' in the act of creation, renders the artist's feeling all the more powerfully.

This leads to the final thought on this stage in Rilke's evolution, and to the most important aspect of the integration of the Rodin and Cézanne experiences. The concentration on 'Sachlichkeit' had begun under Rodin, and, as we saw in the examination of *Der Panther*, Rilke had already achieved a considerable measure of practical success in reconciling the demands of objectivity on the one hand and duty to his feelings on the other.[2] In other words, Rilke appears *already*, four years earlier, to have put into practice the Cézanne revelation which is now put forward as something so new and vital. We may, therefore, ask in what way the impact of Cézanne marks an advance at all. This question has been partly answered earlier in this chapter, where it was pointed out that Rilke was now able consciously and rationally to understand and examine the issue involved.[3] Under Rodin he had proceeded empirically; he had been so content to take Rodin on trust that detached thought was in abeyance; his feelings had been embodied in *Der Panther* in spite of himself, because he was constitutionally incapable of eliminating them,[4] and not, one feels, in obedience to a particular theory of art. This, then, is the crux of the advance made by Rilke under Cézanne: that his artistic concept was now *formulated*; it was a permanent part of him, a goal towards which he could consciously and deliberately strive; he now had assurance, The principle on which, under Rodin, he had worked unconsciously and pragmatically—and therefore necessarily with some degree of uncertainty and hazard—now had 'a local habitation and a name'.

---

[1] In this connexion, we may also recall Rilke's emphasis, in *Auguste Rodin*, on surface, *le modelé*, rather than on shape.

[2] See pp. 58–59.

[3] p. 91.

[4] See particularly p. 59.

The autumn of 1907 thus marked the most theoretical period of Rilke's life, as far as his approach to his own art was concerned. This does not invalidate the earlier suggestion that the Rodin years were his 'intellectual' period.[1] This statement was made in the sense that the Rodin years marked the most extreme swing away from the emotional effusion of the first two parts of *Das Stunden-Buch*; it related to his poetry and to the *externalizing* discipline which he was copying from the sculptor. At the time of the Cézanne experience Rilke was writing little or no poetry—no doubt because he was engrossed in the problems of art theory—and therefore the question of 'intellectual' content in his poetry does not arise. Rilke's energies were instead devoted to taking stock of himself, stabilizing his position, wedding theory to practice—all of which was also intellectual activity, but which, paradoxically, also reveals the beginning of the swing back to a greater measure of subjectivity.[2] If there is no immediate material for appraising the effects of Cézanne on Rilke's art, there is nevertheless no lack of evidence in Rilke's letters that the experience remained with him, its force undiminished, throughout the years.[3]

The Cézanne experience has been treated as one of the great formative episodes in Rilke's career. It may well be asked how such a theoretical and ratiocinative period as was the autumn of 1907 could possibly make any contribution to the tempestuous, almost frenzied creation of the Sonnets and the remainder of the Elegies at Muzot. There need be no sense of contradictoriness. The vigour of old wine does not deny the leisured process of crushing and compounding. Every experience of the past had matured in Rilke, had become organically an integral part of him, until theory perfectly merged with instinct and inspiration in a unified manifestation. Everything which preceded February 1922 had something to give to the grand climax.

---

[1] p. 97.                                                     [2] Cf. p. 97.
[3] In addition to the letter quoted on pp. 100–1, see *G.B.*, Bd. V, pp. 18, 69, and 100. The letter of this last reference was, in fact, written only a month before the composition of the Sonnets and the completion of the Elegies.

# V

## BAUDELAIRE AND THE SYMBOLISTS

THE importance of treating the Rodin and Cézanne experiences successively, as complementary parts of a complete phase in Rilke's artistic development, has, by postponing the examination of Baudelaire's influence until after that of the Cézanne experience, involved a partial, though unavoidable, compromise in the plan to proceed chronologically. This compromise is, however, only partial. It is true that the poems most reminiscent of Baudelaire are in *Das Buch von der Armut und vom Tode* and *Das Buch der Bilder*. These poems, with the latest date of 1906, thus at their nearest point antedate by a year Rilke's contact with the art of Cézanne, and indicate Baudelaire's influence as being at its peak during the Rodin period. On the other hand, Rilke's translation of Baudelaire's *Les Plaintes d'un Icare* was made in 1921, while the earliest date of the translations from Verlaine and Mallarmé, the two figures principally associated with the French Symbolist movement proper, is 1914 (Verlaine's *Agnus Dei*). Rilke's interest in Baudelaire and in the movement of which he was the precursor therefore extends far beyond the first four years in Paris. And if we add the French successor to the Symbolists, Valéry, with whom Rilke was preoccupied from 1921 to the end of his life, we find a continuous thread running through Rilke's literary consciousness, from his arrival in Paris in 1902 until his death. This thread, if at times faint and submerged under other experiences, can thus be seen as the one sustained external literary element in the second half of Rilke's life. It is further worthy of note that, in regard to their impact on Rilke, by far the most important figures in the movement were the two historical extremes—Baudelaire and Valéry, the precursor and the successor; and they in turn are associated with the temporal extremes, the beginning and the end, of Rilke's long immersion in French culture and art.

First, it is necessary to make a few preliminary remarks on the general question of Rilke's relationship to French literature, and to indicate briefly some of the figures who impinged on his artistic

career; but these, because they do not appear to have played a
vital part in his development, will not be examined in detail.
Rilke's eclecticism has been a recurrent phrase in this study,
exemplified, as it is, both in his way of life and in his approach to
art. Even the apparent consistency of his leaning towards Symbolism does not, as will be seen, modify this view. At hardly any stage
in his life is it possible to motivate his career according to any
calculated or calculable plan. At every turn he seems to have been
governed, both in his activities and in his artistic predilections, by
impulse and caprice, and there can be few poets with an evolutionary
process revealing so many fragmentary and apparently unrelated
elements as Rilke's. And yet the remarkable thing is that these
innumerable and disparate elements are fused so perfectly into a
unified whole that one is not conscious of any contradiction or
conflict or hiatus—a point brought out by H. Goertz.[1] Rilke was,
in fact, the supreme individualist, with an instinctive and unerring
ability to extract just what he needed from a place or a person
without surrendering his autonomy or being tempted to linger
longer than the process of assimilation demanded.[2] Unlike George,
Rilke was the poet of the perpetually open mind.

   The eclectic and unpredictable nature of Rilke's tastes is nowhere better illustrated than in the translations, which, besides
embracing some half-dozen languages, reveal a variety of authors,
subjects, and moods which is truly surprising. Even his transcrip-
tions from French range from Louise Labé of the sixteenth century
to Valéry of the twentieth. Some reference to the Valéry translations will be made later, in so far as they bear particularly on the
events of February 1922, but it is not proposed to make a detailed
examination of Rilke's work in this field as a whole, since it is quite
impossible to discover any guiding principle controlling his choices
—except in so far as nearly all the principal names associated with the
French Symbolist movement figure among his translations. In regard
to his most important contemporaries or near-contemporaries,
with the exception of Valéry, Rilke appears to alight on poems
at random like a butterfly: only one of Baudelaire's poems, one of
Verlaine's, and two of Mallarmé's are translated, and it is probably
fair to say that in no case are they among the author's best work.
It would, therefore, be disingenuous to attempt to draw too many
conclusions from this literary sideline. One point, however, does

---

[1] Op. cit., p. 1.                    [2] Cf. p. 39.

need to be made: these translations, and even more the fact that they were undertaken at all, do reveal Rilke's growing familiarity with and feeling for the French language. E. M. Butler is perhaps right when she adjudges Rilke a sympathetic rather than a great translator[1]—it is indeed difficult to imagine how an original writer, especially if he possesses the compelling individuality of a genius like Rilke's, can be a great translator. Faithful reproduction will always be threatened by the urge to create. With Rilke, in any case, the quality of the translations matters little, since they should be regarded primarily as yet another aspect of his self-imposed discipline. They are one more element in the poet's constant struggle for greater mastery over his medium. In enriching his store of impressions, and in making new demands on his capacity to manipulate language, they must inevitably make some contribution to Rilke's own poetry.

The picture of Rilke's literary samplings during the early years in Paris is one of bewildering variety—so much so that Butler, discussing the 'desultory and capricious' nature of Rilke's reading during the years 1902 to 1910, is led to comment that he 'had amassed a heterogeneous collection of authors rather after the fashion of a jackdaw'.[2] If this simile does less than justice to his taste and to his undeniable, if instinctive, sense of artistic purpose, it does epitomize the remarkable diversity of his literary acquisitions. In addition to the figures already mentioned, the combined evidence of translations, letters, and *Malte* indicates acquaintance with, among others, Maurice de Guérin, the Comtesse de Noailles, Jammes, Verhaeren, Flaubert, les Goncourt; and it is unlikely that Rilke was unfamiliar with the French Romantics and the Parnassians. It is therefore necessary, in the task of tracing Rilke's poetic development, to avoid confusion and to select for detailed consideration only those artists whose influence was considerable and is ascertainable. None of the last-named writers had an impact sufficient to warrant more than passing reference, although, inasmuch as they were parts of the complicated mosaic which made up Rilke's experience in France, their cumulative effect should perhaps not be dismissed lightly. With Verhaeren Rilke enjoyed a lasting friendship and he had an enduring admiration for his work. As late as 1919[3] and 1921[4] eulogistic references to him

---

[1] Op. cit., p. 243.
[2] Ibid., p. 230.
[3] *G.B.*, Bd. IV, pp. 228–30.
[4] *G.B.*, Bd. V, pp. 62–64.

occur in Rilke's letters, while the translation of the poem *Les Morts* was also made in 1919. But on the whole this relationship appears to have been limited to friendship and admiration, with no formative significance. One more figure, who has received attention in some of the critical works on Rilke, may be mentioned briefly: Maeterlinck. Rilke's preoccupation with the latter, however, belonged to the period before he went to Paris, and Maeterlinck was in fact superseded in Rilke's interest by Jacobsen. Angelloz even sees Maeterlinck's influence as a second Nordic one, though nevertheless representing a first contact with the French language and literature.[1]

Verlaine and Mallarmé are more important in the context of Rilke's literary evolution, although they do not provide the substance of a detailed discussion. As established subjects of Rilke's reading, their significance lies chiefly in the fact that the direction of their artistic ideals and endeavour followed the same general trend as Rilke's own—a point which will emerge shortly when the nature of the Symbolist movement is considered. One might cite, as possible evidence of direct influence, the interesting parallel between *Das Karussell*[2] in the *Neue Gedichte* and Verlaine's *Chevaux de bois* (*Romances sans paroles*), in both of which, though with very different treatment, the dominant thought is the purposelessness of the ride on the merry-go-round—'dieses atemlose blinde Spiel'. But the idea of the futility of riding round in circles and never arriving anywhere is a natural enough reaction to this subject, and to place too much weight on the comparison would be unjustified. There were two factors which, it seems, would tend to diminish Mallarmé's impact on Rilke. First, as a poet he fell short of his high ideal—a fact hardly likely to inspire the ambitious young Rilke. Second, his theoretical preoccupation—which, as we have earlier noted, was directly responsible for his practical failure— was with music;[3] that is, his artistic and aesthetic concept, while aiming at the same ideal as Rilke's—the ideal of technical and linguistic perfection—was based on an attempted synthesis which was at the opposite pole from that which Rilke was seeking to achieve. In short, in the general picture of the influence of French poetry on

[1] Op. cit., p. 67. The complete section on Maeterlinck in this work is in pp. 67–70. H. Goertz, in the work already quoted, also devotes a chapter to Maeterlinck, pp. 4–19.

[2] *A.W.*, Bd. I, pp. 190–1.

[3] See pp. 19 and 67–68.

Rilke, these two poets were ancillary to Baudelaire (whose successors they both were), with whom we shall be primarily concerned in this chapter. They strengthened and confirmed the Baudelaire experience; and, of course, a Mallarmé transformed into a *poète réussi* will reappear in the person of his disciple, Valéry.

It is appropriate at this point to consider some of the aspects of the French Symbolist movement, especially in view of the suggestion that Rilke's relationship to this movement represented his one sustained link with an outside literary trend; and also in the light of the earlier remark that although Rilke touched against several literary movements, he belonged to none.[1] These two statements are not in conflict. On this last question, it is interesting to note, in passing, Rilke's indignant outburst in a letter to Arthur Fischer-Colbrie, dated 18 December 1925:

Ich weiß (um auf Deinen Artikel zurückzukommen), daß Du jene Version der 'Verstimmung' nur aufgenommen hast um der 'Verständigung' willen, weil dies nun einmal die leichteste Einsicht war, die dem Leser etwa erreichbar gemacht werden konnte. Indessen möchte ich gerade um diesen Preis am wenigsten nachsichtiger behandelt sein. Ich weiß nichts von einem Verstimmtsein, so wenig ich je von einer Ablehnung, von 'einer ablehnenden Haltung deutscher literarischer Kreise' gewußt habe. Meine Produktion ist nur in ihren allerfrühesten Erscheinungen von solchen Rückschlägen bis zu einem gewissen unvermeidlichen Grade abhängig gewesen. Schon mit dreiundzwanzig Jahren, zur Zeit des 'Stundenbuchs', hörte ich auf, mich um Zustimmung oder Ablehnung zu kümmern, und seither haben mich höchstens einzelne persönliche Stimmen erreicht, die, möchten sie zustimmend oder absagend oder unentschieden sein, ins Leben zurückwirken und sich (anders als die bloße Kritik) in ihm lösen. Es wäre traurig um mich bestellt, wenn ich in meinem fünfzigsten Jahr, im Bereich meiner Kunst, irgendeine Erscheinung aus Enttäuschtheit oder 'rancune' zuließe, und es ist das seltsamste Mißverständnis, daß dieser meiner Art so fremde Verdacht gerade auf die Produktion jener französischen Gedichte, die mir das heiterste, glücklichste Beschenktwerden bedeutet, seinen dumpfen Schatten wirft![2]

In this instance, at least, Rilke's ego and critical truth go hand in hand. It is true that the letter is concerned primarily with Rilke's attitude to critics, and that this passage related specifically to suggestions of his aloofness from current German literary

---

[1] p. 60.　　[2] *G.B.*, Bd. V, p. 388.

developments; but his remarks are equally applicable to his relation to any conceptual literary trends, or schools, of any nationality.

If, then, Rilke was in no sense a 'group' man, what was the nature of his link with the Symbolists, and what was the character of this movement with which he could be associated, however loosely, over the whole of the second half of his life without in any way compromising his creative individuality? The answer to the second question supplies the answer to the first. Probably no manifestation in literature has been surrounded by so much indeterminate and inconclusive theorizing as has French Symbolism.[1] Even its name is equivocal, since the use of the symbol was no new thing in the nineteenth century[2]—and is, in fact, by the nature of imaginative writing, as old as literature itself. Whereas it is possible to apply certain general unifying principles to some movements of the past, any attempt to do so in regard to the Symbolists meets with almost insuperable difficulties. A glance at the names of those associated with the movement reveals a list of poets who, by comparison with the Parnassians and even the Romantics, appear as ill-assorted and dissimilar as could be. The conclusion to which we are forced is the paradox that the more we consider these figures, the less are we able to discover any simple correlative artistic concept which can be applied to all, or even, in most cases, to any two together. Individualists, each one working out and plying his art in his own way, they appear rather as the antithesis of a school or movement, in the accepted sense of the definition. Symbolism emerges, in fact, as one of those terms of critical convenience which may be of historical assistance, but which as a means of definitive enlightenment are virtually useless.[3] If, moreover, we consider the historical limits—Baudelaire and Valéry—of the poets linked under the general heading of French Symbolism with whom we are concerned in this study, we are confronted with a span of years considerably longer than that occupied by most artistic schools from the nineteenth century onwards—an additional indication of the diffuse nature of this movement.

---

[1] An extensive examination of French Symbolism is, of course, outside the scope of this study. For a detailed analysis of the theory surrounding the movement, see A. G. Lehmann, *The Symbolist Aesthetic in France, 1885–1895*. It is interesting, in view of the central theme of the present study, to note this critic's conclusion that the key to the Symbolist aesthetic is simply language.

[2] Cf. A. Barre, *Le Symbolisme*, pp. 24–27.                    [3] Cf. p. 60.

The coupling of Rilke with such an ill-defined and amorphous movement, while at the same time insisting on his independence and his separation from 'group' tendencies, does not therefore seem a contradictory or vulnerable proposition. On the contrary, Rilke's eclecticism and desire for freedom, so far from suffering violence from this encounter, found fresh stimulus and nourishment. Rilke, in fact, approached these poets, as he had approached Rodin and Cézanne, as individuals, and with the extraordinary capacity he possessed for isolating his experiences—while always retaining them—in distinct compartments of his imaginative organization. There were, admittedly, certain general elements which gave some unity to these poets and which commended them to Rilke. They had all, in its finest distillation, the veneration for art and beauty which was Rilke's own. In particular, they were all his contemporaries, or nearly so. They were all products of the same age and conditions; an age in which science and industry threatened the citadel of art and in which the speed of material progress strained to the utmost the capacity of art to keep pace in its own development; an age when the traditional values and beliefs were no longer revered as they had been for centuries.[1]

C. M. Bowra, in *The Heritage of Symbolism*, has much to say which touches closely on this subject, the more so as Rilke and Valéry are included among the inheritors. In view of the support he gives to much of what has been said, and because of the lucidity of his exposition, we may, as a supplement to the foregoing remarks, draw attention to the first part of his Introduction.[2] He underlines the danger of speaking of movements in literature, and the impossibility of applying rules to the individual character of the poet's personality and inspiration. But, he points out, there was a change in the European poetry written after 1890, and 'the newer poets had some common qualities which make them look like members of a movement'. Unlike such previous groups as the Pléiade or the Lake School, however, the similarity of these poets 'is not the result of an agreed programme or of an entirely conscious purpose'. But these writers, while seeming different from their contemporaries, 'are found by posterity to be all tinged with the characteristic colour of an epoch'.

[1] Cf. p. 1.
[2] See particularly pp. 1-3 of this work. This section is the general reference for the following extracts.

Bowra, while indicating that the poets with whom he is concerned are a later development of what are variously known as the Symbolists or Decadents, points out that neither of these terms is exact. He lists Baudelaire, Verlaine, and Mallarmé as the chief representatives of Symbolism, who, despite their obvious differences, were united by a common view of life and a single creed which determined the character of their poetry. And this critic significantly adds the corollary to our earlier comment on the decline of the traditional values and beliefs when he states that 'the Symbolist Movement of the nineteenth century in France was fundamentally mystical'. It was a protest against the scientific art of the age, the naturalism of novelists like Zola and the impersonal art of the Parnassians, in which mysticism had no place. Bowra aptly remarks that the religion of the Symbolists was 'a religion of Ideal Beauty, of "le Beau" and "l'Idéal" ', and that they clung to their belief 'with a conviction which can only be called mystical because of its intensity, its irrationality, its disregard for other beliefs, and its reliance on a world beyond the senses'. Bowra sums up by describing Symbolism as 'a mystical form of Aestheticism'.

The relevance of this survey in the Rilke context is readily apparent. Our view is confirmed that French Symbolism in no sense represents a school working to an agreed formula; its unity and the justification for the use of the term 'movement' rest solely on a disillusionment with and a reaction against contemporary values and current artistic trends, and on the common aim of its poets to recover in their poetry the spiritual element which had been discarded by their age—terms of reference general enough to enable to be gathered under one heading poets as different from each other as each of them was from any poet of the past. It is in this artistic *milieu* that Rilke is to be considered. Bowra's clear introduction, in fact, provides an admirable starting-point from which to pass to the particular examination of Rilke's relation to the poetry of France; and when, a little later, this critic writes: 'The essence of Symbolism is its insistence on a world of ideal beauty, and its conviction that this is realized by art', we might almost adopt these words as the expression of the principle which guided Rilke's own creative career.

It seems probable that Rilke had an early contact with contemporary French poetry in Prague. Angelloz notes the popularity there of numerous French nineteenth-century poets, through the translations of Vrchlicky, though it must be recalled that Rilke knew no Czech. This critic even propounds the interesting possibility that the emergence of the 'Dinggedicht' could have owed something to Vrchlicky's partiality to Leconte de Lisle, whose numerous poems devoted to animals 'ont pu montrer au poète allemand qu'une poésie sans lyrisme est possible'.[1]

We are, however, not justified in drawing any conclusions from what is largely conjecture. If Rilke had any interest in French literature at this time, his attention was to be diverted by the successive, and much more consuming, experiences of Renaissance Italy, Russia, and Worpswede. The most that can be said is that when he arrived in Paris he may not have been completely unprepared for the process of assimilation which was to follow.[2] For it was from 1902 onwards that the real impact of French literature on Rilke took place. There can be little doubt that his reading of Baudelaire was actively stimulated by Rodin. In *Auguste Rodin* we find this significant revelation of the French sculptor:

> Und von Dante kam er zu Baudelaire[3] . . . in diesen Versen gab es Stellen, die heraustraten aus der Schrift, die nicht geschrieben, sondern geformt schienen, Worte und Gruppen von Worten, die geschmolzen waren in den heißen Händen des Dichters, Zeilen, die sich wie Reliefs anfühlten, und Sonette, die wie Säulen mit verworrenen Kapitälen die Last eines bangen Gedankens trugen. Er fühlte dunkel, daß diese Kunst, wo sie jäh aufhörte, an den Anfang einer anderen stieß, und daß sie sich nach dieser anderen gesehnt hatte; er fühlte in Baudelaire einen, der ihm vorangegangen war. . . .
> Seit jenen Tagen blieben diese beiden Dichter ihm immer nah. . . .
> Später, als er als Schaffender diese Stoffkreise wieder berührte, da stiegen ihre Gestalten wie Erinnerungen aus seinem eigenen Leben, weh und wirklich, in ihm auf und gingen in sein Werk wie eine Heimat ein.[4]

Even more important than the biographical relevance of these lines to Rodin is the insight they give into Rilke's own sympathy with Baudelaire. If his description of Baudelaire's verses reveals his eager interest in achieving a synthesis between the two arts, it shows even more his awareness that here, at last, he had found a

---

[1] Op. cit., pp. 39 and 218.    [2] See also p. 114, n. 2.
[3] It is interesting to note that the Baudelaire critic S. A. Rhodes regards the French poet as the modern counterpart of Dante. See *The Cult of Beauty in Charles Baudelaire*, p. 182.
[4] *G.W.*, Bd. IV, pp. 313–14.

poet whose consummate mastery of language was something for which he himself had to strive. Later in the same monograph, when Rilke is discussing Rodin's drawings illustrating a copy of *Les Fleurs du mal*, the same instinctive sensitivity to Baudelaire's poetry emerges:

> Man sagt nichts, wenn man da von einem sehr tiefen Verständnis Baudelairescher Verse spricht; man versucht mehr zu sagen, wenn man sich erinnert, wie diese Gedichte in ihrem Mit-sich-Gesättigtsein keine Ergänzung zulassen und keine Steigerung über sich hinaus: und daß man doch beides empfindet, Ergänzung und Steigerung, wo Rodinsche Linien sich diesem Werke anschmiegen, das ist ein Maßstab für die hinreißende Schönheit dieser Blätter. Die Federzeichnung, die neben das Gedicht 'La mort des pauvres' gestellt ist, reicht mit einer Gebärde von so einfacher, fortwährend wachsender Großheit über diese großen Verse hinaus, daß man meint, sie erfülle die Welt von Aufgang nach Untergang.[1]

Even though the appraisal of Rodin's art was the primary concern of this essay, it is impossible to mistake the profound impression which Baudelaire's poetry made on Rilke.

Other references in letters written during the early part of the Rodin period indicate Rilke's preoccupation with Baudelaire and the Symbolist poets. In a letter to Clara of 31 August 1902, only three days after his arrival in Paris, Baudelaire, Verlaine, and Mallarmé are mentioned.[2] Even more revealing is a passage in a letter to Lou Andreas-Salomé, dated 18 July 1903, and written during a visit to Worpswede:

> Und in der Nacht stand ich auf und suchte meinen Lieblingsband Baudelaire, die petits poèmes en prose, und las laut das schönste Gedicht, das überschrieben ist: À une heure du matin . . . Ein Gebet Baudelaires; ein wirkliches, schlichtes Gebet, mit den Händen gemacht, ungeschickt und schön wie das Gebet eines russischen Menschen. — Er hatte einen weiten Weg dazu hin, Baudelaire, und er ist ihn knieend und kriechend gegangen. Wie war er mir fern in allem, meiner Fremdesten einer; oft kann ich ihn kaum verstehen, und doch manchmal tief in der Nacht, wenn ich seine Worte nachsprach wie ein Kind, da war er mein Nächster und wohnte neben mir und stand bleich hinter der

---

[1] *G.W.*, Bd. IV, p. 343.
[2] *G.B.*, Bd. I, p. 246. The early date of this reference may be considered to indicate the probability that Rilke had some knowledge of these poets before he arrived in Paris, though there is no evidence to show when this knowledge was acquired.

dünnen Wand und hörte meiner Stimme zu, die fiel. Was für eine seltsame Gemeinschaft war da zwischen uns, ein Teilen von allem, dieselbe Armut und vielleicht dieselbe Angst.[1]

Even when due allowance is made for Rilke's youthful enthusiasm, which may result in an exaggerated and dramatic mode of presentation, there can be no doubt of the importance of this passage and the sense of kinship with Baudelaire which it demonstrates. At the same time, the likening of Baudelaire's prayer to 'das Gebet eines russischen Menschen' does serve as a reminder, not only that the elemental emotionalism of Rilke's nature was always ready to reassert itself, but also that the experiences of the past were not completely forgotten or discarded. The above passage and the attitude which it betokens are reinforced in the first part of *Malte*, where Rilke reproduces, simply and without referring to Baudelaire by name, the 'prayer' with which *A une heure du matin* ends:

Mécontent de tous et mécontent de moi, je voudrais bien me racheter et m'enorgueillir un peu dans le silence et la solitude de la nuit. Âmes de ceux que j'ai aimés, âmes de ceux que j'ai chantés, fortifiez-moi, soutenez-moi, éloignez de moi le mensonge et les vapeurs corruptrices du monde; et vous, Seigneur mon Dieu! accordez-moi la grâce de produire quelques beaux vers qui me prouvent à moi-même que je ne suis pas le dernier des hommes, que je ne suis pas inférieur à ceux que je méprise.[2]

This is a genuine prayer of the artist, and one which Rilke makes his own, as the preceding lines show:

Da liegt es vor mir in meiner eigenen Schrift, was ich gebetet habe, Abend für Abend. Ich habe es mir aus den Büchern, in denen ich es fand, abgeschrieben, damit es mir ganz nahe wäre und aus meiner Hand entsprungen wie Eigenes. Und ich will es jetzt noch einmal schreiben; denn so habe ich es länger, als wenn ich es lese, und jedes Wort dauert an und hat Zeit zu verhallen.[3]

These references are thus conclusive evidence of the force of Baudelaire's impact on Rilke. In turning to the artistic and aesthetic significance of this impact, we may establish the direction of the investigation and give it precision by posing two fundamental

---

[1] *G.B.*, Bd. I, pp. 360–1.     [2] *A.W.*, Bd. II, p. 50.
[3] Ibid., p. 49.

questions: Why did Baudelaire make such a deep and lasting[1] impression on Rilke, and in what way did he contribute to Rilke's evolution as a poet? Among the Rilke critics, two who have devoted sizeable sections of their work to the influence of Baudelaire are M. Bauer[2] and H. Goertz,[3] while Angelloz, in the work already quoted, makes a number of references of varying length to the subject. But writers on Rilke have not, in general, treated this experience in detail, probably because there appears to have been little disposition to recognize the influence of France as being a continuous and decisive process stretching over the whole of the second half of the poet's life. The result has been that, where France has been considered at all, attention has been confined in the main to Rodin and, to a lesser extent, Valéry.

Both Bauer and Goertz have performed a service in assembling a useful body of evidence relating to Baudelaire and Rilke, and in seeking to establish common factors in their work. The former begins with some unexceptionable remarks on the French poet, stressing his unending quest for beauty. She rightly notes that Baudelaire's whole art springs from his longing for beauty, and makes the further important point that Baudelaire seeks to show that everything horrible in life is made beautiful through art.[4] But Bauer does not avoid the pitfall of doctrinaire criticism, and when she tries to draw moral distinctions between Baudelaire and Rilke she is far less convincing. 'Aber den letzten Schritt zu Gott', she writes, 'tut er [sc. Baudelaire] nicht. Hier bleibt er nur Sucher, denn Gott wird letzten Endes nicht erdacht, nur erfühlt — auf Rilkes Weg erreicht werden können.'[5] It may be true that Rilke did not go to the extremes of depravity and perversion of Baudelaire; and it may be equally true that Baudelaire saw everything through a negative, that for him black was white and white black. But it is an over-simplification to make Rilke play Faust to Baudelaire's Mephistopheles, or to set him forward as the religious positive to Baudelaire's negative. This attempt to canonize Rilke

---

[1] In addition to the fact that *Les Plaintes d'un Icare* was translated as late as 1921, there is a further reference to Baudelaire and Verlaine in a letter 'An Gräfin M.', dated 2 December of this same year. See *G.B.*, Bd. V, p. 60.

[2] *Rainer Maria Rilke und Frankreich*, pp. 25–40. The chapter, which is entitled 'Französischer Geist — Baudelaire, die Symbolisten', also discusses Verlaine, Verhaeren, Mallarmé, and Maeterlinck, and alludes briefly to Rilke's other early contacts with French literature.

[3] Op. cit., pp. 38–51.                    [4] Op. cit., p. 25.

[5] Ibid., p. 26.

leads this critic to make such an equivocal statement as 'Er liebt Gott am meisten, da er es sich versagt, seinen Namen zu nennen . . .'[1]

There are two points arising out of this argument which need clarification. First, Rilke, outside his single-minded application to his art, does not emerge as a man with positive convictions at all; rather was he passive, vacillating, deviating to right and left of the middle road as occasion or advantage demanded—there are many who would regard his way of life as no more admirable than Baudelaire's—and in this lack of positive conviction lies, perhaps, the most noticeable difference between him and Baudelaire. It is basically a difference of personality. For while they shared a similar artistic sensibility with a strong bias towards the morbid and the bizarre, Rilke was psychologically incapable of yielding to the Baudelairean extreme of cynicism and 'satanism' or to the opposite extreme of Christian mysticism. (He may well have been a greater artist for the avoidance of extremes, even if this avoidance sprang fundamentally from an inherent lack of moral decision.)

The second, and much more important, point is that the introduction of this note of comparative virtue into the discussion of Rilke and Baudelaire is unnecessary, and is reminiscent of the dubious hagiographical critical practices referred to in the first chapter. The only relevant consideration is how far Rilke and Baudelaire, with their different viewpoints and different temperaments and habits of life, converged in their artistic ideal; how far there was identity of purpose in their approach to their poetry; how far there were common elements in their poetic concept, in their technique, in their sensibility, in their manipulation of the medium of language; and, above all, how far Baudelaire made a decisive and lasting contribution to Rilke's own artistic development.

It is interesting to note several general features which may be considered to provide strong presumptive evidence that, when once Rilke had made the acquaintance of Baudelaire's poetry, the force of elective affinity would come into operation. Baudelaire, like Rilke, disliked the rise of industrialism and the advance of materialist values.[2] We may also adduce his keen and penetrating taste for the representational arts. He was, of course, a practised

[1] Ibid., p. 28.
[2] Cf. S. A. Rhodes, op. cit. pp. 391 and 396.

art critic;[1] but if Rilke did not pursue this literary sideline to the same extent as Baudelaire, the *Florenzer Tagebuch*, *Auguste Rodin*, and the 'Cézanne-Briefe' give sufficient indication of his capacities in this field and of a sensitivity and receptivity similar to Baudelaire's. It is further interesting to recall the French poet's lasting admiration for Delacroix, which may in some measure be seen, perhaps, as the counterpart of Rilke's regard for Cézanne. Rhodes records Baudelaire's scrupulous attention to language and his meticulous care in choosing the right word[2]—a quality which was to become the keystone of Rilke's poetry, and one with which he became preoccupied during his early years in Paris to a much greater extent than he had been before. Of particular interest, when considering Rilke in the context of the Rodin and Cézanne experiences and in the light of his 'Entwicklung zum sachlichen Sagen', is Rhodes's comment: 'A characteristic in Baudelaire's style is its plasticity, the power to visualize effects, fix colours and forms by means of words.'[3] One quality of Baudelaire's that Rilke did not share was a taste for music; although in so far as Baudelaire's leanings towards this art are primarily associated with his attempt to fit music into his theory of 'Correspondances', and also with the impact on France of Wagner and in particular of the latter's revolutionary doctrines, it is difficult to be certain how far his interest in this field was intrinsically musical. Finally, both Baudelaire and Rilke were individualists, literary aristocrats, keeping aloof from the crowd and from anything which savoured of standardization—a quality which found its outward expression in Baudelaire's 'dandyism' and in Rilke's life of solitude and removal from domestic and social ties.[4]

But the many points at which their tastes and pursuits meet, and their notable receptivity to similar impressions, are merely symptomatic of the deeper inner kinship between the two men. Both were 'pure' artists, with a strong strain of aestheticism; both worshipped the ideal of 'le Beau'; for both the prosecution of their art was the supreme fulfilment, the end and justification of their existence, the only duty and compulsion which they acknowledged. Above all—and this leads directly to the essence of the part played

---

[1] Cf. M. Gilman, *Baudelaire the Critic*, p. 6.
[2] Op. cit., p. 211.
[3] Ibid., p. 226.
[4] An additional common characteristic, their bias towards the morbid and the bizarre, has already been noted on p. 117.

by Baudelaire in Rilke's evolution—both were innovators in language, masters of poetic form, of startling image and searing metaphor.

As with the Rodin experience, although in a different sense, since it was not an association with a living person, there were two ingredients in Rilke's reaction to Baudelaire: the emotional and the artistic. And of necessity, since environment, experience, and the emotional response to circumstances and human contacts are themselves influential and have a formative effect in the development of the artist, the two aspects of Baudelaire's impact on Rilke are interrelated. But if it is not possible—or desirable—to make a complete separation, the dual presence of these elements should be kept in mind, in order to establish some degree of critical priority and to avoid basing judgement disproportionately on those factors which are most obvious and which are not of first importance to our purpose.

The first, and most perceptible, feature of Rilke's reaction to Baudelaire is that it is closely related to the first impact of Paris on the German poet. Angelloz comments on the brutal nature of this initiation and points out that none of the great cities of which Rilke had previously had experience—Prague, Berlin, St. Petersburg, Moscow—had been able to provide him with the revelation which Paris was to give. And, after noting the anguish and terror of the young poet seeking the secret of human existence, this critic pertinently concludes: 'Il devra conquérir Paris pour se conquérir lui-même.'[1] Rilke's early period in Paris was one of the big emotional upheavals in his life, and one which came near to breaking his spirit. It was his first contact with the harsh realities of life in a great city, and he was singularly ill-equipped to adjust himself to his new surroundings and experiences. It was in this mood of disillusionment and despair that he made the acquaintance of Baudelaire's poetry, and it is not difficult to see why there was an immediate response and a spontaneous sense of kinship. *Das Buch von der Armut und vom Tode* (written in Viareggio in April 1903, little more than six months after his arrival in Paris), his correspondence of the period, and the early part of *Malte*, are full of Rilke's early impressions of the French capital; echoes of them persist in the later poems of *Das Buch der Bilder* and even in a few of the *Neue Gedichte*. His new world was one of horror and distress, of

[1] Op. cit., pp. 172–3.

poverty, suffering, disease, of hospitals and beggars—in short, Paris was the 'Leidstadt' of the Tenth Elegy. And it was precisely these things, and the reflection of his own mood and sensitivity, which he found in Baudelaire's poetry. Here was a poet who had seen as he saw, who had felt as he felt, who had been receptive to the same impressions as his own and had sublimated them into art. The poem beginning 'Denn, Herr, die großen Städte . . .'[1] is Rilke's poetic picture of Paris during his first months there; such is the sombre theme which dominates *Das Buch von der Armut und vom Tode*—a strange beginning for such an important and rewarding phase in his artistic education.

One or two examples are sufficient to show the striking parallel between Rilke's poetry of the period and parts of Baudelaire's *Tableaux parisiens*. From Rilke we may take the final section of the above poem and against it set the twelve lines from Baudelaire's *Le Crépuscule du matin* beginning 'Les femmes de plaisir, la paupière livide, . . .' Even closer is the similarity between Rilke's *Eine von den Alten*[2] and the opening three stanzas from Baudelaire's *Les Petites Vieilles*. To these could be added many other examples of the Baudelairean motif in Rilke's writings of the time. Sometimes, particularly if *Malte* and Baudelaire's *Petits Poèmes en prose* are incorporated in the evidence, the resemblance is so marked as almost to convict Rilke of imitation.

This, however, is the most obvious aspect of Baudelaire's impact on Rilke, and, perhaps because it is so apparent, it is not the most important. It must be seen in the context of the acute personal crisis through which Rilke was passing: in other words, its significance was only secondarily artistic, in so far as it provided material for artistic treatment. Rilke, shattered by the repellent discoveries he made in Paris, was understandably impressed to find that another great poet had made them too. In this aspect of his approach to Baudelaire there was a cathartic quality, acting as a kind of safety-valve for the release of his own inner tension; and, inasmuch as there was in Baudelaire, who loved his Paris, no suggestion of revulsion or defeat, Rilke may even have acquired vicarious strength to help him to survive his ordeal and triumph over the instinctive impulse to retreat.

In seeking Baudelaire's real, long-term importance for Rilke, we come nearer to the heart of the matter when we consider the

[1] *A.W.*, Bd. I, p. 91.     [2] *G.W.*, Bd. III, p. 173.

close relation of his study of the French poet with the Rodin experience. It may be wondered whether Rilke would have come to know Baudelaire intimately if Rodin had not been such an avid reader and enthusiastic admirer of his work. It seems unlikely that Rilke, artistically constituted as he was, and activated by the Symbolist ideals, would have remained in ignorance of Baudelaire. But it is possible that, without Rodin, the acquaintance would not have been made at that time (an important point when one considers that the chronological order of Rilke's evolutionary experiences was in itself significant,[1] approximating almost to an organic process of growth); and it is probable that, without the stimulus provided by Rodin, Rilke's application to Baudelaire's poetry might not have been so concentrated. In particular, we may assume that, in the early stages at least, Rilke's interest in Baudelaire was directed along certain lines. We have seen, in a quotation from *Auguste Rodin*,[2] that one of the principal reasons for the sculptor's sympathy with Baudelaire was that he saw in the latter's art something which came near to his own. And Rhodes writes that 'for the poet, the secret of all inspired work, Baudelaire held, is hard work'[3]—another echo of Rodin. Recalling Rilke's artistic preoccupation of the period, it can therefore be seen that, in so far as Rodin was his tutor, his reading of Baudelaire was in some measure associated with his concern to achieve a synthesis between the plastic arts and poetry.

Thus, this second stage in Rilke's assimilation of Baudelaire reveals an advance on the first, the 'Parisian' stage, in that it was purely artistic and aesthetic in its character; and in its integration with the Rodin experience it betokens a consistency in Rilke's purpose and development at that time. But to leave Baudelaire's influence on Rilke as merely an adjunct to the Rodin experience and to dwell exclusively on its 'sculptural' quality would still do less than justice to this important episode in Rilke's career. To take the examination of the episode no further would impose crippling limitations on it, and entangle it in the problems of medium which loomed so large in the Rodin chapter; it would do violence to the fact that Baudelaire was an artist in a 'mobile' medium, Rilke's own medium—a fact which Rilke himself was bound to realize in the end. Nevertheless, just as we have seen that

---

[1] Cf. the remarks on the Cézanne experience on p. 76.
[2] p. 113.                    [3] Op. cit., p. 194.

Rilke's exposure to Rodin's discipline was salutary, this aspect of Baudelaire's impact should not be underestimated, even if it is not the last word. Bearing in mind Rilke's emancipation from the unrestrained emotionalism of the first two parts of *Das Stunden-Buch*, which was the first-fruit of the Rodin experience, and his accompanying efforts to objectivize his poetry, without sacrificing the all-important ingredient of feeling,[1] it is interesting to note E. Starkie's comment in the Introduction to her edition of *Les Fleurs du mal*: 'Baudelaire managed to avoid the two pitfalls of nineteenth-century French literature: the excessive subjectivity of the Romantic movement and the cold impersonality of the Parnassian school.'[2] This was precisely the trend along which Rilke's own poetic concept was evolving, and this thought appropriately leads us to the third aspect of Baudelaire's influence on Rilke.

In order to reach the kernel of the French poet's contribution to Rilke's development, it is necessary to go beyond the context of the Rodin experience, which, for all its great value, imposed too many limitations on Rilke's conceptual freedom to allow him complete and unbiassed receptivity to an artist in his own material. Indeed, it is significant that the full force of Baudelaire's impact and the complete assimilation of his artistic concept into Rilke's own did not occur until after the Rodin years (and, incidentally, after *Auguste Rodin* was finished). The important pieces of evidence upon which the discussion will be based are the two well-known passages referring to Baudelaire in *Malte Laurids Brigge*[3] and the 'Cézanne-Briefe'.[4] Despite the distance in time between their composition, they must be regarded as two parts of a whole, the second, in fact, being a commentary on, and extending the idea of, the first.

In view of the previous suggestion that it was necessary for Rilke to be released from the constraint of his preoccupation with Rodin and the latter's medium before he could reap the full harvest of his contact with the poetry of Baudelaire, some explanatory remarks on the date of the first passage are indicated. The writing of *Malte* was begun in February 1904; and, while the progressive dating of the novel cannot be established with any certainty, since

[1] Cf. p. 59.                    [2] Ed. cit. (Oxford, 1942), p. vii.
[3] *A.W.*, Bd. II, p. 66.
[4] *G.B.*, Bd. II, pp. 432–3 and previously quoted on p. 95.

the Baudelaire passage occurs only half-way through the first part, it may be assumed that it was written some time before the end of the Rodin period. On the other hand, since the passage, as will be seen, clearly indicates a poetic and not a 'plastic' approach to Baudelaire's poetry, it is desirable to reconcile this fact with the obstacle to free assimilation, mentioned in the previous paragraph, inherent in Rilke's concentration on the sculptural medium and technique. We may recall, for this purpose, a letter written to Lou Andreas-Salomé in April 1904.[1] Although in the first part of the letter Rilke vaunts his advance under Rodin, his real dissatisfaction and uneasiness emerge in the final paragraph. Even earlier, in a letter to the same recipient written in August 1903, we found a similar note of incongruence expressed in terms of the 'Unvereinbarkeit zweier Kunstwelten'.[2] Thus, even though the association with Rodin still had more than half its course to run, the strains and stresses were already present. In other words, before this passage in *Malte* was written the process of artistic estrangement and emancipation from Rodin had begun; and the decrease in the power of Rodin's influence implicit in this alienation was logically accompanied by a proportionate increase in Rilke's preoccupation with and receptivity to the fundamentals of his own art, and therefore in his preparedness for Baudelaire's lesson.

The first part of the evidence, the passage from *Malte*, reads:

Erinnerst Du Dich an Baudelaires unglaubliches Gedicht 'Une Charogne'? Es kann sein, daß ich es jetzt verstehe. Abgesehen von der letzten Strophe, war er im Recht. Was sollte er tun, da ihm das widerfuhr? Es war seine Aufgabe, in diesem Schrecklichen, scheinbar nur Widerwärtigen das Seiende zu sehen, das unter allem Seienden gilt. Auswahl und Ablehnung gibt es nicht. Hältst Du es für einen Zufall, daß Flaubert seinen Saint-Julien-l'Hospitalier geschrieben hat? Es kommt mir vor, als wäre das das Entscheidende: ob einer es über sich bringt, sich zu dem Aussätzigen zu legen und ihn zu erwärmen mit der Herzwärme der Liebesnächte, das kann nicht anders als gut ausgehen.[3]

The use of the word 'unglaublich' to describe Baudelaire's poem is eloquent of the impression it made on Rilke. There is, here, the vital recognition that in art there can be no question of selection or refusal in the matter of subject; the poet is not justified in excluding —is even under a compulsion not to exclude—anything. This is

[1] See pp. 69–70.          [2] Ibid. p. 69.          [3] *A.W.*, Bd. II, p. 66.

a flat rejection of a concept which holds that only certain things are fit for treatment by the artist; it is an affirmation that art must be universal in the truest sense, that it must embrace the whole of experience. In the pursuit of artistic truth—'das Seiende' —even the ugly and horrible, even death in its most revolting manifestations, must be confronted and penetrated. And although Rilke does not reiterate in so many words Baudelaire's concept that even 'das Schreckliche, scheinbar nur Widerwärtige' is beautified by the metamorphosing power of art, his agreement with this principle is implicit in his acknowledgement that 'das Seiende' must be sought in everything. We may ask what the Baudelaire revelation means, in plain terms, in its application to Rilke's own poetry and to his development. It signifies, first and foremost, a considerable broadening of the frontiers of his artistic vision, a readiness to extend the scope of his experience, an enrichment of his sensitivity—and withal correspondingly increased demands on his capacity to handle his medium. In short, the contact with Baudelaire left Rilke a more complete poet.

And yet he does not go the whole way with Baudelaire. There remains the interesting question of his rejection of the end of *Une Charogne*:

> Oui! telle vous serez, ô la reine des grâces,
>     Après les derniers sacrements,
> Quand vous irez, sous l'herbe et les floraisons grasses,
>     Moisir parmi les ossements.
>
> Alors, ô ma beauté! dites à la vermine
>     Qui vous mangera de baisers,
> Que j'ai gardé la forme et l'essence divine
>     De mes amours décomposés!

(Although Rilke specifies the last strophe, the last two stanzas have been given, since they are really inseparable.) Goertz seeks to motivate Rilke's aversion from the last stanza by contrasting Baudelaire's 'Blasphemie, Hohn und Spott' with Rilke's 'Liebesbereitschaft'.[1] This critic appears to have adopted the dangerous course of basing his judgement of the poem on his personal opinion of Baudelaire's character. There seems to be absolutely no reason for reading 'Blasphemie, Hohn und Spott' into the last

---

[1] Op. cit., p. 43.

stanza. Whatever may be known or thought about his philosophy of life or credal perversity, Baudelaire was an impeccable artist, and to end his poem with a cynical Heine-like twist would have been to disrupt its aesthetic unity and balance in a way which the artist in him would never have allowed. Even more, there is nothing in the content of these closing lines to justify such an estimate.

More important is Rilke's own reason for his rejection of the stanza. Angelloz records him as telling Mme R. Notons that he did not approve of the strophe 'parce qu'elle est trop spiritualiste'.[1] This at least has the merit over Goertz's interpretation that it is critically more objective. But it is difficult to see how the term 'spiritualiste' can be applied to these lines. Surely, the idea which the poet is conveying in the last two stanzas is that, although the body is mortal, he can perpetuate the beauty of his love through the medium of his art, which will endure. It is a conditional, comparative, not an absolute, immortality with which he is concerned. Thus, Rilke's qualification of *Une Charogne* may well have been due to nothing more than a failure to sense Baudelaire's meaning in the closing lines—a failure not altogether surprising when one recalls that he was still very much a novitiate in the study of the language and literature of France. On this count there seems to have been nothing which need have prevented Rilke from accepting the whole poem. One other possibility remains. Rilke, under the influence of Rodin, was applying himself diligently to the task of 'objectivizing' his poetry and eliminating the subjective effusion of his earlier work. In this mood he may have seen in the last stanza of *Une Charogne* an exaltation of the personal element, an excessive personal intrusion of the poet. His proviso may have been an instinctive rebellion against something which appeared to go against the stream of his current poetic endeavour; in short, it may have been an anticipatory movement towards what was later to be formulated in the principle of 'sagen' instead of 'beurteilen'.

This thought leads to the second, and complementary, piece of evidence. Not for nothing was this subject reopened in the 'Cézanne-Briefe', the more so as the leaven of Baudelaire's poetry —and French poetry as a whole—had had more time to work, and also because the autumn of 1907 was one of the most theoretical and contemplative periods in Rilke's life.[2] The passage, which

[1] Op. cit., note to p. 244.    [2] Cf. p. 104.

was only partially quoted in the chapter on Cézanne, occurs in the letter dated 19 October 1907:

Du erinnerst sicher . . . aus den Aufzeichnungen des Malte Laurids, die Stelle, die von Baudelaire handelt und von seinem Gedichte 'Das Aas'. Ich mußte daran denken, daß ohne dieses Gedicht die ganze Entwicklung zum sachlichen Sagen, die wir jetzt in Cézanne zu erkennen glauben, nicht hätte anheben können; erst mußte es da sein in seiner Unerbittlichkeit. Erst mußte das künstlerische Anschauen sich so weit überwunden haben, auch im Schrecklichen und scheinbar nur Widerwärtigen das Seiende zu sehen, das, mit allem anderen Seienden, *gilt*. Sowenig eine Auswahl zugelassen ist, ebensowenig ist eine Abwendung von irgendwelcher Existenz dem Schaffenden erlaubt; ein einziges Ablehnen irgendwann drängt ihn aus dem Zustande der Gnade, macht ihn ganz und gar sündig. Flaubert, als er die Legende von Saint-Julien-l'hospitalier mit so viel Umsicht und Sorgfalt wiedererzählte, gab ihr diese einfache Glaubwürdigkeit mitten im Wunderbaren, weil der Künstler in ihm die Entschlüsse der Heiligen mit beschloß und ihnen glücklich zustimmte und zurief. Dies Sich-zu-dem-Aussätzigen-Legen und Alle-eigene-Wärme-, bis zu der Herzwärme der Liebesnächte, mit-ihm-Teilen: dies muß irgendwann im Dasein eines Künstlers gewesen sein, als Überwindung zu seiner neuen Seligkeit.[1]

(We may wonder whether there is any significance in the fact that this time there is no reference to the last stanza of Baudelaire's poem. Despite the concept of 'sagen' instead of 'beurteilen', we may also recall the earlier suggestion that Rilke, during this period, was passing through a stage of personal readjustment which was leading him to a greater measure of subjectivity.)[2]

This passage does more than repeat the earlier one in *Malte*. It is more precise, more categorical. Rilke's aesthetic and artistic concept was now more mature; he was more sure of himself. The italicized '*gilt*' reveals the emphatic and unhesitating nature of Rilke's assurance. Where, before, he had simply acknowledged the artist's duty to embrace 'das Schreckliche' in his art, the affirmation is now much more positive: it is that 'das Seiende', the essence, the vital artistic truth in the horrible and repugnant has *equal validity* 'mit allem anderen Seienden'. There can, in fact, be no such thing as revulsion for the artist. All things and all experiences have equal beauty under the transforming power of art, and to select or reject is to commit an act of destruction rather than

---

[1] *G.B.*, Bd. II, pp. 432–3.          [2] Cf. p. 104.

creation, since by so doing one shatters the unity, the indivisible validity, of all being.[1] Rilke uses strong words to condemn the culpability of such an act—'ein einziges Anlehnen irgendwann drängt ihn [sc. den Schaffenden] aus dem Zustande der Gnade, macht ihn ganz und gar sündig'. And Rilke finds the symbol of this unity in the incident described by Flaubert.[2]

Of particular interest is Rilke's opinion 'daß ohne dieses Gedicht die ganze Entwicklung zum sachlichen Sagen . . . nicht hätte anheben können'. Even if this is an exaggerated view—or, rather, a view arrived at *a posteriori* when he learnt that Cézanne knew *Une Charogne* by heart[3]—it does establish beyond doubt Baudelaire's participation in the complicated formative process which was taking place in Rilke's creative constitution during these important early years in Paris. And it does correlate the Baudelaire revelation with that of Cézanne, indicating the remarkable integration and common direction of the influences operating on Rilke during these years—a factor to which we have already drawn attention.[3] It is noteworthy that here again is something which was begun with Rodin and completed with Cézanne. The preoccupation with Baudelaire, linked in the first place with the ordeal of Rilke's first contact with Paris, and continued with the 'sculptural' and 'architectural' flavour imparted to it by Rodin's reading of the French poet, reached its climax, its final precipitation, under Cézanne. It would, therefore, be more accurate, perhaps, to modify Rilke's judgement that the development marked by the Cézanne experience would have been impossible without prior knowledge of Baudelaire's poetry by submitting that neither influence would have been complete without the other. In addition to providing Rilke with an enriching aesthetic and artistic experience in its own right, Baudelaire fulfilled a further interesting function in this crucial period of Rilke's evolution: he was the one unifying factor in the complicated pattern of these years. Like Ariadne's thread, he helped to guide

[1] It is perhaps not inappropriate to note, especially in the context of Baudelaire, that Rilke is unwittingly expressing a corollary to Goethe's emphasis, in *Faust,* on the common origin and indivisibility of good and evil.

[2] In August 1909, in a letter to Jakob Baron Uexküll, Rilke returns to the subject of 'das Schreckliche' in art. His views remain unchanged with the passage of two years—a fact which indicates the consistency of his evolution. It may, however, appear a little strange that his comments here emerge from references to *Das Stunden-Buch.* See *G.B.,* Bd. III, p. 71.

[3] See p. 95.

Rilke along the labyrinthine progress through the representational arts, ensured that his contact with his own art and with the poet's instrument of language would not be severed, and finally helped to bring him to the clear light of day, or at least to the point where, henceforth, his whole attention would be given to his own medium and to artists of his own kind. For this purpose Baudelaire, who, with his admiration for Delacroix, had his own link with the representational arts, was a singularly appropriate guide.

The nature and implications of Rilke's 'Entwicklung zum sachlichen Sagen' were discussed at length in the previous chapter.[1] Recalling E. Starkie's comment on Baudelaire,[2] we can see how well the latter fits into this phase in Rilke's development. For there can be little doubt that, of all the poets with whom recorded evidence shows Rilke to have been familiar at this time, Baudelaire most nearly approached the ideal for which Rilke was striving. Historically and artistically, Baudelaire had contacts with the Romantics and the Parnassians, and he succeeded in finding a middle course between them. His artistic problem bore a remarkable resemblance to Rilke's own, his solution was a striking counterpart to that which Rilke was himself evolving. Baudelaire succeeded in extracting something from both movements and welding them into a characteristic unity: the emotional, subjective element of the Romantics and the technical perfection of Le Parnasse. He showed Rilke the way to the perfect merger between subjectivity and objectivity, with all the demands it made on the poet's control over his material. In technique, mastery of language, immaculateness of form, artistic taste and integrity, in his power of evocation, in his capacity to assault the emotions with the sudden arresting image or metaphor, in his unalloyed love of 'le Beau' and 'l'Idéal'—in all these Baudelaire could not fail to loom large in Rilke's preoccupation with his own artistic fulfilment.

[1] See particularly pp. 90–92.        [2] p. 122.

# VI

## GIDE

THE years 1902 to 1907 were, from the point of view of the vital influences which contributed to Rilke's evolution as a poet, the most crowded in his life—and at the end of the Cézanne experience the Sonnets and the completed Elegies were still more than fourteen years away. Into these first five years after his arrival in Paris was compressed the rich assortment of contacts with Rodin, Cézanne, and Baudelaire: though each was representative of a different art, the three yet formed a closely interwoven pattern in the complicated and ever-growing fabric of Rilke's artistic personality. In the autumn of 1907 Rilke was still not 32 years of age, and the logical sequel to such a rapid succession of formative experiences was a period in which they could be fully assimilated and brought to maturity. The years which followed were ones of comparative quiescence; for those investigating Rilke's development they are far less spectacular than the preceding period, and at first sight they may, perhaps, seem unrewarding.

But the process of fermentation went on within, even if outwardly Rilke seemed to be marking time; and if he himself was to come to know the depths of despair, after the exaltation of the revelations of Rodin, Cézanne, and Baudelaire, we, in retrospect, can see how necessary it was that he should have a prolonged period of gestation, in which the seeds already planted would have time to grow and adapt themselves to the harsh climate of the winter of creative trial and disappointment before finally bearing fruit in the high summer. Certain it is that Rilke could not have continued to absorb major fertilizing experiences at the rate at which they had occurred in the early Parisian years without sacrificing something of their full potential. All this should be borne in mind if the years which followed 1907 appear, on the surface, to be inconclusive and something of an anti-climax. Rilke pursued his reading, and on a much broader basis—under the influence of Kippenberg his interest in German literature was widened considerably, and the publisher was notably instrumental in stimulating

his study of Goethe; in particular, his knowledge of the French
language and literature was consolidated and extended. His frequent and varied travels continued. He worked on his translations,
which, as well as being a linguistic exercise, reveal the all-important
persistence and strengthening of his ties with the Symbolist poets.
*Malte Laurids Brigge*, which in itself is in such a large measure a
reflection of, as well as a contribution to, Rilke's evolutionary conflict, was finished in 1910. This remarkable piece of writing, which,
because it partakes of the qualities of both, cannot properly be
classified either as a novel or as an autobiography, was, more than
anything else, the means by which Rilke kept himself moving
forward, pouring into it the elements of his struggle towards realization. And, of course, he went on writing poetry—but for the most
part poetry which, if much of it was good, was not the real fulfilment for which he was waiting. Above all, he was thinking, slowly
disentangling and putting into order, uncertainly and experiment-
ally, the complicated strands of his experience, and painfully
evolving his poetic personality.

   To Rilke, however, anxious for quick results, there seemed little
sign of positive progress. The period which followed the completion of *Malte* marked the most serious and sombre crisis in his life[1]
—a crisis severe enough to make him wonder at times whether he
had been right to choose the profession of poet, and to make him
hanker after those formal qualifications which would have enabled
him to pursue a conventional career. This mood of gloom and
uncertainty, relieved only occasionally (for example, during the
visit to Spain in 1912–13), was to last until after the end of the
First World War. Even the intermittent work on the Elegies after
their beginning at Duino in 1912 seemed rather to increase than to
allay the sense of failure and frustration. (It should not be forgotten
that quite a sizeable portion of this great series was written before February 1922.)[2] Thus for well over a decade the picture we
have of Rilke is one of watching and waiting, of probing and self-
examination, of doubt and despondency punctuated by barely
enough achievement to sustain faith in himself and to keep him
steadfast in his purpose.

   [1] Cf. p. 10. It is interesting to observe that, although somewhat different
in nature, the crisis of the artist came in the same period of Rilke's life as in
Goethe's, when they were both in their middle thirties.
   [2] For the chronology of the Elegies, see *A.W.*, Bd. I, p. 423.

It is against this background that the figure of André Gide
emerges. Rilke's contact with Gide was unlike any other experience
in his life, and it is important to examine the exact nature of the
latter's influence. Certainly, in the purely literary sense, Gide's
significance in Rilke's development is not as great as that of the
artists who had preceded him in Rilke's experience, or of Valéry,
who was to come after; but neither is it by any means so small as to
warrant ignoring it. Gide's contribution to Rilke's evolution was,
in fact, different from that of the other figures appearing in the
earlier chapters in that it was not strictly formative; he brought to
Rilke no new revelation which was essentially artistic or aesthetic
in its character. His importance is to be seen in the light of the
introductory remarks of this chapter, and can be estimated only
against the circumstances of Rilke's life between 1908 and the early
post-war years. Rilke, as we have noted, had already had a rich
intake of artistic experience, the integration of which into his own
poetic concept was far from complete. This process was slow and
hard, and, as with every other gain in the poet's gradual advance,
was not to be prevailed over 'mit Gewalt'. It obeyed what was
almost an organic law of growth. In the event, Rilke was destined
for years of waiting far longer than he can have anticipated—a
period in which his faith was to be assailed nearly to breaking-
point, and in which he would be sorely tempted to relax in his
purpose and abdicate from his high calling. He needed, above all
else, someone who would help to keep him anchored to his task
and, in particular, to the country and culture which (as has become
increasingly clear) alone could infuse into him the element of
discipline and control which would enable him to emerge finally as
the complete artist.

It was Gide who, more than any other single figure, provided
this stabilizing force in Rilke's life; it was he who helped to focus
Rilke's attention and concentrate his energies at a time when they
might easily have been dissipated through sheer hopelessness and
inability to see the way ahead. His function in Rilke's pilgrimage
was thus primarily one of confirmation and support. The relationship between the two men was, first and foremost, one of warm
personal regard and friendship—a friendship which was maintained until the end of Rilke's life, though in the last years, when
Rilke's purpose was accomplished and Gide's part in that purpose
therefore at an end, the intercourse between them decreased

considerably. In the length of its duration we can see the index of
how this relationship differed from the previous ones, which were in
the main characterized by comparatively sudden and brief periods
of intense revelation and were then stored away deep in the poet's
consciousness. This was, moreover, Rilke's only association with
a creative artist which produced a large body of letters.[1] Before
passing to a critical assessment of Gide's contribution to Rilke's
evolution, we may once again comment on the remarkable pattern
of the latter's career and the manner in which in every crisis and
need of his life the appropriate figure or experience unfailingly
emerged to help him resolve his problems.

We have spoken of the process of the correlation of his fertilizing
experiences and the maturing of his artistic concept which lay
before Rilke after the revelations of Rodin, Cézanne, and Baudelaire. It is fitting to remind ourselves that this was inseparable from
the achievement of progressive mastery over his medium, in which
France had such an important part to play. The requisite that this
vital link with French language and literature should not be broken
is implicit in Lang's remarks in the Introduction to her edition of
the correspondence between Rilke and Gide:

> Est-il encore nécessaire de dire ce que Rilke vint chercher en pays
> latin? La vision sûre et précise, l'expression contrainte, le métier im-
> peccable et la volonté du travail superposée au hasard de l'inspiration,
> tout cela il le trouva chez Rodin aussi bien que chez Cézanne, Gide ou
> Valéry. Aussi la correspondance . . . est-elle bien plus que l'histoire
> d'une amitié; elle est une parfaite illustration des rapports de Rilke
> avec la France.[2]

If 'la volonté du travail' has been found to be an equivocal term in
the context of Rilke's creative activity, this passage nevertheless
summarizes concisely his task. Gide's part in the accomplishment
of this task, and the lines along which we may profitably consider
his significance in Rilke's evolution, are further indicated by the
same writer. Commenting on the fact that Rilke was at the mercy of
his emotions and his facility, she notes his awareness that he needed
the hard discipline of the art of France. And if, at first, certain affinities attracted him to Gide, he soon realized that he could learn

---

[1] These letters have been edited, with a useful introduction, by R. Lang,
under the title *Rilke et Gide, Correspondance.*

[2] Ed. cit., p. 7.

both from Gide's 'limpid writing' and from his attitude to life. She goes on, in the same passage, to refer to Rilke as 'l'éternel apprenti'.[1] There is little in the content of this correspondence which relates to the present study; its primary importance for us is that it exists, strengthening Rilke's bond with France and (not least, since it was all in French) increasing his intimacy with a language which in itself had so much to give him. Rilke's first letter to Gide was written in 1910, though he was already familiar with the latter's work and had an admiration for it.[2] Gide's *Le Retour de l'enfant prodigue*, which Rilke translated in 1913, had appeared in 1907, and it is significant, bearing in mind the theme with which *Malte Laurids Brigge* closes, that the correspondence between the two men should open in the year of the completion of this work. In his letter to Gide, in fact, Rilke offers him *Malte*. This date and the theme of the Prodigal Son provide the most significant key to Rilke's association with Gide, especially when we remember that 1910 marked the beginning of Rilke's most serious crisis—albeit a crisis which, in the very pain of its struggle, may be regarded as a point of transition, the start of the emergence from the chrysalid stage and of the poet's 'Reifwerden' which was to lead to the vision of the Elegies and the Sonnets. Rilke's awareness that he was at a turning-point in his life is revealed in a letter to Lou Andreas-Salomé, dated 28 December 1911, in which, writing of *Malte*, he says: 'Je weiter ich es zu Ende schrieb, desto stärker fühlte ich, daß es ein unbeschreiblicher Abschnitt sein würde, eine hohe Wasserscheide . . . ; aber nun erweist es sich, daß alles Gewässer nach der alten Seite abgeflossen ist und ich in eine Dürre hinuntergeh, die nicht anders wird.'[3] Rilke's diagnosis was accurate; it is hardly surprising if his prognosis was not. Rilke's equation of the completion of *Malte* with a watershed in his life is illuminated by a further significant feature. From the end of 1910 there was a marked reduction in the hitherto plentiful stream of letters to his wife—a further retreat from family ties and social responsibilities. If this may be construed as the logical accompaniment of his onward march as an artist, it also invites correlation with the Rilkean version

---

[1] Ed. cit., p. 11.
[2] The first letter in Lang's series, from Rilke to Georg Brandes and dated 28 November 1909, contains commendatory references to *La Porte étroite*. The letter is taken from *Briefe aus den Jahren 1907–1914*, pp. 88–90, but is not in the *Gesammelte Briefe*.
[3] *G.B.*, Bd. III, p. 157.

of the story of the Prodigal Son. Thus, while Rilke was conscious
only of impotence and perplexity, the instinctive mechanism which
controlled so much of his life was operating, as so often before,
with inexorable efficiency.

That Rilke saw himself as the modern counterpart of the Prodigal Son is evident. That, in this mood, he should be drawn to the
writer who had written his own version of the story, and in the very
recent past, is understandable. More interesting, and more useful,
are the variations in the treatment: if the common choice of theme
explains Rilke's association with Gide, the difference in their approach to it will help to define the relationship between the two
men and, in particular, will demonstrate the limits beyond which
Gide's influence could not pass. Rilke had already treated the subject in the *Neue Gedichte*, in the poem *Der Auszug des verlorenen
Sohnes*,[1] the last lines of which are:

> Und dann noch fortzugehen, Hand aus Hand,
> als ob man ein Geheiltes neu zerrisse,
> und fortzugehn: wohin? Ins Ungewisse,
> weit in ein unverwandtes warmes Land,
> das hinter allem Handeln wie Kulisse
> gleichgültig sein wird: Garten oder Wand;
> und fortzugehn: warum? Aus Drang, aus Artung,
> aus Ungeduld, aus dunkler Erwartung,
> aus Unverständlichkeit und Unverstand:
>
> Dies alles auf sich nehmen und vergebens
> vielleicht Gehaltnes fallen lassen, um
> allein zu sterben, wissend nicht warum —
>
> Ist das der Eingang eines neuen Lebens?

It will be noticed that there is no hint here of the interpretation of
the parable which was to distinguish his later version. The poem is
on the whole in keeping with the Biblical story. In *Le Retour de
l'enfant prodigue* Gide, while adding his own adornments, also con-
forms in general to the spirit of the Biblical account. Rilke's departure from the accepted version is radical in the closing pages of
*Malte*, in which, with a twist worthy of Nietzsche, he conceives the
story as 'die Legende dessen . . . , der nicht geliebt werden wollte',[2]
and which ends with the bleak and sombre commentary: 'Was
wußten sie, wer er war. Er war jetzt furchtbar schwer zu lieben,

[1] *A.W.*, Bd. I, pp. 166–7.        [2] *A.W.*, Bd. II, p. 211.

und er fühlte, daß nur Einer dazu imstande sei. Der aber wollte noch nicht.'[1]

A more revealing picture of Rilke's own feelings would be difficult to find. The difference in their approach to this common subject is of fundamental significance in assessing the relationship between Rilke and Gide. The latter, like Rilke, was a great traveller and hungry for experience; each could find in the story of the Prodigal Son something which matched a part of himself. But Gide's Prodigal Son returned—and was glad to return—because his 'aspirations were thwarted and finally tamed by dangers and hardships',[2] because his courage and endurance were not sufficient to sustain him. Of Rilke's, on the other hand, we read: 'Wir wissen nicht, ob er blieb; wir wissen nur, daß er wiederkam'[3]—the inference, based on Rilke's conception of the parable, surely being that there could be no permanent return. The implication in the closing lines of *Malte* is unmistakably that the resumption of normal family life was impossible. This leads us to the essential contrast between Rilke and Gide. The latter, for all his journeying and adventure, was firmly rooted in his own soil and home. He belonged inseparably to the environment and conditions from which he originated; there was no intention or desire to sever those ties. His travels were merely an interlude, and he returned from them exhausted and satisfied, ready to resume his normal existence where it had been interrupted. For Rilke it was not even a question of travelling; it was one of *exile*, of complete severance, a social and domestic withdrawal which was absolute. For him the problem was altogether deeper, bound up indissolubly with his whole approach to life and with his dedication to his calling: his Prodigal Son is the symbol of his belief that his art was paramount and that there was no room for two loyalties. Where, for Gide, absence from country and home was no more than a temporary fructifying experience, for Rilke it was an article of faith, allowing no compromise or retracing of steps.[4]

Many critics have sought to correlate Gide's *Les Nourritures terrestres* with *Malte Laurids Brigge*. Lang notes such apparent resemblances as 'les thèmes du déracinement, de la disponibilité, du dénûment et l'intense communion avec la nature et les choses'.[5]

[1] Ibid., p. 218.                    [2] E. M. Butler, op. cit., p. 209.
[3] *A.W.*, Bd. II, p. 217.           [4] Cf. R. Lang, ed. cit., pp. 20–21.
[5] Ibid., p. 15.

But here, again, the dissimilarity between the two men soon becomes clear. This critic contrasts 'un ravissement tout sensuel' in Gide's work with 'un univers d'outre-tombe . . . les ténèbres de l'angoisse . . . la misère et l'obsession de la mort' in *Malte*; and she further remarks: 'Contrairement à Rilke qui s'arrêtait malgré lui à ce qui allait dans son sens ou ce qu'il croyait aller dans son sens,[1] Gide se sentait surtout sollicité par ce qui différait de lui et de son entourage.'[2] The same differentiation emerges, therefore, in relating Rilke's concept to that of *Les Nourritures terrestres* as in the case of *Le Retour de l'enfant prodigue*. The most obvious affinity between Gide's earlier work and *Malte* is that each, since it was a kind of confession-cum-manifesto of the young literary artist, served a similar purpose, chronological and functional, for its author. More questionable is the statement by Bauer: 'Gides Einfluß ist in den Sonetten, aber er hat nur gesteigert, was in Rilke war, was Rilke selbst erleben mußte, um es zu gestalten . . .'[3] Apart from the fact that this sets too high and too aesthetic a valuation on Gide's impact—his was not essentially a fertilizing or 'creative' influence at all—such attunement as had existed between Rilke and Gide's work no longer existed when the Sonnets were written. Angelloz, commenting on Rilke's refusal, in December 1921, of the task of translating *Les Nourritures terrestres*, writes: ' . . . nous pensons qu'à cette époque il s'est trop éloigné de Gide pour traduire une œuvre où s'exprime une pensée qui, chez l'auteur lui-même, est déjà dépassée.'[4] This same 'distance' from Gide makes it improbable that the latter made even the most vague and indirect contribution to the content of the Sonnets: for by 1922 Rilke's interest in Gide had diminished, although he continued to read his work. (The Gide experience was not, in fact, in the artistic sense, so deeply and permanently enshrined in Rilke's consciousness as were the other great influences in his life.) The most that can be said is that there are themes in the Sonnets which are not contrary to the spirit of Gide; but such affinity appears to be no more than incidental.

Gide did not *initiate* anything in Rilke's artistic consciousness; he had nothing new to give him, as had Rodin, Cézanne, and Baudelaire. His function was confirmatory and cohesive. He was,

[1] Cf. the remarks on influence on p. 94.
[2] Ed. cit., pp. 15–16.
[3] Op. cit., p. 66.
[4] Op. cit., p. 353.

moreover, singularly fitted to perform this function, since, unlike Rodin and Valéry, he knew German and understood the German character. Lang records the interesting fact: 'A plus d'une reprise Gide avait identifié l'esprit allemand avec la musique, l'esprit français avec le dessin'[1]—a sentence which admirably epitomizes the duality of the poet of the first two parts of *Das Stunden-Buch* and the poet of the *Neue Gedichte*. And perhaps in this perspicacious judgement by Gide we may see the symbol of his part in the development of Rilke, the success of whose whole art was bound up with his ability to achieve a synthesis between the two cultures. Thus, if Gide's influence on Rilke was not a fertilizing one, if we see his role as more human than artistic, as the psychological one of providing Rilke with a kind of anchorage and some measure of emotional and moral stability and assurance, the indirect importance of this role in Rilke's evolution as an artist can be readily recognized. For if the man had disintegrated under the oppression of his crisis, the artist would have been lost as well. Gide fulfilled the double purpose of helping to sustain Rilke's will and of keeping his attention turned towards France, its language, and its literature.

If, however, Gide was not associated with any fresh formative activity or conceptual revelation in Rilke's life, he nevertheless did make one direct and positive contribution to Rilke's art. This lay in the latter's translation of *Le Retour de l'enfant prodigue*. We are not primarily concerned with Rilke's merits as a translator;[2] also, an extensive examination of his rendering of Gide's work is outside the scope of the present study.[3] But, in so far as Rilke's work as a translator must be regarded as an element in his long struggle for language-mastery, one or two general comments are indicated. First, *Le Retour de l'enfant prodigue* was quantitatively one of Rilke's biggest undertakings in this field, representing a sustained effort on a piece of writing which differed radically from his own treatment of the same subject. Secondly, it is necessary to underline the truism that all literary translation is a compromise, that there is no such thing as a perfect rendering. With the inhibiting factors involved

---

[1] Ed. cit., p. 25. Gide's view, which is a general one, does not clash with the fact that Rilke was not interested in music as an art in itself (see p. 118). His capacity to create, in essentially German fashion, his own brand of Orphean 'music' in the Sonnets underlines the validity of Gide's perception.

[2] Cf. pp. 106–7.

[3] A detailed and useful analysis of Rilke's translation of *Le Retour de l'enfant prodigue* has been made by Adrien Robinet de Clery in *Rilke traducteur*, pp. 39–83.

in translation, it is therefore necessary to make certain reserva-
tions when comparing the prose of Rilke's version of this work
and that of his original writings. This said, however, it is impossible
to ignore the fact that in this translation the reader's general
impression is one of much greater terseness, restraint, and austerity
than in Rilke's original prose. While due regard must be paid to the
limitations imposed by Gide's own style—the greater part of *Le
Retour de l'enfant prodigue*, for example, is in dialogue, a device
seldom used by Rilke in *Malte* and one which in itself has the effect
of making a style more succinct—there is a further consideration
which is of particular importance in this study. It is that Rilke was
translating into a language which was richer and more flexible than
that of the original (this question will emerge even more prominently in the next chapter). In other words, by transposing from a
more into a less restricting medium Rilke was forced to exercise
with greater restraint an instrument the use of which would naturally tend more towards expatiation and virtuosity. The significance
of this exercise as a factor in his development becomes readily
apparent when we recall that the dominant need and function of
his 'Lehrjahre' was the imposition of that discipline and control
which were so lacking before he came to France and without which
the Elegies and Sonnets could never be realized.

There will, inevitably, be some conflict of purpose when the
translator is also a man of Rilke's fertility and creative imagination.[1]
A. R. de Clery aptly points out that Rilke's translations are denomi-
nated 'Übertragungen' and not 'Übersetzungen'.[2] The use of this
term implies that Rilke was not prepared completely to sacrifice his
originality—a fact further indicated by his occasional variations of
meaning and, even more, by the subtle stylistic modifications he
applies to Gide's text by delicate adjustments in balance and emphasis. We may profitably draw attention to de Clery's summing-
up of this translation.[3] Of especial relevance is his reference to
Rilke's preference for simple terms and monosyllables—a sign of
the growing terseness and concision which were at the heart of the
linguistic discipline he underwent in France and which will loom
larger in the context of Valéry. The value and importance to Rilke's

---

[1] Cf. p. 107.
[2] Op. cit., pp. 8 and 135. The writer uses the word 'nachdichten' to describe
Rilke's technique.
[3] Op. cit., p. 82.

progress of this notable translation is thus clear: while advancing the process of increasing and refining his knowledge of French, it also, although a prose work, furthered the development of his powers to express himself artistically in his own instrument.

Although the friendship between the two men lasted for the rest of Rilke's life, by its nature the crucial period of Gide's impact was in the years which preceded the war. During the war Rilke's intercourse with France was completely cut, although even then Gide generously exerted himself in an unsuccessful attempt to recover Rilke's possessions in Paris. After the war Rilke began a new life, and the mood which had prevailed after the completion of *Malte* had passed. In the words of Angelloz: 'Si nous pouvions matérialiser les lignes suivies par les deux écrivains nous les verrions converger, se confondre, puis diverger.'[1] But if Rilke had moved away from Gide, they continued to correspond, and Rilke pursued his French reading. There was, however, one more function for Gide to perform. Among the French writers whom Rilke read, which included Gide himself, Proust, Schlumberger, Giraudoux, one took precedence over the rest: Valéry. Gide, who was a friend of Valéry, was delighted, spurred Rilke on, supplied him with more of Valéry's writings, and finally acted as intermediary between the two poets.[2] Thus, as the figure of Gide, his part played, retires into the background, he leaves Rilke with someone far more important —and unobtrusively leads us to the last great contact of Rilke's life and to the most significant and spectacular period of his career.

[1] Op. cit., p. 352.
[2] See R. Lang, ed. cit., pp. 29–30.

# VII

## VALÉRY AND THE POETIC CLIMAX

For last year's words belong to last year's language
And next year's words await another voice.
But, as the passage now presents no hindrance
To the spirit unappeased and peregrine
Between two worlds become much like each other,
So find I words I never thought to speak . . .

T. S. ELIOT, *Little Gidding*

'J'ÉTAIS seul, j'attendais, toute mon œuvre attendait. Un jour, j'ai lu Valéry, j'ai su que mon attente était finie.'[1] With these words of Rilke in mind, and as we enter the most important creative period in his life, it is appropriate, first, to recall the central aims of this study, as set out in the first chapter; secondly, to indicate Rilke's situation at the end of the war, what remained to be done, and how the events which led up to the final fulfilment fit into the process of development which has been traced in the foregoing chapters. It will be remembered that we have suggested that the key to the aesthetic and artistic appreciation of Rilke is to be found in the medium of poetry itself: language; and, further, that the impact of France—language, culture, and individual influences —was the vital factor which contributed to the final realization of his full powers.[2]

After a first wave of emotional enthusiasm, the war years were painful ones for the poet, partly because of the mood of disillusionment which grew out of the war itself, but even more because he felt that the pattern of his life, built up over a period of twelve years and which he regarded as indispensable to his purpose, had been shattered, and that he was cut off from the environment which mattered most. In this he was right, though it would be a mistake to assume that he was not still moving forward during these comparatively quiescent years; and equally it would be a mistake to assume that the final consummation would necessarily have come sooner

[1] Quoted by Monique Saint-Hélier in *A Rilke pour Noël*, p. 21.
[2] See p. 23.

had the war not intervened. Rilke, perhaps more than any other poet, depended on the moment of readiness, when every force within him, with a tremendous and concerted intensity, was concentrated on the supreme act of creation. As we have seen, the great fertilizing experiences, which were of crucial importance in moulding his artistic concept and which set in motion the process of developing the 'complete' poet, were tightly compressed into his early Parisian years: an embarrassment of riches, the full possibilities of which could be realized only by a long and hard period of readjustment. Nothing comparable to these experiences occurred after the Cézanne revelation in the autumn of 1907. At the same time, the impetus given to his evolution by these experiences was maintained by the continued preoccupation of his thoughts with the art of Rodin and Cézanne and, in the field of literature, by his continued reading of those writers with whom he felt a kinship— a glance at the dates of his translations shows clearly that his reading, notably of the French Symbolist poets, was sustained all through, even during the war years; so that, even while he was suffering physical separation from France, the leaven was still working.

The Elegies were begun in 1912. Thus, between their beginning and the last major fertilizing experience, that of Cézanne, more than four years had elapsed. It is significant that Rilke was able to start this great series in 1912—a fact which indicates that, critical and unhappy though they were, the years 1907 to 1912 were of far greater importance than might at first appear. We may conceive them as being a period of great formative activity in Rilke's artistic development, during which, with the sustaining and stabilizing liaison with Gide to help him, he was able to digest the rich nourishment of the earlier years until it merged completely and organically with his own being. The fact that Rilke could begin the Elegies in 1912 indicates that one aspect of his development, the formative aspect, was virtually complete by this date: his ability to conceive and plan the Elegies and start work on them shows that his artistic concept had reached an advanced stage of maturity, the more so as the broad vision of the series, if with the addition of material suggested by subsequent experience, remained unchanged through the following decade, and the lines written in 1912 were in tune with what emerged from the far greater act of creation which occurred in 1922.

But if the formative experiences had been assimilated and integrated and his general poetic concept was formulated, there was
another side of him which was not yet mature. It is true that from
1912 Rilke worked at the Elegies at intervals and that a considerable
portion of them already existed before February 1922. But, so far
from being content with what was accomplished and with the fact
that, at last, a start had been made, Rilke was deeply aware that he
was still far from the final fulfilment. The very limits of his success,
considerable though it was in itself, seemed to augment his sense of
failure and despair. On 6 January 1913 he wrote to Lou Andreas-
Salomé from Spain: 'Ja, die zwei Elegien sind da —, aber mündlich
kann ich Dir sagen, ein wie kleines und wie scharf abgebrochenes
Stück sie bilden, von dem, was damals in meine Macht gegeben
war.'[1] He was acutely conscious that something was impeding the
full and free operation of his poetic powers. Why, we may ask—
and the question is fundamental to the consideration of the impact
of Paul Valéry—was Rilke condemned to the long years of frustration and delay? Why did the Pentecostal wind of Duino die out
prematurely? When once the series was started, when once the
impetus was there, what prevented Rilke from rapidly gathering
creative momentum and finishing his work in one great effort? We
have suggested that one side of Rilke's evolution was effectively
complete by 1912. We may, therefore, see the stream of his poetic
experience as having built up to a point of pressure sufficient for it
to exert considerable force; the channel was full. But something was
hindering its flow; the flood-gates were down. Almost everything,
perhaps, which was to make up the 'content' of the Elegies was
there. All that was needed was that the torrent should be released.
At intervals from 1912 the pressure was so great that something
seeped through, but it was little more than a trickle at a time. What,
then, was the obstacle to the free flow of Rilke's genius? The
answer lies in the instrument of language itself. Rilke still lacked
the full mastery over his medium which would enable him to give
adequate and uninhibited expression to the great vision of the
Elegies. One of the objects of this chapter will be to consider how
the release of his creative energies came about—and it is not ir-
relevant to note that we are concerned, not only with the completion of the Elegies, but also with the composition of the other great
series, the Sonnets. These have the particular interest in the present

[1] *G.B.* ,Bd. III, p. 287.

context that, unlike the Elegies, there is no evidence that they were even contemplated before the actual moment of their creation.

If our repeated contention that the influence of the French language itself was of vital importance to Rilke is correct, we may perhaps regard the fact that his enforced stay in Germany during the war years isolated him from intimate and continuous contact with his adopted tongue as a most serious deprivation in this period. For even with his reading, his use of French was minimal compared with what it would have been had he been able to pursue, uninterrupted, his pre-war mode of life. With the thought in mind of Rilke's frustration at what the war was costing him, and with the knowledge of his longing to resume the ties and the way of life which he regarded as vital to his artistic destiny, it is appropriate to consider in what way, and to what extent, the link with France was re-established after the war. Surprisingly, perhaps, he did not return to Paris; partly, no doubt, because of currency difficulties, but chiefly, it would appear, because the pre-war mood had passed. Whatever Rilke needed had to be found in an environment quite different from that of Paris. In 1919 he went to Switzerland, where he spent two years of indeterminate wandering before deciding on a permanent residence. He made the acquaintance of Valéry, through the latter's poem *Le Cimetière marin*, in the spring of 1921; and within a few months he was installed in his final home in the Château de Muzot. In less than a year the Elegies and the Sonnets were completed. Such are the bare facts, and it may seem strange that Rilke's greatness was brought to fruition in the solitude and tranquillity of Muzot, far from the bustle and throb of Paris which had given him so much. But it is possible to correlate these last events with what had gone before and to show that, so far from being a complete departure from the old way of life, the final years were really the crown and culmination of the experience of France and Paris.

Above all, Muzot was in the French-speaking canton of Valais, so that such local intercourse as Rilke had was again in the language in which he was now almost as proficient as in his own. Moreover, he quickly availed himself of the opportunity to immerse himself in French literature to an extent not possible during the war. Angelloz, noting Rilke's renewed preoccupation with France, lists the authors whom he admired, including, of course, Valéry.[1] This leads us directly to examine the exact nature of the latter's impact on Rilke

[1] Op. cit., p. 351.

and the part he played in the emergence of Rilke's greatest work. This was the last great artistic contact of his life; and, once again, the remarkable manner in which, throughout Rilke's career, the experience appropriate to his need always occurred at the opportune moment invites comment. In a passage which bears very closely on the previous remarks in this chapter, Angelloz points out that Rilke would have been less likely to admire Valéry twenty years earlier. Where, under Rodin, the question had been how to live, now it was how to create, to fulfil his mission of poet. And he quotes Rilke's telling comment to Charles Vildrac: ' . . . "que penserait-on d'un horloger qui, ayant devant lui toutes les pièces d'un mécanisme, se trouverait incapable de le monter?" '[1] This confirms our suggestion that a part of Rilke was already mature; the ingredients of his poetry were already present, needing only to be brought to utterance.

If Rilke was spontaneously captivated by *Le Cimetière marin*, he followed his familiar practice of wasting no time in informing himself on the author's history and circumstances. We are at once confronted by the paradox that, although it would be difficult to find two personalities more unlike than Rilke and Valéry, it was a point of similarity upon which Rilke immediately seized. This was that Valéry had also been poetically silent, for more than twenty years.[2] It mattered not that in the case of Valéry the silence had been calculated, deliberately self-imposed while he pursued his scientific studies. It was sufficient to give Rilke's despairing spirits the same sort of moral encouragement they had drawn from the examples of Rodin and Cézanne. The knowledge gave him fresh hope and, in Butler's words, 'the achievements and destiny of another artist seemed to explain and justify his own poetical existence'.[3] This psychological element does mark a point of resemblance between Valéry's impact and Rilke's earlier experiences, different though they were in other respects. It no doubt had its value in giving Rilke a measure of the strength he sorely needed, but its chief importance is probably that his acceptance of Valéry as a kindred spirit cemented the attachment and promoted the extensive reading and translation of the latter's work.

More helpful in estimating Valéry's impact is a consideration of the differences between the two men. Some of these differences,

[1] Angelloz, op. cit., pp. 318–19.
[2] Cf. E. Buddeberg, op. cit., p. 474.        [3] Op. cit., p. 309.

as well as the fact that Valéry played a decisive part in enabling Rilke to reach poetic fulfilment, have been recognized by a number of critics; few, however, have taken the discussion to its conclusion and investigated exactly how and why Valéry could have such an unleashing effect on Rilke's art. Valéry had been, as a young man, a disciple of Mallarmé. Two interesting points arise from this, neither of which appears to have attracted critical notice. First, Valéry had thus received his poetic grounding at the feet of a man whose whole poetic concept—though not his artistic ambition—had been turned in the opposite direction from Rilke's, in so far as he had been concerned with a synthesis between music and poetry, whereas Rilke had been preoccupied with the representational arts.[1] Secondly, Mallarmé, Valéry, and Rilke had all experienced poetic silence (with Rilke it was less complete than with the others), but in each case for a different reason. With Mallarmé it had been due to the fallacy and deception inherent in his aesthetic theory; in Valéry's case it had been intentional; in Rilke's it had been due to his failure to match an artistic concept which was fundamentally viable and, since 1912, mature with comparable power over his instrument. We are left with the intriguing paradox that Rilke, at the crucial moment in his life when he was poised and longing for utterance and when success or failure hung in the balance, was brought, at one remove, into closer contact with a poet whose aesthetic abstraction made creative impotence inevitable. The contradiction may be taken a stage further when we recall Gide's analysis of the French and German character.[2] Yet Rilke, a great part of whose concept of art stemmed from his preoccupation with 'le dessin', and into whose aesthetic thought music had never entered as a formative element, was about to revert to the true character of his native genius; and, despite the long years of patient assimilation of Rodin and Cézanne, the final strains of his greatest poetry were touched off by the impact of Valéry, whose early association had been with a poet whose approach had been in complete contrast to Rilke's and who, by the nature of his art theory, was foredoomed to failure.

But Valéry, the intermediary, unlike his master, did succeed fully, though this may seem surprising in view of his pursuits and his personality.[3] Angelloz calls him 'poète par jeu',[4] while Goertz

---

[1] Cf. p. 108.                                [2] See p. 137.
[3] Cf. Bowra, op. cit., pp. 19–20.            [4] Op. cit., p. 65.

reminds us that Valéry himself declined the title of 'poeta' in favour of 'artifex'.[1] The fundamental difference between Rilke and Valéry is of particular interest in the light of the vital contribution which the latter is generally agreed to have made to the completion of the Elegies and the composition of the Sonnets. For Valéry was precisely what Rilke was not: a highly trained intellect, a disciplined, deductive thinker, a mathematician and logician. And his greatest poetry, *Charmes*, so far from being stifled by cold, clear reason, was written *after* he had spent a great part of his life in academic exercises. Several critics have commented on the antipodal difference between the two men. Angelloz calls Valéry 'fils de Descartes . . . [il] vit dans le réel, qu'il soumet, sans angoisse apparente, à une analyse impitoyablement lucide. Rilke, sensitif, hypernerveux, est un visionnaire et un intuitif, qui ne subit qu'avec angoisse le contact du réel . . .'[2] Goertz points to the same contrast and stresses Rilke's refusal to allow his consciousness to intrude and interfere with the immaculate artistic conception.[3] Bassermann remarks on the illuminating fact that such an extremely different poetry should have this effect on Rilke.[4] And Buddeberg notes that the juxtaposition of Rilke's translations and the originals of Valéry reveals the polar antithesis between the two poets.[5] Most interesting of all, perhaps, are Valéry's own words on Rilke:

> Si le mot *magique* a un sens, je dirai que toute sa personne, sa voix, son regard, ses manières, tout en lui donnait l'impression d'une présence magique. On eût dit qu'il sût donner puissance de charme à chacune de ses paroles.
>
> C'est peut-être pourquoi il me semblait souvent si différent de moi et si difficile parfois à concevoir. Sans doute avait-il développé sa pensée tout à l'opposite du sens dans lequel j'avais orienté et longtemps entraîné la mienne? Peut-être une question de race?[6]

These passages forcibly underline the great gulf between Rilke and Valéry, a gulf which is scarcely lessened by the fact that Valéry, more complete and balanced than Mallarmé, also had his 'plastic' and 'architectural' side. For the most part, however, critical expositions of this vital period in Rilke's life have been content to catalogue the differences between the two men and to state the importance of the timing and the intensity of Rilke's application

[1] Op. cit., p. 92.              [2] Op. cit., p. 317.
[3] Op. cit., pp. 91–92.         [4] *Der späte Rilke.* See pp. 413–14.
[5] Op. cit., p. 473.            [6] Published in *Rilke et la France*, p. 217.

to the translation of Valéry, without investigating how the association with Valéry could have the effect it did and without seeking to resolve a situation which bristles with apparent contradictions. No examination of Rilke's poetic development can be complete without an attempt to probe thoroughly, and answer the problems posed by, the Valéry experience. Butler writes that Valéry's poems 'aroused that kind of enthusiasm which releases the creative instinct; and, by transferring Valéry's rhythms into his own modes, Rilke set his mind vibrating with an energy which developed into sound'[1]—an accurate assessment, as far as it goes. This critic moves nearer to the heart of the matter when she comments:

His present belief that music alone could transform the world seemed to demand that Rilke, like Socrates before he came to die, should devote himself to music in a special sense and must discover a new instrument, if those symbols which had appeared and reappeared in so many different guises since he first began to write were to be sung to sleep in this world that they might enter the next. There was such an instrument to hand: the language of Villon, Racine and Valéry, which can produce the purest and most intellectual music ever formed.[2]

Buddeberg comes nearest to our purpose. She notes Rilke's possible awareness of the danger his intuitive approach spelt to control over his medium, to lucidity, to the capacity to render his perceptions with the exact word, and continues:

So ist nicht eigentlich ein 'Einfluß' Valérys auf Rilke zu verzeichnen; wie wäre das bei der schon vollkommen geprägten Persönlichkeit, die unmittelbar vor der Dokumentation ihrer letzten Reife stand, auch nur möglich gewesen. In der Begegnung mit der auf eine äußerste Höhe geführten disziplinierten Wortkunst wurde Rilke ein hohes Wahrzeichen vollkommener Poesie gegenübergestellt. . . .[3]

The same critic, pursuing the all-important question of language and discussing, in particular, the 'equivalence' of Rilke's translation of *Le Cimetière marin*, paves the way for the closer examination of Valéry's impact which we shall shortly undertake:

Das Verwandelte — wenn es von der gleichen 'Valenz' sein soll wie das, was verwandelt worden ist — kann nicht Gleichartigkeit, sondern muß Andersartigkeit meinen. Die Äquivalenz hier liegt einzig in der gleichen Schwergewichtigkeit und Reichweite innerhalb der je zwei

---

[1] Op. cit., p. 309.       [2] Ibid., p. 402.
[3] Op. cit., p. 475.

verschiedenen Sprachräume und der so grundsätzlich anders gearteten beiden Dichterpersönlichkeiten.[1]

Before passing to a detailed attempt to arrive at the linguistic implications of Rilke's contact with Valéry, some general preliminary remarks on the distinctive features of the Valéry translations may be helpful. First, they were for Rilke the most satisfying exercise of this kind he ever undertook.[2] Secondly, they were his most intensified and prolonged exercise in this field, continuing from 1921 until the end of his life and including most of the *Charmes*, as well as *Narcisse*, *Eupalinos*, and *L'Âme et la danse*. Thirdly, they encompassed Rilke's own greatest creative period.[3] It is clear that the key to the part Valéry played in the release of Rilke's creative flood lies in the very contrast between them. Rilke was 'formed' in the conceptual sense, the material of his poetry was within him, pressing for escape. The intellectual and intuitive personalities met, and because Valéry approached from the opposite direction of experience, he was able to effect the clearance in Rilke's creative channel which the latter could not achieve from his own side. We can, therefore, see how, although Valéry's impact was not a formative one, this last great contact of Rilke's life fits firmly and logically into the process of development which has been followed throughout the course of this study.[4] For this was not Rilke's first exposure to the forces of the intellect. It will be recalled that, in the early days when his artistic concept was being moulded, the Rodin years were noted as being his most 'intellectual' period, in the sense that they marked the most extreme swing away from the hyper-subjectivity of Russia and Worpswede.[5] The process initiated by Rodin and continued by Cézanne and Baudelaire now had its culmination in the function performed by Valéry: what the earlier artists had done for Rilke during his formative period, Valéry now did in the no less important phase of achieving utterance and attaining Orphean mastery over the poetic instrument. It is true that we cannot make a complete separation between these two aspects of Rilke's development, since, as we have seen, the earlier process of forming his artistic concept was also accompanied by ever-increasing control over language. But something more was needed, and, because Valéry could bring no new element to a poet

---

[1] Op. cit., p. 476.     [2] See *G.B.*, Bd. V, pp. 107–8 and 188.
[3] Cf. p. 42.     [4] Cf. p. 140.
[5] See pp. 97 and 104.

who was already conceptually mature, his function was that of a catalytic agent; the whole force of his impact was brought to bear on bringing about the tremendous release which, by their nature, the earlier influences could not accomplish.

All this is in keeping with the picture of Rilke which has emerged in the earlier pages. Just as Russia, as Rilke saw it, was the least vital of his influences because it ministered to those qualities with which he was already richly endowed,[1] so it was always the 'opposite' or the different which contributed most to his progress. For the history of his evolution is the history of a poet struggling for 'completeness'. He entered as one with great natural gifts, but one for whom the disequilibrium caused by the one-sidedness of his talents constituted a real and serious danger. With his intense sensitivity and sensibility, his fertility, the creative power of his imagination, and the undisciplined effusion of his early work, he resembled the rich profusion and luxuriance of a tropical forest which has not been brought to order and whose potential has been exploited unselectively. Intuition and imagination, which he already possessed, must be wedded to intellectual control, which had to be acquired. Thus, Valéry, the artist-intellect *par excellence*, can be seen as the crowning figure in Rilke's long and hard passage towards the perfect merger, the figure who resumed and set the seal on the contribution made by France to Rilke's poetic fulfilment. In the protracted and exacting task of translating the poetry of a man in diametric contrast to himself, Rilke found his own voice.

It is now possible to turn to a closer examination of how this great climax came about and how it fits into the main course of the poet's development; and also to attempt to estimate the nature of Rilke's achievement in the Elegies and the Sonnets. Rilke was 36 when he began the Elegies, 45 when he discovered Valéry, and 46 when the Elegies were completed and the Sonnets written. We may consider how well he conformed to Herder's ideal of slow, gradual maturing. The Elegies and the Sonnets are the product of his ripeness, the highest peak to which he could attain; and, although the Sonnets were not contemplated before 1922, the two collections must be regarded as the parts of a whole. Into them we may expect to find poured the sum of Rilke's feelings and experience; and, artistically, we may expect them to represent an amalgam of all the influences he had undergone, albeit compounded

[1] See p. 30.

by the distinctive character of his own imagination in such a way as to emerge as a completely personal, individual art.

In considering the accomplishment of this, Rilke's greatest creative period, we may profitably recall, with brief textual illustration, the main course of his poetic development from his earlier work through the modifications in his artistic concept and practice which occurred during his first years in Paris; thence passing on through the Valéry experience (with an examination of Valéry's language in *Le Cimetière marin* against that of Rilke's translation) to the final poetic consummation in February 1922. At the time of, and stimulated by, the Russian journeys, Rilke was unashamedly Romantic, subjective, emotional, making no attempt to subordinate self:

> Was wirst du tun, Gott, wenn ich sterbe?
> Ich bin dein Krug (wenn ich zerscherbe?)
> Ich bin dein Trank (wenn ich verderbe?)
> Bin dein Gewand und dein Gewerbe,
> mit mir verlierst du deinen Sinn.[1]

Such is the mood of *Das Buch vom mönchischen Leben*—a mood which is maintained in *Das Buch von der Pilgerschaft* of the Worpswede period:

> In tiefen Nächten grab ich dich, du Schatz.
> Denn alle Überflüsse, die ich sah,
> sind Armut und armseliger Ersatz
> für deine Schönheit, die noch nicht geschah.

> Aber der Weg zu dir ist furchtbar weit
> und, weil ihn lange keiner ging, verweht.
> O du bist einsam. Du bist Einsamkeit,
> du Herz, das zu entfernten Taten geht.[2]

The early Paris years saw a radical change—almost a complete reversal—in Rilke's approach. Under Rodin's influence, Rilke embarked on a conscious effort to externalize his poetry. The subjective element was not eliminated altogether, but it was subordinated with the most extreme control of Rilke's whole career. Typical of his artistic endeavour during this phase are the poems which were quoted and commented upon in the Rodin chapter: *Der Panther*[3] and *Die Fensterrose*.[4] As regards the studied attempt to objectivize,

[1] *A.W.*, Bd. I, p. 29.   [2] Ibid., p. 85.
[3] See pp. 57–58.   [4] See p. 65.

the *Neue Gedichte* represent the poet's furthest swing away from
the character of the first two parts of *Das Stunden-Buch*.[1] Cézanne
and Baudelaire, while not denying the influence of Rodin, took
Rilke a stage further, modifying his concept so that it came to rest
between the two earlier extremes. The Cézanne and Baudelaire
revelations became crystallized in the formula of 'sagen' instead of
'beurteilen'—a formula which implied a marriage between subjectivity and objectivity by which the character of both would be
preserved in the poetry. It was, moreover, suggested in the
Cézanne chapter that the attempt to achieve in practice the merger
of two such seemingly irreconcilable qualities was essentially a
problem of language, and one which presented considerable difficulties.[2] It is, in fact, hardly surprising that Rilke had to wait so
long for the final accomplishment of such an exacting task. Thus,
by the end of 1907 Rilke's artistic concept was, in effect, complete,
as far as external influences were concerned. There followed years
of digesting his earlier experiences and of adapting himself to his
new outlook, but there were no fresh revelations or changes of a
major order. What remained for Rilke was to translate his art theory
into practice, and if, at least from 1912, there were sporadic moments of success, the full realization of his purpose still confronted
him, like an almost unscalable peak, in 1921.

This brief recapitulation of the trend of Rilke's evolution has
been necessary in order to establish precisely his position at the moment of his encounter with Valéry. It is important to bear in mind
that, conceptually, he was fundamentally the same in 1921 as he had
been at the end of 1907. He continued to develop after this date, as
we saw in the Gide chapter, but it was the development of self-
adjustment, not the acquisition of new theoretical elements. Above

[1] It is worth noting that the last section of *Das Stunden-Buch*, *Das Buch von der
Armut und vom Tode*, was written in 1903—that is, after the beginning of the
association with Rodin and in the year of the composition of *Der Panther*. Rilke
was thus confronted with a problem of compromise: on the one hand was the
urge to write the 'new poetry' emerging from the Rodin experience, on the
other was the no less compelling obligation to preserve a measure of artistic
unity with the first two sections—which implied a retrogression. The difference
between this section and the earlier two is, in fact, easily discernible, betraying
the uneasy struggle between the two compulsions. In a sense, therefore, *Das
Buch von der Armut und vom Tode* may be seen as a first faltering attempt by
Rilke to solve the problem of 'sagen' instead of 'beurteilen', but without the
guidance of the Cézanne and Baudelaire revelations and without the advantage
of having formulated his poetic concept.

[2] See pp. 90–91.

all, the concept of 'sagen' instead of 'beurteilen' had never been renounced: in other words, in Rilke's creative consummation we must look for the practical realization of the concept formulated in the autumn of 1907; we must seek the quintessential use of the instrument of language by means of which the poet may reconcile the opposing demands of subjectivity and objectivity, by means of which emotion is 'ohne Rückstand . . . aufgebraucht in der Aktion des Machens'.

We can now attempt to estimate how the reading and translation of Valéry helped to bring Rilke to utterance in the great poetic climax of 1922. *Le Cimetière marin*, perhaps Valéry's finest poem, has been chosen for examination in this context because the date of its translation has been definitely established as preceding that of the completion of the Elegies and the Sonnets.[1] The first stanza contains a number of the features which characterize Rilke's technique:

> Ce toit tranquille, où marchent des colombes,
> Entre les pins palpite, entre les tombes;
> Midi le juste y compose de feux
> La mer, la mer, toujours recommencée!
> Ô récompense après une pensée
> Qu'un long regard sur le calme des dieux![2]

which Rilke renders:

> Dies stille Dach, auf dem sich Tauben finden,
> scheint Grab und Pinie schwingend zu verbinden.
> Gerechter Mittag überflammt es nun.
> Das Meer, das Meer, ein immer neues Schenken!
> O, die Belohnung, nach dem langen Denken
> ein langes Hinschaun auf der Götter Ruhn![3]

It is, of course, inevitable that the different syllabic sound values

---

[1] Although the bulk of the Valéry translations were executed after February 1922, it is known that Rilke became acquainted with Valéry's poetry in the winter of 1920–1. And since it is reasonably probable that Rilke formed the intention of translating a number of the poems at that time, we can surmise that he approached them with the translator's eye and ear—he may even have carried out some preliminary work on them at that time. We can, therefore, claim that Valéry's effective value was not confined to the action of this one poem, convenient though it is for our purpose. And even as it stands, the translation of this difficult and fairly long poem is a piece of work considerable enough for the validity of the argument as to the importance of Valery's impact to be sustained.

[2] For a fuller analysis of this translation, see de Clery, op. cit., pp. 105–16.

[3] *G.W.*, Bd. VI, p. 288.

and metrical principles in the two languages produce a different rhythmic effect in any translation from one to the other. In any case, it was no part of Rilke's purpose to sacrifice the music and cadences of German, which is rightly acknowledged as one of the finest poetic instruments. Since, here, we are primarily interested in Rilke's translation work as a preparation for, and as a factor contributing to, his original writing, it must be stressed that it was vital for the realization of the creative consummation of the Elegies and the Sonnets that Rilke, while achieving utterance and striving for articulateness, should not jettison any of the incomparable poetic qualities of his own language. This question will be referred to again when some general comments are made on the importance of the French language to Rilke's linguistic development. It is, however, important to remember, when appraising Rilke's translation of *Le Cimetière marin*, that, however little he realized it at the time, this exercise was essentially a means and not an end.

The opening stanza of this poem at once establishes Valéry's style. The reader is immediately struck by its terseness, its compression, by the extreme, almost elliptical, economy of the language. Not a word is superfluous, and yet nothing of the sense or power is sacrificed—rather are they increased by the poet's verbal austerity. This is poetry which is an even higher linguistic distillation than that of the Parnassians and the Symbolists—in short, it is the nearest thing possible to the manifestation of Mallarmé's poetic ideal of the 'œuvre pure'. It is the result of the application of the intellect to Mallarmé's poetic conception; Mallarmé himself refused to allow the intellect any part in the act of creation. This extreme astringency and economy of expression is indicative of the magnitude of the task with which Rilke was faced. The first impression given by Rilke's version is, in fact, of a loosening of the tight compression of Valéry's lines. This, it is true, is in part due to the rhythmic, syllabic expansion inherent in the Germanic instrument. More interesting is the expansion resulting from Rilke's syntactical method. In the second line, for instance, Valéry's main verb 'palpite' is rendered by the present participle 'schwingend', and a completely new principal verb 'scheint . . . zu verbinden' is added which takes the place of Valéry's simple preposition 'entre'. In the fourth line the 'toujours recommencée' of the original is translated by the more extended phrase 'ein immer neues Schenken'. In the fifth line 'après une pensée' becomes 'nach dem langen

Denken'. Moreover, four times in this stanza—in the words 'Schenken', 'Denken', 'Hinschaun', 'Ruhn'—Rilke uses infinitives as substantives, a device which has a lengthening effect.

We may further compare Valéry's eleventh stanza:

> Chienne splendide, écarte l'idolâtre!
> Quand solitaire au sourire de pâtre,
> Je pais longtemps, moutons mystérieux,
> Le blanc troupeau de mes tranquilles tombes,
> Éloignes-en les prudentes colombes,
> Les songes vains, les anges curieux!

with Rilke's version:

> Hündin aus Glanz, verjag mir den Beirrten!
> Siehst du mich so, mit Mildigkeit des Hirten,
> bei meinen Lämmern stehn, wie eingepflockt;
> laß mich an meine Herde Gräber glauben,
> halt von ihr ferne die zu klugen Tauben,
> die Grübelei'n, die Engel, die es lockt![1]

Here Rilke departs considerably from the original. Sometimes a facet of Valéry's meaning is discarded altogether, as with 'solitaire' in the second line and 'tranquilles' in the fourth; but mostly Rilke alters and expands, as with 'Mildigkeit' for 'sourire' in the second line, 'zu klugen' for 'prudentes' in the fifth, and 'die es lockt' for 'curieux' in the sixth. In addition, Rilke's verbal construction in the second, third, and fourth lines is quite different from Valéry's.

We may finally quote the twelfth stanza of Valéry's poem:

> Ici venu, l'avenir est paresse.
> L'insecte net gratte la sécheresse;
> Tout est brûlé, défait, reçu dans l'air
> A je ne sais quelle sévère essence . . .
> La vie est vaste, étant ivre d'absence,
> Et l'amertume est douce, et l'esprit clair.

which Rilke translates:

> Kommt sie hierher, so wird die Zukunft träge.
> Der harte Käfer ist des Trocknen Säge;
> alles ist aufgebrannt, verzehrt —, geht ein
> in irgendwie gestrengere Essenzen . . .
> Der Rausch des Nicht-Seins sprengt des Lebens Grenzen,
> und Bitternis ist süß, und Geist ist rein.[2]

[1] *G.W.*, Bd. VI, p. 290.    [2] Ibid., p. 291.

This stanza has been cited because it provides a notable illustration, in the fifth line, of those variants which are an emphatic reminder that in this case the translator is also an original artist. Less important than the considerable modification which Rilke imposes on Valéry is the quality of his rendering. His line, particularly his 'sprengt des Lebens Grenzen', appears a majestic piece of composition in its own right, the work of a powerful creative imagination. Already, perhaps, in such a line as this, we may see Rilke moving towards the great climax of the language of February 1922.

It must be emphasized that in this brief and incomplete examination of Rilke's version of Le Cimetière marin we are not concerned with the merits of Rilke's translation as such. Our purpose is to follow his progress towards his own poetic fulfilment, and we have sought to isolate the main features of his technique of translation which seem to be leading him towards his goal. As de Clery points out, Rilke's rendering of this poem would not satisfy the academic examiner; but neither is it fitting that Rilke should be judged by such a standard.[1] Not only was he confronted with the problem of translating from a concise language (and, in particular, from the works of a poet whose style was remarkable for its economy and compression) into a richer and more flexible one;[2] he was further subject to the limitation imposed by rhyme—a limitation upon which, by following Valéry's rhyme scheme, he refused to compromise. And overriding all was the natural impulse of the original poet to create. At the same time, despite the tendency to loosen and expand the extreme terseness and severity of Valéry's style, it is possible to see, in the language of this translation, the condensation and restraint which betoken Rilke's submission to the control and self-discipline so vital to his artistic well-being—a control reminiscent of that of the Rodin days. For this was the beginning of his last great struggle with his medium, a medium which, if it had not the physical hardness and resistance of Rodin's, was none the less recalcitrant.

Some remarks remain on the subject of the French language itself. Throughout this study, repeated reference has been made to Rilke's growing familiarity with his adopted tongue. It will be recalled that the question was earlier posed whether there was not some quality in the French language itself which was able to contribute directly to Rilke's mastery over the German poetic instrument,

[1] See de Clery, op. cit., pp. 134–7.          [2] Cf. p. 138.

however contradictory this may seem at first sight.[1] And it was indicated that this subject would emerge more prominently in the context of Rilke's translations from the French—it was touched on in the previous chapter in connexion with his translation of Gide —and would come under particular discussion when the impact of Valéry was considered.[2] It is not without interest and significance that the great bulk of Rilke's translation work was undertaken after 1912, the year of the beginning of the Elegies and the date which marked the attainment of conceptual maturity. In other words, it was after his formative period was over that Rilke turned in earnest to pursuits which, in so far as they related intimately to the problem of learning control over the means of expressing himself, would help to make good the remaining major limitation in his artistic equipment. His work on the poetry of Valéry is by far his most important venture in this field, not only because of its timing, and not only because of the unprecedented intensity of Rilke's interest and effort, but above all because of its nature. It is impossible to dissociate Valéry's art from the language in which it is written, since it exists only through the medium by which it is expressed; and it is impossible to disregard the nature of the French language itself, which, of all European languages, is perhaps the most terse, lucid, and exact. It has, as we have mentioned, none of the flexibility of German; it is a language which, by its very exercise, imposes its own character of concision, directness, and restraint on the user.[3]

When to this intrinsic character of the language are added the implications for its use inherent in Valéry's intellectual, Cartesian personality, when account is taken of the fact that in Valéry the French poetic instrument reaches its purest distillation in precision, ellipsis, and control and economy of expression, we can see the monumental demands which translation made upon Rilke. And is not this exactly what Rilke needed? This was the climax of the process of training which had been going on sporadically, and at times apparently capriciously, for a decade. And herein lies the

---

[1] p. 43.                                                          [2] p. 42.

[3] In a letter to Merline, dated 23 March 1921, Rilke makes the interesting comment: 'C'est admirable comme la poésie française des dernières années par ses moyens s'est rapprochée des nôtres, jamais elle n'a été aussi traduisible.' (Lettres françaises à Merline, p. 122.) We would suggest that Rilke has unwittingly reversed what has, in fact, taken place. What has happened is rather that Rilke's own language-consciousness has developed to the point where he can achieve the happy blend between the qualities of his own and his adopted instruments. It is he who has drawn nearer to the character of the French language.

answer to the question how Valéry was able to contribute to the release of the golden stream of Rilke's genius. The qualities of the French language could not be transferred absolutely and entirely into German, but Rilke could appropriate something of its character for his own use. It is at least conceivable that the very wealth and flexibility of his own language was in part responsible for choking the creative flow. Somehow, without sacrificing the richness, the music, and the majesty of German, he had to bring order to his medium, and this was done by passing it through the fine and exacting filter of Valéry's poetic thought and expression. Once again, the thought of the perfect merger forces its way forward, and we may ponder the remarkable integration of Rilke's whole evolution. For this climax of release was but the fulfilment of what had been postulated in the early, formative years. The revelation, under Cézanne, of 'sachliches Sagen' led directly to the formulation of Rilke's concept of the perfect merger between subjectivity and objectivity. This was the last major modification in Rilke's art theory, and the problem posed was essentially one of language.[1] Thus, the continuity of Rilke's development is unmistakable; from formation, through translation, to the final creative consummation. And from Rodin to Valéry runs the unbroken thread of the language of France.

.    .    .    .    .

This, then, was Rilke's position when he approached the great culmination of his work at Muzot at the beginning of 1922. He still adhered to the cardinal principle of 'sagen' instead of 'beurteilen' which he had formulated in 1907. This remained the keystone of his art theory, and the obstacle to its realization in practice had been his inability to exert the mastery over his medium which such an exacting concept demanded. The problem postulated a treatment somewhere between his two earlier extremes: the excessive effusion of the first two parts of Das Stunden-Buch—an excess to which Rilke was the more prone because of his 'romantic-intuitive' nature and also, even, because of the great richness and flexibility of the German instrument and his natural facility and virtuosity in it—and the antipodal, ascetic, 'intellectual' method of the Rodin years. It implied a handling of his medium which combined selection and restraint on the one hand with the fullest exploitation of the immense poetic potential of German on the other: in other

[1] p. 91.

words, so far from sacrificing the enormous wealth and the genius of his native instrument, his task was to achieve its maximum power by means of a quintessential linguistic discipline. We have attempted to show that, in translating Valéry, Rilke was engaged in an exercise which led him towards the middle path which he was seeking: while relaxing the uncompromising austerity, the near-elliptical style of Valéry's lines, he yet brought his own medium and mode of expression under the restraint and control which would eliminate the danger of effusion and extravagance. If, therefore, we see Valéry's significance as the culmination of the long process of French influence which had been going on since 1902, we may see Rilke's final task of achieving utterance as involving a synthesis of the best characteristics of both languages. With these thoughts we can turn to discussion of the Elegies and the Sonnets.

The Fifth Elegy is of particular interest, since it is the only one in the series which has its inspiration in a work of visual art—a fact which immediately prompts thoughts of the Rodin days. How, in the light of all that has happened since the early Parisian years, will Rilke's treatment of Picasso's picture show an advance on his handling of similar subjects nearly twenty years before? This Elegy, admittedly, has the elements of a verbal portrayal of *Les Saltimbanques*, and on this level alone the poem could be justifiably regarded as notable. And it is true that Rilke never forgot the Rodin experience; the technical advance made during that period was never lost. But it is soon apparent that Picasso's picture is being used by the poet as a vehicle for the expression of something much broader and deeper than the mere presentation in words of the acrobats. Where, under Rodin, Rilke went out and sought visual impressions *for the purpose of making his poetry out of them*, here the visual element is an accessory; Rilke uses it to illustrate and transmit *something which he already has to say anyway*. The difference between the two approaches is thus clear: he now uses the visual as a means, where before it had been very near to being an end in itself, with the result that, as we suggested, 'however happy the result, the control over the success of the poem was vested, at least in part, in the subject instead of belonging wholly to the poet'.[1]

> Wer aber *sind* sie, sag mir, die Fahrenden, diese ein wenig
> Flüchtigern noch als wir selbst, die drängend von früh an
> wringt ein *wem*, *wem* zu Liebe

[1] p. 72.

niemals zufriedener Wille? Sondern er wringt sie,
biegt sie, schlingt sie und schwingt sie,
wirft wie und fängt sie zurück; wie aus geölter,
glatterer Luft kommen sie nieder
auf dem verzehrten, von ihrem ewigen
Aufsprung dünneren Teppich, diesem verlorenen
Teppich im Weltall.[1]

It should be said at once that Rilke does not even 'describe' the picture, for Picasso's figures are not in action; they are standing or, in one case, sitting. Nevertheless, even if one allows that the extension of the idea of the painter's subject justifies the use of the term 'description', these opening lines at once establish the wider sweep of Rilke's purpose. It is immediately clear that this is no mere recital of a physical performance; the poet is not just a disinterested spectator of a series of imagined happenings. Something is powerfully and deeply exercising his feelings. There is something of urgency and import which he wants to communicate and for which the routine of the acrobats will provide the symbols. They are not simply going through a number of skilled movements. He sees them as wrung by 'ein *wem, wem* zu Liebe niemals zufriedener Wille'. Rilke, with this subtle touch, thus motivates their performance by a personal act of interpretation, just as, by the phrase 'auf . . . diesem verlorenen Teppich im Weltall', he expands the whole conception of the poem into something of general, universal application.

This technique of description which is more than description is characteristic of Rilke's solution of the problem of 'sachliches Sagen'. While going on to depict the members of the troupe and their routine, he accompanies his portrayal with this delicate, controlled commentary which personalizes the whole scene and lifts it into the realm of all human experience.[2] And sometimes, with a sudden, unexpected stroke, as in

> Und dennoch, blindlings,
> das Lächeln . . .[3]

he, with something of the terseness culled from Valéry, assaults the

[1] *A.W.*, Bd. I, p. 259.
[2] If these remarks are reminiscent of the commentary on *Der Panther* (see particularly pp. 63–64), they reinforce our view that, so far from denying any experience of the past, Rilke's creative climax embodied all the influences which had operated on him.
[3] *A.W.*, Bd. I, p. 261.

emotions in a way that is all the more powerful for the restraint and simplicity of his linguistic devices. Gradually, Rilke's canvas broadens out even beyond the scene suggested by Picasso:

> Plätze, o Platz in Paris, unendlicher Schauplatz,
> wo die Modistin, *Madame Lamort*,
> die ruhlosen Wege der Erde, endlose Bänder,
> schlingt und windet und neue aus ihnen
> Schleifen erfindet, Rüschen, Blumen, Kokarden, künstliche
>     Früchte —, alle
> unwahr gefärbt, — für die billigen
> Winterhüte des Schicksals.[1]

These lines, impregnated though they are with Rilke's own feelings and memories of Paris, embrace symbolically every arena in which a troupe of performers has gone through its mechanical, joyless motions—indeed, they embrace the whole world stage. It is noteworthy how, in the suggestive transition from 'Plätze' to 'o Platz . . . , unendlicher Schauplatz', Rilke performs the remarkable feat of immeasurably expanding his thought when, by changing from the plural to the singular, he would appear to be contracting and confining it. This shows his mastery over his medium at its best. He concludes by extending his poetic conception still further, with the vision of the limited perfection of human endeavour as displayed by the acrobats translated into the boundless perfection of the infinite:

> Engel!: Es wäre ein Platz, den wir nicht wissen, und dorten,
> auf unsäglichem Teppich, zeigten die Liebenden, die's hier
> bis zum Können nie bringen, ihre kühnen
> hohen Figuren des Herzschwungs,
> ihre Türme aus Lust, ihre
> längst, wo Boden nie war, nur aneinander
> lehnenden Leitern, bebend, — und *könntens*,
> vor den Zuschauern rings, unzähligen lautlosen Toten:
>     Würfen die dann ihre letzten, immer ersparten,
> immer verborgenen, die wir nicht kennen, ewig
> gültigen Münzen des Glücks vor das endlich
> wahrhaft lächelnde Paar auf gestilltem
> Teppich?[2]

Again we see how, by such simple but telling devices as the subjunctive 'Es wäre', by the coupling of the adjective 'unsäglich' with

---

[1] *A.W.*, Bd. I, p. 262.    [2] Ibid., pp. 262–3.

'Teppich', by the italicized '*könntens*', and by the delicate emphasis
on the 'wahrhaft' in 'das wahrhaft lächelnde Paar', the poet achieves
an optimum expression and evocation of feeling by means of
subtle, finely balanced suggestion.

We are less concerned, here, with interpreting the meaning of
this poem—the private domain of subjective appreciation is perhaps better left uninvaded with such poetry as this—than with investigating the manner of Rilke's creative climax and seeking to
establish how the work of Muzot demonstrates the attainment,
through the marriage of concept and technique, of the goal of his
long pilgrimage. The reader is struck by how little the personality
of the poet obtrudes—the use, twice, of the first person singular is
little more than a figure of speech and almost passes unnoticed—
and yet how present he is. There is no 'judging', no protestation;
there is, ostensibly, 'objective' presentation; and yet the poem is
redolent of the poet's feeling, into which the reader is irresistibly
drawn. Here, in the subtle and suggestive exploitation of the technique of 'sagen' by means of complete mastery over his instrument,
Rilke can offer the perfect merger between creator and object,
between subjectivity and objectivity, between the compelling surge
of his inspiration and fertile imagination and the intellectual control
which was his inheritance from France; he can claim that feeling
is 'ohne Rückstand . . . aufgebraucht in der Aktion des Machens'.

If the Fifth Elegy exemplifies the practical realization of the kind
of poetry which Rilke had conceived in 1907, as well as the unbroken continuity and the fundamental viability of his artistic
concept, we can also see how the reading and translation of Valéry
contributed towards bringing Rilke to articulateness. As a comparison of the examples in this study of the various phases in his evolution will show, his handling of his material in the creative climax of
1922 differs markedly from that of his previous work. If the first
lessons of the Rodin years were never rejected, and if we can still
perceive how deeply and firmly the method cultivated during that
early period was embedded in Rilke's poetic personality, this poetry
nevertheless differs qualitatively from that of the earlier collections.
It even differs, though in another way, from the portions of the
Elegies which already existed before Rilke went to Muzot. For,
while there is no aesthetic disharmony between the sections written
before and during the war and those completed in 1922 there was
a significant difference in the manner of Rilke's creation. Before

February 1922, he had written about half the total product of the
Elegies. But this had been accomplished only over the long period
of ten years, and the evidence of corrections and alternative versions
in Rilke's notebooks is indicative of the poet's lack of assurance and
the tentative nature of his efforts. Against the intermittent, desultory, groping character of his work hitherto—however successful it
was in the result—the achievement of Muzot stands in remarkable
contrast. The remaining half of the Elegies was written in seven
days. It was still a tremendous struggle with his medium, certainly,
but the swiftness and completeness of the victory and the unmistakable confidence which carried Rilke along his triumphant path
speak for themselves. From the nature of this consummation it is
impossible to dissociate the impact of Valéry. Apart from the timing of Rilke's acquaintance with the great French poet, the language
of the Fifth Elegy supports our earlier inferences regarding the
effect which the translation of *Le Cimetière marin* had on Rilke and
regarding the quality of the control over his instrument which it
developed. He has clearly profited from Valéry's linguistic discipline. The directness and economy of words in this poem are notable,
and yet, so far from there being any diminution in the emotive
power, the effect is enhanced. Sometimes the lines writhe with the
movements of the tumblers or with the feelings of the poet, sometimes they strike with a sudden, short thrust; but every word is
laden with meaning. Two dominant impressions emerge from this
Elegy: first, that Rilke achieves the saturation point in his use of
language by which the fullest power and value and virtue of each
word is utilized; secondly, that there is not one word too many or
too few, and that every phrase is perfectly balanced and attuned to
the idea which it is employed to convey. We may, therefore, see Rilke
finding the middle way between the two languages which occupied
his poetic consciousness; between the extreme, elliptical essence
to which Valéry had reduced French and the tendency towards
dilation inherent in German. While advancing from the ultra-
austerity of Valéry, he yet avoided the diffuseness and turgidity to
which German is such an easy prey. In short, he drew upon the
qualities of his adopted tongue while retaining the best of his native
instrument.

The Fifth Elegy was one of only three, the others being the
Seventh and Eighth, written in entirety at Muzot. This, as well as
its association with a work of visual art and the tempting link with

the history of Rilke's development to which this association points, has made it an obvious object of examination. The surging, soaring assurance which enabled the poet to write the remaining half of the Elegies in the short space of a week has been noted. It is, therefore, interesting to compare this Elegy with the previous one, written in 1915 and, incidentally, the only part of the cycle to be written in Germany. Stress has been laid on the artistic harmony and qualitative unity of the whole series, and, without the evidence of dating, it would be a dangerous exercise to attempt a definitive critical separation of those portions written at Muzot and those written before. Account has to be taken of the fact that, in poetry as intensely personal as this and demanding an equally personal response in the reader, the substance is so delicate that one is as far removed as it is possible to be from any question of hard proof. Moreover, in a cycle which explores every experience of the poet and which reflects almost every mood, feeling, and thought, there is bound to be a wide range of treatment, with wide variation of rhythm, style, and all the devices at the poet's command. And the continuity and wholeness of Rilke's vision must not be forgotten. It is, therefore, impossible to say with certainty that the Fourth Elegy would have differed greatly had it been written in 1922. Nevertheless, it is possible to wonder whether the poet is less at ease here, whether the sureness of touch, the almost instinctive sense of language with which the work of Muzot throbs, is less evident in this poem:

> Wer saß nicht bang vor seines Herzens Vorhang?
> Der schlug sich auf: die Szenerie war Abschied.
> Leicht zu verstehen. Der bekannte Garten,
> und schwankte leise: dann erst kam der Tänzer.[1]

And again:

> Ich will nicht diese halbgefüllten Masken,
> lieber die Puppe. Die ist voll. Ich will
> den Balg aushalten und den Draht und ihr
> Gesicht aus Aussehen. Hier. Ich bin davor.[1]

It is perhaps not too fanciful to detect here, in the *staccato* rhythm and the broken style of statement, the evidence, not only of intentional effect—which must not be discounted—but also of a certain groping and probing in Rilke's search for language fit to clothe his feelings and ideas.

[1] *A.W.*, Bd. I, p. 256.

Such thoughts, however, can be no more than conjectural, especially when one contemplates his impressive control in the closing lines:

> ... Aber dies: den Tod,
> den ganzen Tod, noch *vor* dem Leben so
> sanft zu enthalten und nicht bös zu sein,
> ist unbeschreiblich.[1]

Moreover, the nature of the poem, with its prevailing mood of assertion and debate, could be said to justify, and even impose, the ejaculatory style and the changes of pulse of oratory—an impression which is reinforced by the thrice repeated 'Hab ich nicht recht?'[2] In this connexion we may recall the remarks in the first chapter as to the manner in which Rilke came to terms with the linguistic demands and characteristics of his age.[3] At most, then, any qualifying considerations of Rilke's handling of his medium in this Elegy do not go beyond suspicions. Above all, it must be emphasized that the *quality* of Rilke's language is not in question. We are concerned here with the confidence and immediacy of the control which he acquired as the result of his encounter with Valéry. We may perhaps attempt to resolve any doubt that may exist in the suggestion that, whereas, qualitatively, the language of the whole series shows no sign of umbalance, there are indications in some of the sections written before Muzot of the poet's struggle to prevail over his medium—indications that the creation of his effect required more effort. There is an interesting clue in the already quoted lines:

> Wer saß nicht bang vor seines Herzens Vorhang?
> Der schlug sich auf: . . .[4]

This is curiously reminiscent, both in language and rhythm, of the section in *Der Panther*:

> Nur manchmal schiebt der Vorhang der Pupille
> sich lautlos auf — . . .[5]

Without pressing the comparison too far, it does offer a possible diagnosis of the difference between Rilke's creative process in the storm of 1922 and that at work in some of the earlier portions of the Elegies. It indicates that the poet, lacking the liberating effect of the Valéry experience and enjoying only intermittent mastery over his instrument, may have reverted at times, however unconsciously

---

[1] *A.W.*, Bd. I, p. 258.  [2] Ibid., p. 257.  [3] p. 22.
[4] *A.W.*, Bd. I, p. 256.  [5] Ibid., p. 189.

and however satisfying the result, to the 'intellectual' approach of
the Rodin days; that what, at Muzot, came about through the
'Orkan im Geist' had sometimes had to be achieved in the past by
more deliberate means.

An even more interesting example, because of the fragmented
nature of its composition, is the shorter Sixth Elegy, on the theme
of the 'hero'. Lines 1–31 and the closing three lines were written in
Spain in 1912 and in Paris in 1914, while lines 32–41 were inserted
at Muzot. In order to place the Muzot section in the context of
what had been completed earlier, we may quote lines 26–44:

> Hör ich doch keinen wie *ihn*. Auf einmal durchgeht mich
> mit der strömenden Luft sein verdunkelter Ton.
>
> Dann, wie verbärg ich mich gern vor der Sehnsucht: O wär ich,
> wär ich ein Knabe und dürft es noch werden und säße
> in die künftigen Arme gestützt und läse von Simson,
> wie seine Mutter erst nichts und dann alles gebar.
>
> War er nicht Held schon in dir, o Mutter, begann nicht
> dort schon, in dir, seine herrische Auswahl?
> Tausende brauten im Schooß und wollten *er* sein,
> aber sieh: er ergriff und ließ aus —, wählte und konnte.
> Und wenn er Säulen zerstieß, so wars, da er ausbrach
> aus der Welt deines Leibs in die engere Welt, wo er weiter
> wählte und konnte. O Mütter der Helden, o Ursprung
> reißender Ströme! Ihr Schluchten, in die sich
> hoch von dem Herzrand, klagend,
> schon die Mädchen gestürzt, künftig die Opfer dem Sohn.
>
> Denn hinstürmte der Held durch Aufenthalte der Liebe,
> jeder hob ihn hinaus, jeder ihn meinende Herzschlag,
> abgewendet schon, stand er am Ende der Lächeln, — anders.[1]

This Elegy and the Tenth are the only ones the creation of which
took place at three different times and places, though in the latter,
a much longer poem, the great bulk was written at Muzot, only the
opening having been completed earlier, in 1912 in Duino and in
1914 in Paris. We might, therefore, expect the Sixth Elegy to be-
tray, more than any other, signs of the prolonged and broken
nature of its genesis. The impression, however, is one of remarkable accord; there is a smoothness and consistency throughout,
which contrasts with the difficulties which confronted the poet in

---

[1] *A. W.*, Bd. I, p. 265.

his triple attempt to accomplish his purpose. And, as the section quoted above shows, despite the long years of silence and frustration, the lines written at Muzot fit into their environment without any hint of roughness or jarring or hiatus.

An examination of the text, then, with a view to differentiating between the parts of the Elegies written in 1922 and those written before, is at best inconclusive; the only 'proof' of Rilke's creative problems lies in the incidental knowledge of dating and of his notebooks. It is even impossible to be sure that the occasional inference that is drawn is genuinely the result of textual analysis and is not weighted more by this incidental knowledge. We are, in fact, left wondering at the homogeneity of the whole cycle, and at the extent to which the poet succeeded in concealing his spasmodic effort. It is evident that his vision was so comprehensive and compulsive that it was able to overcome the fissile tendencies and warring factions inherent in such a protracted and agonized act of creation. And it is this very evenness, this absence of hard edges, this concord of concept and technique, which underlines the anguish of Rilke's dilemma and the vital importance of Valéry. For the standard Rilke set himself—a standard born of long years of discipline and preparation—was so high and consistent, and his refusal to compromise on it so absolute, that any prospect of completing the series without a change in the manner of composition as startling as that which occurred at Muzot did not exist.

The sureness with which Rilke handles the varied resources of his material, and the skill with which he modulates his style to suit his subject, are remarkable, and override any differences of valuation which personal taste may apply to different parts of the cycle. He ranges from the more-than-description of a visual scene in the Fifth Elegy to the declamation of the Seventh, from the calm, almost conventional mood of discussion in the Eighth to the allegorical narrative of the Tenth. And always words and form are appropriate to his purpose. Sometimes the poet himself emerges more prominently:

> Engel, und würb ich dich auch! Du kommst nicht. Denn mein
> Anruf ist immer voll Hinweg; wider so starke
> Strömung kannst du nicht schreiten. Wie ein gestreckter
> Arm ist mein Rufen . . .[1]

in the Seventh Elegy. But he always remains in the territory

---

[1] *A.W.*, Bd. I, p. 269.

between the two extremes of his early poetic endeavour, adapting but not violating the principle of 'sachliches Sagen'. Sometimes a striking image or a piece of word-magic challenges the imagination:

> Und wie bestürzt ist eins, das fliegen muß
> und stammt aus einem Schooß. Wie vor sich selbst
> erschreckt, durchzuckts die Luft, wie wenn ein Sprung
> durch eine Tasse geht. So reißt die Spur
> der Fledermaus durchs Porzellan des Abends.[1]

The Eighth Elegy, from which this comes, is a remarkable piece of poetic thinking, contrasting the outward-looking animal, which has its 'Untergang' behind it and God and eternity before, and ourselves, backward-looking and impeding the animal's free outlet, backward-looking and living an eternal leave-taking. But even the animal has its memory of the security of the womb which it has left, its first home, a part of that eternity of which this present existence is but an interruption. The lines quoted above are by any standards an arresting piece of writing: the idea of a creature flashing through the air like a crack streaking across a cup; then, developing this thought, likening the trace of the bat to a crack darting across the porcelain of the evening sky. Rilke takes something we have all seen many times and, with a few simple strokes, transmutes it into an image of passing beauty.

Sometimes the symbolism is complex, as in the journey through the 'Leidland' of the Tenth Elegy. Sometimes the most evocative and powerful effect is achieved in a near-whisper, as in the quiet, moving simplicity of the closing lines of this last Elegy:

> Aber erweckten sie uns, die unendlich Toten, ein Gleichnis,
> siehe, sie zeigten vielleicht auf die Kätzchen der leeren
> Hasel, die hängenden, oder
> meinten den Regen, der fällt auf dunkles Erdreich im Frühjahr.
>
> Und wir, die an *steigendes* Glück
> denken, empfänden die Rührung,
> die uns beinah bestürzt,
> wenn ein Glückliches fällt.[2]

This Elegy may indeed be regarded as the summit and summary, not only of this great series, but also of Rilke's own long poetic pilgrimage.

---

[1] Ibid., p. 272.    [2] Ibid., p. 280.

Freilich, wehe, wie fremd sind die Gassen der Leidstadt,
wo in der falschen, aus Übertönung gemachten
Stille, stark, aus der Gußform des Leeren der Ausguß
prahlt: der vergoldete Lärm, das platzende Denkmal.[1]

These lines and those following, in which he pictures the scene as
that of a fair, with its din and hustle and artificial values, invite the
thought of the poet's early memory of Paris, with all its pain and
bitterness. This is not reality; this is just a façade, with no more
substance than a stage set. Reality lies behind:

... Oh aber gleich darüber hinaus,
hinter der letzten Planke, beklebt mit Plakaten des 'Todlos',
jenes bitteren Biers, das den Trinkenden süß scheint,
wenn sie immer dazu frische Zerstreuungen kaun ...,
gleich im Rücken der Planke, gleich dahinter, ists *wirklich*.[2]

Reality is close at hand, just as it was for Rilke, for it was here that
his real journey began. Here, under Rodin, was the start of his
voyage of discovery; and it is here that the young Lament takes
charge of the youth, leading him onward to her own land. Not for
nothing has Rilke chosen this personification as the young man's
guide, a choice appropriate both to the sorrow and anguish of the
way ahead and to the title of the series. But

... — Mit Jünglingen geht sie
schweigend.[3]

When they reach the 'Leidland' an older Lament, one who is not
silent, takes over his guidance, symbolizing, perhaps, his growing
maturity and awareness. She it is who tells him the history of their
race and shows him their country, its temples, its ruins, its memo-
rials, and finally the constellations in the heavens, pointing the way
to the stars. It is significant that the youth is one of the 'young
dead', reminding us of Rilke's preoccupation with the idea of early
death and of his belief that only in death is there completeness,
fulfilment.

But the Lament can take him only so far. The last part of his
journey he must make alone:

Doch der Tote muß fort, und schweigend bringt ihn die ältere
Klage bis an die Talschlucht,
wo es schimmert im Mondschein:

[1] *A.W.*, Bd. I, p. 276.        [2] Ibid., p. 277.
[3] Ibid., p. 278.

die Quelle der Freude. In Ehrfurcht
nennt sie sie, sagt: — Bei den Menschen
ist sie ein tragender Strom. —[1]

She can bring him to the foot of the mountain; no one can accompany him on the final climb. She can show him the spring, the source of joy, and there is promise in her parting words, with the double significance of 'tragend', in the sense of 'bearing', 'sustaining', and in the sense of 'yielding', 'productive'. The poet, after his own years of formative experience, had to reach the summit alone, but always having in sight 'ein tragender Strom', the stream of his own creative consciousness directed inalienably by his link with France.

Einsam steigt er dahin, in die Berge des Ur-Leids.
Und nicht einmal sein Schritt klingt aus dem tonlosen Los.[1]

How well Rilke suggests the arduousness of the ascent, with the repetition of the long vowels, and how poignant is the second line, with its reminder of his own familiarity with poetic silence!

Then come the remarkable closing lines, quoted earlier,[2] the 'dying fall' of such peace and tranquillity that it almost seems to belie the idea of a climax. Yet climax it is, of dramatic impact. Once again, as we saw in the Fifth Elegy, Rilke intensifies his effect by completely reversing his poetic thought. In the earlier example we noted that, while seeming to limit his scope by changing from the plural to the singular in

Plätze, o Platz in Paris, unendlicher Schauplatz,

he nevertheless succeeds in extending the vision.[3] Here, the transition is even more astonishing and unexpected. Throughout the poem, with its long lines and their slow tempo, and with its mood of gradual and painful progression, we have become conditioned to thinking in terms of the long journey onwards and upwards. Then, suddenly and with subtle manipulation of rhythm, Rilke directs our thought to the very opposite of the previous trend of the poem. In place of happiness conceived in terms of ascent, of rising experience—'steigendes Glück'—we are invited to think of those things which hang and which fall, the hazel catkins and the spring rain, and to ponder that this is the way of happiness. The last four lines, short and restrained, have a concision worthy of Valéry himself. And in this hushed ending to the poem and the cycle lies the

whole world of Rilke's contentment. Perhaps, in this closing antithesis, he is expressing the culmination of his own great purpose.
After his own long, hard, questing pilgrimage, consummation has
come, not in the way expected, but as a gift, as something falling
into his possession. Certainly, we may see significance in this antithesis in the context of Rilke's encounter with Valéry, and may
recall the earlier comment that the release of Rilke's creative flow
was accomplished because Valéry approached this encounter from
the opposite direction of experience.[1]

· · · · ·

The Sonnets, in so far as they were conceived and executed in
their entirety at Muzot, do not present the same critical compli-
cations as the Elegies. But, even though they bring a marked change
in mood and in the use of the poet's material of language, they are
still the product of the same creative release which completed the
Elegies, and we may seek in them evidence of the same artistic
approach and the same influences operating on the poet as we have
found in the Elegies. Rilke handles the sonnet form with considerable variation and with great subtlety and suggestiveness. But these
poems are, by their nature, much more homogeneous and more
compactly constructed than the Elegies. The general uniformity of
mood and theme produces an effect of much greater evenness,
which is enhanced by the rhymed form and the more easily perceptible syntactical structure. Technically, they are for the most
part light and lilting; their lines have none of the agonies, the sudden, dramatic pauses, and the violent fluctuations of tension which
characterize those of the Elegies. In the latter the poet's spirit is
imprisoned and seeking by every means to escape; in the Sonnets
it is liberated and able to move freely and smoothly along the path
of its choice. The two series are complementary, showing the two
sides of the poet's nature and emotions, and revealing, according
as one or the other was in the ascendancy, the remarkably contrasting effects which they had on his poetic consciousness and technique. Our principal concern, however, is how the Sonnets fit into
the climax of Rilke's development, and how far they conform to the
principles which informed his creative activity. They were com-
posed in the great outpouring which accomplished the remainder
of the Elegies and which lasted only a matter of days. It would,
therefore, be illogical to expect to find any fundamental difference

[1] p. 148.

in Rilke's concept of his art, or to imagine that the results of Valéry's impact, if they have been satisfactorily established as being
present in the Elegies, could be absent from the Sonnets. Added
weight is given to this point when we recall that the greater part of
the remaining work on the Elegies intervened between the writing
of the two parts of the Sonnets.[1] In the event, the concept of 'sagen'
instead of 'beurteilen' still controls Rilke's approach, and the linguistic competence and flow which emerged from the contact with
Valéry are still present.

The poet's personality may sometimes seem more to the fore in
these poems, for 'Rühmung' is the dominant theme of the Sonnets,
but he never lapses into the excessive, cloying subjectivity of the
Russian and Worpswede days. The particular interest of the Sonnets in our examination is that, besides confirming Rilke's fidelity
to the concept which he had guarded for so long, they are further
convincing testimony of the absoluteness, the immediacy, the
surging confidence of his control over his artist's material. There
now appears to be no faltering, no hesitation—a view which, if we
believe Rilke's own record, is supported by the letter to Xaver von
Moos referred to earlier.[2] Most noticeable are the range of Rilke's
technical skill, within the more restricted limits of the sonnet form,
and the seeming ease with which he manipulates his language.
There is the compelling simplicity of the Twenty-second Sonnet of
Part I:

> Wir sind die Treibenden.
> Aber den Schritt der Zeit,
> nehmt ihn als Kleinigkeit
> im immer Bleibenden.
>
> Alles das Eilende
> wird schon vorüber sein;
> denn das Verweilende
> erst weiht uns ein.
>
> Knaben, o werft den Mut
> nicht in die Schnelligkeit,
> nicht in den Flugversuch.

---

[1] The chronology of Rilke's work on the two series is interesting. The whole of
the first part of the Sonnets was written before a word was added to the Elegies,
while only the Fifth Elegy was written after the second part was begun.

[2] See p. 52.

Alles ist ausgeruht:
Dunkel und Helligkeit,
Blume und Buch.[1]

Here, again, we may note the dexterity and assurance with which
Rilke matched rhythm and form to the idea. The poem is reduced
to its essence—not the austere, elliptical essence of Valéry, but to
an essence that remains true to the character of German while strip-
ping it of all superfluous matter. This is a further telling reminder
that, just as his concept of 'sagen' was a middle way, so the solution
to his problem of utterance took him between the two extremes of
his linguistic consciousness: the terseness of French, and in particular the ascetic severity of Valéry, and the weltering, luxuriant
potential of German. It is not difficult to see how the contact with
Valéry made the writing of a poem such as this an easier and more
instinctive process. As we read it, the feeling is inescapable that the
poet is aware of his powers as never before, that the accord between
idea and execution is immediate.

Sometimes the structure of the poem is more elaborate, as in the
Twentieth Sonnet of Part II:

Zwischen den Sternen, wie weit; und doch um wie vieles noch weiter,
was man am Hiesigen lernt.
Einer, zum Beispiel, ein Kind . . . und ein Nächster, ein Zweiter —,
o wie unfaßlich entfernt.

Schicksal, es mißt uns vielleicht mit des Seienden Spanne,
daß es uns fremd erscheint;
denk, wieviel Spannen allein vom Mädchen zum Manne,
wenn es ihn meidet und meint.

Alles ist weit —, und nirgends schließt sich der Kreis.
Sieh in der Schüssel, auf heiter bereitetem Tische,
seltsam der Fische Gesicht.

Fische sind stumm . . ., meinte man einmal. Wer weiß?
Aber ist nicht am Ende ein Ort, wo man das, was der Fische
Sprache wäre, *ohne* sie spricht?[2]

This is a more reflective, more contemplative poem. Like a number
of the Sonnets, especially in the second part, with their longer lines
and the more expansive treatment, it illustrates how flexible and
versatile was Rilke's handling of the sonnet form. With its greater
complexity, its slower tempo, and its mood of meditation, it takes

[1] *A.W.*, Bd. I, p. 295.     [2] Ibid., p. 311.

our thoughts back to the Elegies. But it is easy to see the difference between the two series. Here, the lines, though they are longer and more involved, have none of the writhing torment and the sudden spasms and stresses which are so often present in the Elegies. The poet, certainly, is in serious vein, but the mood is essentially calm and peaceful, the pulse even. And yet, in this poem, it is not difficult to sense that the two series are the product, not only of the same poetic imagination, but also of the same surge of creation. The closing lines of the sestet again reveal Rilke's arresting use of antithesis, his capacity to take an ordinary image or experience, one that we commonly take for granted, and, with a few delicate, almost imperceptible strokes, completely change our awareness of it and transform it into something of supreme significance. The last two lines, with their question form and their haunting suggestion of a place, somewhere, where those things which here are commonplace and bounded by limitations may have their own infinitude and perfection, recall the last lines of the Fifth Elegy, written in the middle of the second part of the Sonnets.

The Eighth Sonnet of Part I is of interest in that it introduces us again to the Lament:

> Nur im Raum der Rühmung darf die Klage
> gehn, die Nymphe des geweinten Quells,
> wachend über unserm Niederschlage,
> daß er klar sei an demselben Fels,
>
> der die Tore trägt und die Altäre. —
> Sieh, um ihre stillen Schultern früht
> das Gefühl, daß sie die jüngste wäre
> unter den Geschwistern im Gemüt.
>
> Jubel *weiß*, und Sehnsucht ist geständig, —
> nur die Klage lernt noch; mädchenhändig
> zählt sie nächtelang das alte Schlimme.
>
> Aber plötzlich, schräg und ungeübt,
> hält sie doch ein Sternbild unsrer Stimme
> in den Himmel, den ihr Hauch nicht trübt.[1]

It is of particular interest when we remember that it was written before the greater part of the Tenth Elegy which was written at Muzot. And yet, poetically, it appears quite clearly as a sequel to the

---

[1] Ibid., p. 287.

Elegy, it seems to carry on where the Elegy left off—or, more accurately perhaps, it presents the positive, the more optimistic side
of the same theme. It is difficult to believe that the two poems were
not close together in Rilke's mind. Much of the symbolism and
imagery is the same, albeit with subtle change of emphasis. The
'stars' in the Elegy are 'die Sterne des Leidlands',[1] the constellations images of the long, questing journey, milestones and sign-
posts on the way ahead:

> . . . den *Reiter*, den *Stab*, und das vollere Sternbild
> nennen sie: *Fruchtkranz*. Dann, weiter, dem Pol zu:
> *Wiege; Weg; Das Brennende Buch; Puppe; Fenster.*
> Aber im südlichen Himmel, rein wie im Innern
> einer gesegneten Hand, das klar erglänzende *M*,
> das die Mütter bedeutet. . . .[1]

Significantly, they are the last thing the Lament shows the youth;
they are there with their message of promise, yet at the same time
symbolical of the fact that the end of the road is not yet. In this
Sonnet, however, the Lament is linked with another 'Sternbild':

> hält sie doch ein Sternbild unsrer Stimme
> in den Himmel, den ihr Hauch nicht trübt.

This is the final constellation, betokening arrival, fulfilment; a
constellation of the poet's voice; one which she can receive and
hold up into the highest heaven; one which, in the clear pouring
forth of its radiance, not even her breath can cloud or dim.

One other Sonnet, the First in Part II, may be cited for the
illustration it gives of the extreme flexibility of Rilke's handling of
this form and for the strange, compelling penetration of his poetic
thought:

> Atmen, du unsichtbares Gedicht!
> Immerfort um das eigne
> Sein rein eingetauschter Weltraum. Gegengewicht,
> in dem ich mich rhythmisch ereigne.
>
> Einzige Welle, deren
> allmähliches Meer ich bin;
> sparsamstes du von allen möglichen Meeren, —
> Raumgewinn.
>
> Wieviele von diesen Stellen der Räume waren schon
> innen in mir. Manche Winde
> sind wie mein Sohn.

[1] A.W., Bd. I, p. 279.

Erkennst du mich, Luft, du, voll noch einst meiniger Orte?
Du, einmal glatte Rinde,
Rundung und Blatt meiner Worte.[1]

Here, with his elusive and suggestive imagery, with his lines of un-
even length which yet achieve remarkable balance and harmony,
with the alchemy which transmutes the simple word into gold, and,
above all, with the utmost delicacy of touch on his Orphean instrument, Rilke seems to be resuming the creative act as he has
come to know it. This is the concentrated essence, the free-flowing
stream of his art enriched by every tributary of the past. The poem,
in its 'invisibility' now a part of the universe itself, is an act of
breathing. In the unusual phrase 'eingetauschter Weltraum' we
may perhaps detect Rilke's awareness of the completeness of his
fulfilment. Revealing, too, is

> . . . Gegengewicht,
> in dem ich mich rhythmisch ereigne.

His whole life had been spent in reconciling the discrepant elements, making good the unbalance, supplying the parts of his creative
whole which he lacked, bringing harmony to contradiction and conflict, and finally, through the fine mesh of Valéry's poetic thought,
accomplishing the untroubled union of concept and practice, the
untrammelled ease of utterance which had so stubbornly opposed
him. Now, at last, he is aware of this 'equipoise' in which, in a
striking figure, he can just 'rhythmically happen'. Now his poetry
belongs to the sea, fluid, 'gradual'; and to the air, non-resistant, the
'smooth shell, the rounding, and the leaf' of his words.

Throughout the Sonnets, whether the structure be simple or
more complicated, whether the central idea be less or more serious,
Rilke constantly achieves the perfect harmony between form and
content. He realizes throughout the whole series the optimum use
of language, the true economy of words which extracts the maximum effect from each and in which none is superfluous, and, above
all, the uninhibited freedom and facility of voice which had eluded
him for so long—all of which may be said to epitomize the impact
of Valéry. We may borrow the imagery of the Seventh Sonnet of
Part I and apply it to Rilke's own creative consummation:

[1] Ibid., p. 299.

Nie versagt ihm die Stimme am Staube,
wenn ihn das göttliche Beispiel ergreift.
Alles wird Weinberg, alles wird Traube,
in seinem fühlenden Süden gereift.[1]

The poetic fulfilment of February 1922, marked by the completion of the *Duineser Elegien* and the *Sonette an Orpheus*, may therefore be summarized as the culmination of the long and complex evolutionary process which we have attempted to follow throughout this study. Not only was this poetry the crown of Rilke's struggle; in it every artistic and aesthetic experience and influence of the past met. In particular, it embodied all the ingredients which he owed to France—the country which, as Russia did not, offered him the possibility of acquiring those elements which he did not already possess and which had to be grafted on to his natural endowments if he was to become the complete artist. The work of Muzot may be seen as the outcome of a complicated process of synthesis: it incorporated the fusion of Rilke's intuitive and inspirational nature and the intellectual discipline which he learnt first, and in its most extreme form, from Rodin; it embraced the formulated expression of this fusion, the concept of the perfect merger between subjectivity and objectivity which emerged in 1907 as the result of the Cézanne and Baudelaire revelations; it reflected, if not the synthesis of the 'static', representational arts and the mobile, dynamic art of poetry—for this, as we have seen, was impossible—at least the assimilation into his poetry of those by-products of his sojourn with the plastic arts by which his own concept and medium could be enriched; and finally, it exemplified the resolution of the most difficult creative problem of all—the achievement of the marriage between concept and execution, the setting in motion of the poetic flood the release of which was the direct and swift sequel to the exacting exercise of translating Valéry. In other words, Rilke's great creative climax embodies the blending of the finest cultural and linguistic qualities of his own and his adopted countries, by means of which he forged a new instrument—an instrument of language which, as H. W. Belmore, writing of the Elegies, remarks, 'comes from great depths, purified of all dross during its long way up through hardest rock'.[2] We may use of Rilke, in a different sense, his own description of Orpheus:

[1] *A.W.*, Bd. I, p. 286.          [2] *Rilke's Craftsmanship*, p. 209.

Ist er ein Hiesiger? Nein, aus beiden
Reichen erwuchs seine weite Natur.[1]

And it is symbolical that he attained the summit of his powers in
the country which partakes of the national heritage of both Germany and France.

·     ·     ·     ·     ·

It is now possible, with the evidence of his greatest poetry at
hand, to attempt a general assessment of the nature of Rilke's art
and achievement. Despite the cyclic conception of the Elegies and
the Sonnets, Rilke is essentially a lyric poet, and it is not inappropriate to return briefly to some of the comments in the first chapter.
Lyric poetry was there described as the poetry of mood and emotion; and, although the variations in the manner of expression are
endless, there are certain common elements in the lyric poetry of
all ages. For certain facts of existence, and the feelings which those
facts arouse, are eternally manifest. At the root of all lyric poetry
are the inescapable realities of life and death, the whole adventure
of living from the cradle to the grave; its stuff is the whole range
of human emotions with which life throbs, the ever-recurrent stir-
rings of the heart, from love and hope to fear and despair. It was
further suggested that the function of the lyric poet is to re-express
the eternal and unchanging fundamentals in the light of the
changed conditions of his time, and in language applicable to his
age.[2] When to this we add the important factor of the age in
which Rilke lived and for which he wrote,[3] we have come nearer to
establishing our critical position in relation to his greatest poetry.
    In Rilke we are confronted with a poet whose personality and
whose natural approach to his art were intuitive and subjective, and
yet who, through long years of self-discipline, had sought to objectivize—but not, be it noted, sacrifice or eliminate—his feelings.
We may, therefore, distinguish two elements in Rilke's poetry: the
reflection of his age and civilization, and the personal testimony of
his own pilgrimage and struggle. C. M. Bowra comments that the
Elegies may be read at two levels, the personal and the universal.
The Elegies and the Sonnets are thus an intimate revelation of
Rilke's own soul, and yet 'as a poet he speaks for humanity'.[4] And
it is ironical that his acute sensibility, which was in such a large

[1] *A.W.*, Bd. I, p. 286.          [2] See p. 20.
[3] See pp. 1 and 21.               [4] Op. cit., pp. 75–76.

measure responsible for the greatness of his poetry, was the quality which rendered him unfit to cope with the conditions of the modern world—which he recorded and to which he appealed with such evocative power.

In seeking to estimate the nature of Rilke's art, it will be profitable to bear in mind some of the critical problems which were discussed in the first chapter. We are confronted, in lyric poetry, with the most personal of all literary forms; and, while refraining from violating the personal nature of appreciation, we yet must seek an approach which is generally valid and acceptable. No two people will capture the same impressions or experience exactly the same emotions from any work of art. Is it, therefore, possible to arrive at some guiding principle which reconciles, on the one hand, the individuality of appreciation with, on the other, the eternal aspiration of critic and reader to enrich that appreciation by establishing some common ground of discussion? If this is to be accomplished—within the context of the basic argument of this study that language is the key to an appraisal of lyric poetry—there appears to be one prerequisite: while allowing full play to his feelings and thoughts, the reader must nevertheless move *on the same plane* as the poet; that is, his consciousness, if less sensitive and refined, must be of the same kind and tuned in the same way as that of the poet. With such considerations in mind, we can now attempt briefly some final suggestions.

What is his achievement in this, his greatest poetry, and what critical standards are we to apply in judging it? Much has been written about Rilke's 'thought' and 'message' and about the strange, compelling symbols he uses, particularly in the Elegies. What are the angel, the hero, the lovers? Are they the icons of a new religion, the vehicles of a new, Messianic revelation? Are they the keys to a new philosophy, capable of logical, systematized analysis? We may profitably draw attention to what Holthusen has to say about Rilke's thought. In an eloquently reasoned section[1] he underlines the falsity of Rilke's 'ideas' in the abstract, philosophical sense— a falsity comparable, he says, with that of the great prophetic theses of Nietzsche and of the so-called 'Satanism' of Baudelaire. If this argument, which links up with our remarks in the first chapter,[2] is accepted, it demonstrates the dangers courted by some of the critical expositions of Rilke's work; and it gives us useful guidance in

[1] Op. cit., pp. 58–63.    [2] pp. 12–15.

determining our own approach. For Rilke was essentially a *subjective* thinker, however much he presented his thoughts objectively— a fact emphasized by Holthusen.[1] But, as this critic acknowledges, this is not the whole of the picture. Quite clearly Rilke has created something new and worth while, and something, moreover, which has been able to arrest and enthral a great number of people. What value, then, are we to set on Rilke's thought? Holthusen places his finger on the truth. Pointing out that truth has a relative and an absolute aspect, he says: 'Wo Rilke den Menschen überhaupt in der Situation des Menschen seiner Zeit zum Sprechen bringt, da ist er wahr, hinreißend wahr.'[2]

Rilke was not a thinker, in the accepted sense of the word, he was not a prophet, or the high priest of a new orthodoxy. He was a poet, a poet of the twentieth century, and it is as a poet that he must be judged. 'Seine Einbildungskraft schuf sich eine Welt, in der das Phänomen der Zeit gleichsam ausgeklammert war, und alle Dinge, denen fühlbare Wirklichkeit zuzuschreiben war, in magischer Gleichzeitigkeit nebeneinander bestanden.'[3] From this approach the whole elaborate symbolism and imagery of his greatest work becomes clear, not intellectually but *poetically*. He represents the 'eternal spirit of the chainless mind' of art. Endowed with truly remarkable sensibility and sensitivity, Rilke was born into an age and lived in an environment which seemed to militate against everything towards which his fundamentally mystical imagination reached out. Like Nietzsche, he reflects 'die offene Wunde der Epoche . . . , die objektive Manifestation der gewaltigen Krise der europäischen Kultur'.[4] Inheritor of the Symbolists, he was deeply conscious of the lost values and of the shallow, artificial, materialistic character of an age which is spiritually bankrupt and dispossessed. The Elegies and the Sonnets are the product of his profound inner conflict, just as they are the mirror of the great spiritual conflict of our time. In them Rilke is fighting, in his own highly distinctive and personal way, a rearguard action to defend something which he regards as of supreme value and which he believes is slipping out of the grasp of a world too indifferent and insensitive to hold it. These poems are his tremendous struggle to

[1] Op. cit., p. 40. The realization that Rilke's thought was subjective is a reminder that his weakness as a thinker was his strength as a lyric poet.
[2] Ibid., p. 64.
[3] Ibid., p. 33.
[4] Ibid., p. 63.

recapture what has been lost, to recover 'Le Beau' and 'l'Idéal' and the things of the imagination and the spirit, to re-create the Golden Age, to re-establish the glory and the majesty of the Renaissance in the twentieth century.

In the light of his greatest poetry and of the contribution of France both to his experience of life and to his artistic development, we may ask how Rilke has accomplished his task, by what means he has achieved his effect. That he has created something new is not in question; and that his use of language is the key to an artistic and aesthetic appreciation of his work has been one of the underlying themes of this study. It must be emphasized again that, for all his sense of estrangement from the world and age in which he lived, the fulfilment of Rilke's purpose depended, in the last analysis, upon his ability to adjust and accommodate himself to his time. If, as was his overpowering inner compulsion, he would communicate with his age and reflect and minister to it, he must, in some measure at least, meet it on its own terms. And yet he must avoid the trite, banal, utilitarian utterance which has become the hall-mark of a cliché-ridden century. Holthusen, who was earlier noted as one of the few Rilke critics who have paid attention to this important problem of language,[1] speaks of 'die reine Eigentümlichkeit seiner Sprache, . . . das ganz und gar Einseitige, Unverwechselbare, das völlig in sich selbst Beruhende, aus sich selbst Gespeiste, das intensiv Idiomatische, ja zuweilen Idiopathische dieser Lyrik'.[2] And, drawing a notable comparison between Rilke and Klopstock, he comments: 'Wie dieser überrennt er eine ganze Generation von Spätlingen einer versinkenden Zeit, durchbricht er einen dichten Kordon von sprachlichen Requisiten, Konventionen oder sterilen Neuerungen, wirft seine Fahne weit hinaus in den feindlichen Bereich des Ungesagten, vermeintlich Unsagbaren und — holt sie ein.'[3] How has Rilke achieved this remarkable and incontrovertible distinction and individuality, while at the same time exerting his hold over an epoch the idiom of which has become 'conventional and sterile'?

The first important consideration relates to his vocabulary. O. F. Bollnow writes: 'Eine gewisse Armut drängt sich auch bei der Betrachtung von Rilkes Sprache auf.'[4] He expands this

---

[1] See p. 22.
[2] Op. cit., p. 10. See also the extracts quoted on pp. 22–23.
[3] Ibid., pp. 24–25.                                                        [4] *Rilke*, p. 13.

thought with a commentary which is particularly appropriate in view of our examination of the operation of French influence on Rilke's art. He notes that this linguistic austerity is not accidental but deliberate: '. . . denn im Verlauf seiner Reifung wird seine Sprache immer nüchterner, klarer, präziser.'[1] This judgement fits in with the trend of Rilke's development which we have noted in this study. Bollnow continues: 'Erstaunlich klein ist schon Rilkes Wortschatz. Die seine Jugendstil kennzeichnende ästhetisierende Freude an kostbaren und gewählten Worten verschwindet im Verlauf einer immer strengeren Disziplinierung.'[2] He goes on to remark the constant recurrence in Rilke's writings of his favourite words in new associations. We may object that this critic goes too far in making the statement that Rilke's vocabulary is 'astonishingly small', but his general observations regarding the increasingly disciplined moderation and precision of Rilke's language coincide with our own findings. Belmore, too, comments on the change which the poet's vocabulary undergoes in the Elegies and records the frequent recurrence of certain words—'plain words of the type that stand for much, embodying a wealth of common experience and therefore of poetic associations'. But he also points out that some of these words 'have become imbued with special meanings peculiar to the poet, and to him alone; his emotions and experiences have, to some extent, been superimposed on them'.[3] The relevance of this judgement to the problem of how Rilke reconciled individuality with universality is readily apparent.

Although we cannot go so far as Bollnow, and while it would be idle to pretend that some of the symbolism of the Elegies is not complex, the poet's constant recourse to certain simple words is nevertheless notable. The most obvious examples are the well-known symbols about which so much has been written—'der Engel', 'die Puppe', 'die Liebenden', 'der Held', 'die Toten'. But throughout the Elegies and the Sonnets one meets repeatedly a host of words which, for all the subtle shading and weighting with which Rilke uses them, are among the most unpretentious in the language—words like 'Baum', 'Raum', 'Rose', 'Quelle', 'Blume', 'Ohr', 'Stern' and 'Sternbild', 'Frucht', 'Schooß', 'Erde'. Indeed,

---

[1] Bollnow, *Rilke*, p. 13.
[2] Ibid. This critic, however, does not make this line of research the main issue of his work.
[3] Op. cit., pp. 128–9.

though his allusions are not always common property, one seldom, if ever, finds a word which is not known to people with normal reading habits. Even more important—and this was remarked in the discussion of the Elegies and the Sonnets—is the fact that Rilke again and again achieves his most powerful and telling effects by the simplest verbal means. We may cite, as a particular example, the skilful and arresting antithesis of 'das reine Zuwenig' and 'jenes leere Zuviel'[1] in the Fifth Elegy. Here Rilke produces an image of great force and suggestiveness while using everyday words which can be easily understood by everyone.

This feature of Rilke's use of language is an important factor in assessing him in the context of contemporary conditions. For it is arguable that, in the artistic sense, the vocabulary of the present age is more limited than that of the past. Although the great increase in education in the last hundred years has resulted in a much higher proportion of literacy, it has also meant, with the dilution produced by expansion, an overall lowering in the standard of language-consciousness. The latter has evened out on a plane inferior to that of the cultural *élite* which constituted the reading public up to the nineteenth century. There has also been the vast increase in popular means of communication, each of which has tended to evolve its own technique and idiom,[2] thereby imposing a further restriction on linguistic variety and shading. Above all, the ever-increasing tempo of modern life has militated against the leisured assimilation and savouring of words which was possible in the past. The result is that vocabulary has become characterized by a repetitive economy of words and phrases. All this could not fail to have its impact on one of Rilke's sensitivity, and could not be ignored if he was to achieve his purpose. The problem was a difficult one. If he was to be the poet of his age—and no great artist can sever himself from his time and environment—he had to meet it, and triumph over it, on its own ground. He had to make some concession to modern linguistic trends and yet preserve his own poetic personality and, above all, that distinctive quality which makes art the highest, the quintessential manifestation of human creative endeavour. Rilke's solution in his greatest poetry is interesting. His vocabulary is not difficult or recondite, a great proportion of the words he employs are among the most familiar, and, in particular, a number of the simplest words are frequently repeated. But he

[1] *A.W.*, Bd. I, p. 262.        [2] Cf. pp. 21–22.

does, by subtle placing and association and by unexpected compounding, invest these words with a special value which, while leaving them readily intelligible, lifts them out of the ordinary and makes them obedient to his poetic aim.[1]

There is a second aspect of Rilke's use of language which is significant. This relates notably to the Elegies, in which the conflict and conditions of his time are so powerfully portrayed. Bowra points to Rilke's use of a new form, the *vers libre*, and to its remarkable effect.

The element of song is entirely lacking. Its place is taken not by quiet meditation but by nervous, excited, discursive thought in which sensibility plays a large part. It is hard to find a label for this kind of poetry. It is undeniably full of thought, even of argument, but it does not prove a thesis or move to a regular plan or appeal directly to the understanding. It appeals to the nerves and the emotions.[2]

Again, when we consider the nature of the present age, we can see how well Rilke has adjusted himself to the character and mood of his time. 'Nervous, excited, discursive thought' is precisely the description which may be applied to the mode of expression of the twentieth century: the century of argument and debate, of social and political awareness and struggle, of controversy, of rapid changes of circumstances, of tension, of competition. It is an age in which discussion and altercation thrive in conditions of strain and under the pressure of the more complicated mechanics of living. This is what was meant when it was earlier suggested, while agreeing with S. K. Langer that poetry is not genuine discourse,[3] that Rilke, far removed though he is from deductive thinking, does adopt the technique of argument and discourse.[4] And we may remind ourselves that it was in Paris that Rilke came face to face with twentieth-century Western civilization and the stresses of modern living in their most clamant form.

Finally, we may note another feature of Rilke's technique which again brings into relief his debt to France. We have traced his 'Entwicklung zum sachlichen Sagen'—the great artistic concept which emerged from the contact with Cézanne and Baudelaire and

---

[1] We may recall, in this connexion, the remarks in the first chapter indicating that the same words have different values in different associations. See pp. 17–18.

[2] Op. cit., p. 74.

[3] p. 18. We may, however, also recall that this critic, in the extract quoted, does acknowledge that poetry uses the means of 'discursive language'.

[4] p. 22.

which was brought to practical expression under the impact of Valéry. Here again, in remarkable fashion, Rilke fell into step with the demands of his age. To all the latter's other qualities must be added the emergence of science and technology as dominant conditioning factors. The emphasis is on factual assimilation and presentation and rational explanation. Even those most intimate and personal things, human feelings and impulses, are critically detached and objectively examined—and this is the method which Rilke pursues. We can thus see how significantly the intellectual, objectivizing discipline which he underwent in France conduced, not only to the realization of his own personal poetic fulfilment, but also to the emergence of an art which proclaimed, and belonged indissociably to, the time and conditions in which it was written.

These, then, are the means by which Rilke, through the use of language and under the influence of France, comes to terms with his age and with the demands of his high calling; by which he achieves the merger between intuition and intellectual control, between subjectivity and objectivity, between his instinctive hostility to and suspicion of the manifestations of his epoch and the overwhelming inner compulsion to portray it and speak to it, between the spiritual aspirations of a mystical personality and the dictates of a factually minded, cynical, and sceptical society around him. If the present era would do away with the age of miracles by explaining them, Rilke has performed the greater miracle by fulfilling the dual task of bringing his own sensitive and incomparably creative imagination to full fruition while at the same time representing the civilization in which he lived.

# VIII

## CONCLUSION

W E have sought to follow Rilke through the varied phases of his development and to trace the successive stages in the progress which culminated in his becoming the complete poet. We have also attempted to avoid the dangers inherent in some of the critical methods applied to this poet and to adhere to an approach which recognizes and does not encroach upon the personal nature of the appreciation of lyric poetry. That Rilke's poetic career was one of the most unusual in the history of literature is indisputable. But that he did attain 'completeness' is no less certain. In some ways the climax of his achievement prompts the thought of the ideal combination of Schiller's 'naïve' and 'sentimental' poets. If this comparison may not be pressed too far, we can nevertheless see in Rilke's creative consummation the end of a struggle which went on for twenty years to reconcile and blend different and opposing elements.

Underlying all the complexities of his evolution, encompassing, as it did, vital contacts with widely differing personalities, different arts, and different countries, was the fundamental disequilibrium of Rilke's own artistic personality. He possessed from the start extreme sensibility, a fertile imagination, and, within the limits prescribed by his intuitive, inspirational nature, considerable facility in the use of his medium. But the richness of his gifts on the one side was inhibited by the lack of an intellectually imposed control, without which the full possibilities of his natural talents could never be realized. The magnitude of Rilke's problem was increased, moreover, by his strong antipathy to any formal discipline or systematized training; in short, the quality which he needed most was precisely that which his temperament rendered the most difficult of acquisition. If it is a well-worn truth that intellect and inspiration are often uneasy partners in the realm of creative art, and if in lyric poetry especially the dominant role of emotion and mood must be acknowledged, it is none the less certain that the degree of Rilke's unbalance was a major deficiency in his artistic equipment.

It was imperative that, without sacrificing the fertility of his imagination and without frustrating the compelling surge of his feelings and instincts, some measure of external control should be learnt and applied, or he would remain the poet of the first two parts of *Das Stunden-Buch*. It is with these thoughts that we can briefly expand our earlier remarks on influence.[1]

It seems to be frequently forgotten that the transmission of 'influence' involves a positive act on the part of the recipient. He may deliberately frequent places and people with whom he feels in sympathy and from whom, because of that sympathy, he expects to derive stimulus and encouragement. And where the association is unpremeditated or where there is no initial attraction, there must still be conscious choice and acceptance by the recipient before 'influence' can operate. From this it follows, as we suggested in the earlier reference, that there can be no influence except where potential response already exists. And it is also logical to infer that where there is a strong sense of kinship to start with, the influence is less likely to be of the first importance, since the very awareness of affinity implies a parity of attributes in giver and receiver. Rilke's evolution is characterized by both kinds—or degrees—of influence, and it is significant that by far the most fructifying and vital associations in his life were those which offered him the opportunity of developing powers the ultimate exercise of which was unforeseen and seemed unlikely at the outset. His progress was earlier seen, in the reference just quoted, as a process of germination. Obviously the capacity to write the Elegies and the Sonnets was always there in seminal form. Whether the seed came to bear fruit depended, first, on the cultural soil in which it was planted—or, in this case, into which it was transplanted—and, secondly, on the care with which the early tender shoots and, later, the growing branches were pruned and tended.

In the second chapter we examined the part played by Russia in Rilke's career. Whilst it was seen that Russia did have a powerful emotional effect on him, the artistic influence was found to belong to the lower of the two categories. That there was 'influence' is demonstrated by the first two parts of *Das Stunden-Buch*, but it was essentially limited. There was too great a kinship between Russia and Rilke for the poet to be able to acquire anything comparable to what was to come later. Russia, as Rilke experienced it,

[1] See p. 94.

represented and offered the qualities with which he was already adequately furnished; it promoted an artistic nostalgia; it evoked poetry which presented the poet with no great difficulty and which merely involved giving free rein to those attributes which he already possessed. It is impossible to dissociate Rilke's failure to return to Russia from the latter's limitations as a fertilizing agent.

His experience in France was very different, and it is noteworthy that his first reaction to Paris was as antipathetic as his response to Russia had been enthusiastic. In France, with few exceptions, Rilke was preoccupied with artists who, in various ways, from Rodin to Valéry, were in marked contrast to himself. His long sojourn with the representational arts in particular, with all the problems emerging from the insurmountable barrier of medium, remains one of the most intriguing episodes in Rilke's development. But his consistent association with artists who differed from him so widely is indicative of the nature of the influence which he underwent in France. For he was now at grips with the stern task of cultivating those aspects of the poetic personality which he did not possess, or which at any rate were present within him only in the most rudimentary form. Rilke's development from the year 1902 falls under two headings: the formative and what may be called the creative—the latter being used here with particular reference to the consummation of the Elegies and the Sonnets. We have seen that the formative period belonged to the first decade after his arrival in Paris. Rilke's artistic concept was complete by the end of 1907 in the sense that no fresh elements were to be added, and mature by 1912 in the same sense that the various elements were fully assimilated and integrated—this conclusion being based on the fact that he was able to begin the Elegies in this year. As we turn to the creative phase of Rilke's evolution, however, we are confronted with an interesting point. We notice that the more mature he became conceptually, the harder it became for him to produce poetry. This is of particular significance when we recall the facility and virtuosity of the Russian period, when he was working according to no particular principles of art theory and when, in effect, the only obedience he acknowledged was to impulse and inspiration.

It is a natural consequence of advance in any field of human endeavour that more problems are posed and execution becomes more difficult. The relevance of this truth to our examination of Rilke is that the progressive, and finally desperate, crisis of utterance which characterized his career after 1902 was, paradoxically, a sure index of the fact that he was advancing. What this crisis meant was that, as his experience widened and as his concept became crystallized in a definite formula, his whole approach to his art was lifted to a higher plane; with the result that the mode of expression and the quality of his use of language which had sufficed for the un-inhibited outpourings of the early writings were no longer adequate. The sublimated vision of poetry which now emerged demanded the forging of a new instrument, refined and ennobled to match the exalted concept for which it was to be the vehicle. If one accepts, as most critics of Rilke do, that the vision of the Elegies and the Sonnets was one of impressive grandeur and nobility—and tower-ing far above anything in his previous work—it can be understood why the last great creative release was so difficult of achievement and so long delayed. The attainment of mastery over his medium of language, which has been the central theme throughout this study, was the categorical imperative in Rilke's life. The problem began to loom right from the beginning of his stay in France—as soon, in other words, as his attitude to his art embraced the ele-ments of intellectual and critical judgement. For, although the supreme crisis of utterance occurred after his formative period was over, it is clear that any conceptual modification was inseparable from a modification in the means by which the concept had to be expressed. Rilke himself soon began to suspect where the root of his problem lay. Even as early as August 1903, long before he was conceptually mature, he wrote to Lou Andreas-Salomé: 'Liegt das Handwerk vielleicht in der Sprache selbst, in einem besseren Erkennen ihres inneren Lebens und Wollens, ihrer Entwicklung und Vergangenheit?'[1] And in the same letter he says: '... darum tut es mir so furchtbar not, das Werkzeug meiner Kunst zu finden, den Hammer, meinen Hammer, daß er Herr werde und wachse über alle Geräusche.'[2] If his thought and terminology are very much the product of the Rodin experience, the inference is nevertheless plain.

That the major crisis of creation came after Rilke's formative period was over is logical. For it was only when his concept had attained its highest form that the full extent of the resulting de-mands on his control over his material became apparent. During the Rodin period, when, although his approach to his art changed

[1] G.B., Bd. I, p. 387.                    [2] Ibid., p. 385.

radically, he was not really concerned with theoretical matters, but proceeded empirically,[1] Rilke achieved a considerable measure of success within the prescribed limits of the *Neue Gedichte*, even if success no longer came so easily as it had come earlier. It was when the Elegies were begun in 1912, however, that the magnitude of his task really emerged. For here was a poetic vision on a much vaster scale than anything he had before attempted, to the realization of which only the purest distillation of language would be adequate. The question was no longer what kind of poetry he should write, but how and whether utterance could be accomplished. If the intermittent work on the Elegies in the following years offered a measure of promise and hope, there was still no certainty at the beginning of 1922 that the great cycle could be completed; even less could the swift, sudden, confident nature of its completion be anticipated. The contrast between the tremendous creative storm of Muzot and the laboured, piecemeal efforts of the previous decade is indeed remarkable. Why was it that what had proceeded with difficulty, uncertainty, and delay now swept without hindrance to its triumphant conclusion? As we have seen, the influences which operated on Rilke in the pre-war years were essentially formative; and, while they inevitably had a modifying effect on his use of language, they were not, by their nature, able to impart the last creative impetus. They could help him to build up the vision of the kind of poetry he wanted to write, but something more was needed before the full and free release of what was within him could be realized—something which was not formative but practical, something which, by physically establishing in Rilke a rhythm of work and expression, would set in motion his own stream of utterance and give to concept its visible form. This final impetus came from his acquaintance, on the eve of his poetic fulfilment, with Valéry. In his whole-hearted application to the task of rendering in German a poet whose artistic thought was completely different from his own, and in his tenacious determination to wrestle with a linguistic exercise far more exacting than anything he had before attempted in this field, Rilke achieved the release of his own poetic torrent.

In this vital last stage of Rilke's development, it is difficult to imagine anyone who could have served his ends better than Valéry. In this connexion, two points need to be re-emphasized. First, the

[1] Cf. p. 103.

French language itself is notable for its concision and precision and
for the rigid discipline it imposes on anyone handling it. Second,
in Valéry's poetry these native attributes of the language are reduced to an absolute, in which the maximum meaning and effect
are extracted from every word; in which the quality, the power, the
virtue of every word are completely used up. Here was the core of
Rilke's own problem, a problem which had bestridden the years
since 1907. We have not found, and we should not seek, imitation
of Valéry in Rilke's greatest poetry. Their concepts and the genius
of their respective languages were too different for that, and in any
case Rilke was no imitator. What Rilke needed, and what he found
in Valéry, was something the validity of which applies to all languages and to all concepts of literary art. It was the optimum use of
his instrument; the quintessential concentration and condensation
of the poet's material by which every word is made to bear and
yield its fullest value and by which alone the great vision of the
Elegies and the Sonnets could be fittingly expressed. And this use
of his medium, refined and distilled to its purest and most pregnant
essence, was nothing else than the giving of practical effect to the
theoretical conclusions of 1907, whereby everything within the
poet is 'ohne Rückstand . . . aufgebraucht in der Aktion des
Machens'.

We may see the many facets of Rilke's long association with
France, from his arrival in Paris in the summer of 1902 at the age of
26, as a series of syntheses, all of which have their root in the overriding need to accomplish the great central synthesis within himself. The task of attaining completeness did not, by definition,
involve the denial or sacrifice of his innate qualities; it meant the
addition of the element of discipline which would bring these qualities to order and make them fully effective. We can, therefore, see
why the idea of a marriage between intuition and intellect, between
subjectivity and objectivity, has recurred so insistently throughout
this study. It dominated Rilke's formative period. Under Rodin,
with the externalized approach implicit in the plastic arts, his
poetic technique underwent the most extreme change of his whole
career. The introversion of the earlier writings was replaced by the
extraversion of the *Neue Gedichte*. There were good reasons why
this phase could be only temporary: there were fundamental decep-
tions in any attempt by an artist in a living, organic medium to
draw too heavily on an artist whose medium was both inanimate

and physically resistant; and Rilke's swing in the opposite direction went too far for it to be the final answer to his problems. But the extent of this *volte-face* was its principal value as a corrective. Having experienced the two extremes, Rilke was equipped to find the middle path between them.

With the contact with Cézanne, which though prolonging the sojourn with the representational arts did not confront the poet with the obstacle of medium in quite such uncompromising terms as did sculpture, the pendulum of Rilke's poetic concept came to rest. In the formula of 'sagen' instead of 'beurteilen', which, as we saw, posed the formidable task of achieving a merger between subjectivity and objectivity, he finally decided on the kind of poetry he wanted to write; it was a formula which implied a fusion of his native gifts with the intellectual control which he had lacked and had had to acquire. And throughout these early Parisian years ran the Baudelairean thread, linking him with Rodin and Cézanne and, above all, correlating his experiences in the field of 'static' art with his literary evolution and keeping him from straying too far from his own domain of poetry. There were no more revelations or theoretical modifications. The years which followed were spent in assimilating fully the experiences which had come in such rapid succession during the first five years in Paris and in adjusting himself to his new poetic outlook. During this difficult and at times critical period, Gide was a pillar of strength. It was not until ten years after his arrival in France that Rilke can be said to have reached conceptual maturity. But his problems did not end with the beginning of the Elegies, and another decade was to pass before, with the aid of Valéry, he realized the final synthesis which resulted in the free and uninhibited utterance for which he had waited so long. This was a synthesis of language—a synthesis which united the richness, the flexibility, the music of his own instrument with the clarity, the precision, the concentrated control of French in general and of Valéry's condensed use of it in particular. In this last contact with one of the outstanding figures in French letters, we may see, not only the crowning point of Rilke's own artistic endeavour, but the culmination of a process of absorption of a foreign culture and language, with which, in its duration and in the degree of saturation achieved, there is perhaps nothing comparable in the whole history of poetry.

After the consummation of the Elegies and the Sonnets came the

192        CONCLUSION

*diminuendo.* Rilke pursued, with notable pertinacity, his translations of Valéry. He wrote his original French poems, but these, if
not without academic interest, scarcely add to his reputation. They
may be regarded as the almost recreational exercise of a poet whose
toil was over, a modest memorial of his debt to France. He also
continued to write poetry in his own language, but there was no
longer the dynamism or the compelling urgency which throbbed
through the Elegies and the Sonnets. If some of these poems are
among his most beautiful, they offer no suasive evidence to justify
the inference of any fresh evolutionary trend. All the information
we possess points convincingly to the conclusion that the year 1922
was the grand climacteric in Rilke's life. It is possible, as J. B.
Leishman suggests in the Introduction to his translations of the
*Gedichte 1906 bis 1926*, that, had he lived out a full span of years,
'this eternal beginner might long have continued to surprise us
with new possibilities of expression',[1] but it is difficult to dismiss
the thought that Rilke appears essentially as an artist whose creative organism was directed above all else towards one supreme act
of production and whose life centred on this one great artistic event.

One final question remains. It was earlier suggested that, although it is not possible to make a complete separation between the
influence of the parts and that of the whole, some distinction can
nevertheless be made between Rilke's individual experiences from
1902 onwards and his more general relationship to France as a
cultural and artistic environment. We drew attention, in this connexion, to the contrast between the permanence of his link with
France as a whole and the more transient nature of his individual
contacts. More detailed comment on this interesting question was
then deferred until the whole of the French experience could be
considered in retrospect.[2] We can now ask why the enduring and
infrangible bond in Rilke's life was with France and not with
another country, especially when we remember the bitterness and
anguish of his first impressions of Paris. Two points in particular
stand out. First, although it is a Latin country, and although it is
capable of passionate feeling and intense enthusiasms, France is
known as the practitioner *par excellence* of the logical approach, of
clear, rational analysis and exposition. Part of the native genius of
the French race is the capacity to find the shortest route to the
heart of a problem and to concentrate its intellectual energies

[1] Op. cit. (London, 1957), p. 53.        [2] See pp. 39–40.

unerringly on the relevant, the essential. The significance of this
national characteristic can be understood when we recall the in-
completeness of Rilke's personality when he went to Paris, and the
nature of his deficiency. If any country could help him, belatedly,
to acquire the intellectual control which was indispensable if he
was to move forward, it was France. That he persevered in his new
environment, despite his initial sense of revulsion and despite
his natural antipathy to any formal discipline, is noteworthy. For,
however unpalatable was the task of submitting to restraint and of
modifying a poetic approach which had hitherto placed absolute
reliance on the sufficiency of inspiration, something within Rilke—
instinctive, perhaps, rather than conscious—must have convinced
him that his destiny as an artist depended on his readiness to accept
the hard schooling which confronted him and in which, in their
different ways, the influential figures with whom he was associated
were his masters. Angelloz sees the process in terms of the acquisition by Rilke of something of the French temperament.[1] This admirably epitomizes the role played by France in the prolonged
process of synthesis, of fusion of inspiration and intellect, which
was the ineluctable condition upon which the creation of the
Elegies and the Sonnets rested. For, paradoxical though it may
seem, it was by the integration into his own personality and temperament of an element which was foreign that Rilke became a
great poet of Germany.

The second aspect of the general cultural significance of France
in Rilke's career, if more indeterminate, is perhaps no less important. Rilke has already been described as a 'pure' artist.[2] There was
in his outlook none of the narrow nationalism which has been such
a consistent feature of German letters, and which was so evident in
his contemporary Stefan George. Probably in no other country has
the ideal of 'le Beau' been cherished and pursued as an end in itself
as it has in France. Art for art's sake is no mere slogan, but the expression of a way of life and cast of thought which, over the centuries, have become a national tradition. In France there is the true
aristocracy of talent; the artist is a prince among men and enjoys
authority, respect, and freedom equalled probably nowhere else.
It is not difficult to see why Rilke sensed that his genius could
flourish in this climate, the more so when we recall his close affinity
with French Symbolism, which of all literary movements was the

---

[1] Op. cit. p. 273.                    [2] p. 118.

most dedicated to the ideal of Beauty and the most hostile to anything *bourgeois* or philistine. Rilke, for whom his art was the beginning and the end of living and who sacrificed everything to it, needed constantly to be able to justify himself. He needed a cultural environment which was tolerant of his way of life and benevolent to his aspirations; in which he could pursue his course untrammelled by the necessity even to consider the demands of orthodox, conventional living; in which everything was countenanced for the sake of art. We may point these thoughts with the interesting and penetrating judgement of Rudolf Kassner, one of the few intimate friends of Rilke who could admire him without illusions:

In dem Kampf zwischen Art und Gesinnung, der auch ein Kampf ist, den der Sohn kämpft, entschied Rilke für die Art. Von Deutschlands bedeutenden Dichtern war niemand unbürgerlicher als er. Und nur insoweit, als der deutsche Geist in jeder Hinsicht der bürgerlichste Geist Europas ist, war Rilke undeutsch. In keiner anderen Rücksicht. Er liebte Frankreich, weil er darin die höhere Art sah. Es wäre verfehlt, in Rilkes Liebe zu Frankreich nichts anderes als die deutsche Liebe zum Fremden zu sehen.[1]

[1] *Buch der Erinnerung*, p. 249.

# SELECT BIBLIOGRAPHY

## A. RILKE'S WRITINGS

*Gesammelte Werke* (6 Bde.), Leipzig, 1927.
*Ausgewählte Werke* (2 Bde.), Wiesbaden, 1951.
*Gedichte 1906 bis 1926*, Wiesbaden, 1953.
*Poèmes français*, Paris, 1935.
*Gesammelte Briefe* (6 Bde.), Leipzig, 1936.
*Briefe über Cézanne*, Wiesbaden, 1952.
*Rilke et Gide, Correspondance* (with introduction and commentaries by R. Lang), Paris, 1952.
*Lettres à Merline*, Paris, 1950.
*Tagebücher aus der Frühzeit*, Leipzig, 1942.

## B. CRITICAL AND OTHER WORKS

S. ALEXANDER: *Beauty and other Forms of Value*, London, 1933.
E. ANDREAS-SALOMÉ: *Rainer Maria Rilke*, Leipzig, 1928.
J. F. ANGELLOZ: *Rainer Maria Rilke — l'Évolution spirituelle du poète*, Paris, 1936.
A. BARRE: *Le Symbolisme*, Paris, 1911.
D. BASSERMANN: *Der späte Rilke*, München, 1947.
M. BAUER: *Rainer Maria Rilke und Frankreich*, Bern, 1931.
H. W. BELMORE: *Rilke's Craftsmanship*, Oxford, 1954.
O. F. BOLLNOW: *Rilke*, Stuttgart, 1951.
C. M. BOWRA: *The Heritage of Symbolism*, London, 1942.
E. BUDDEBERG: *Rainer Maria Rilke. Eine innere Biographie*, Stuttgart, 1955.
E. M. BUTLER: *R. M. Rilke*, Cambridge, 1941.
A. R. DE CLERY: *Rilke traducteur*, Genève, 1956.
F. DEHN: *Rainer Maria Rilke und sein Werk*, Leipzig, 1934.
M. GILMAN: *Baudelaire the Critic*, New York, 1943.
H. GOERTZ: *Frankreich und das Erlebnis der Form im Werke Rainer Maria Rilkes*, Stuttgart, 1932.
R. GUARDINI: *Rainer Maria Rilkes Deutung des Daseins. Eine Interpretation der Duineser Elegien*, München, 1953.
F. W. VAN HEERIKHUIZEN: *Rainer Maria Rilke. His Life and Work*, Bussum, 1946. (Translated from the Dutch by Fernand G. Renier and Anne Cliff. London, 1951.)
E. HELLER: *The Disinherited Mind*, Cambridge, 1952.
H. E. HOLTHUSEN: *Der späte Rilke*, Zürich, 1949.
R. KASSNER: *Buch der Erinnerung*, Zürich, 1954.
K. KIPPENBERG: *R. M. Rilke, ein Beitrag*, Leipzig, 1935.

S. K. Langer: *Feeling and Form*, New York, Toronto, London, 1953.

A. G. Lehmann: *The Symbolist Aesthetic in France, 1885–1895*, Oxford, 1950.

E. C. Mason: *Lebenshaltung und Symbolik bei R. M. Rilke*, Weimar, 1939.

H. Meyer: *Zarte Empirie*, Stuttgart, 1963. *Vide* the essays *Rilkes Cézanne-Erlebnis*, pp. 244–86, and *Die Verwandlung des Sichtbaren*, pp. 287–336.

R. Mövius: *Rilkes Stunden-Buch. Entstehung und Gehalt*, Leipzig, 1937.

C. K. Ogden and I. A. Richards: *The Meaning of Meaning*, London, 1923.

S. A. Rhodes: *The Cult of Beauty in Charles Baudelaire*, New York, 1929.

M. Saint-Hélier: *A Rilke pour Noël*, Berne, 1927.

C. Sieber: *René Rilke. Die Jugend Rainer Maria Rilkes*, Leipzig, 1932.

E. Simenauer: *Rainer Maria Rilke: Legende und Mythos*, Bern, 1953.

J. Steiner: *Rilkes Duineser Elegien*, Bern, 1962.

L. de Sugar: *Baudelaire et R. M. Rilke*, Paris, 1954.

M. von Thurn und Taxis-Hohenlohe: *Erinnerungen an R. M. Rilke*, München, Berlin, Zürich, 1932.

E. M. Wilkinson: *Johann Elias Schlegel*, Oxford, 1945.

—— *Rainer Maria Rilke. Aspects of his Mind and Poetry* (edited by William Rose and Gertrude Craig Houston, with an introduction by Stefan Zweig), London, 1938,

—— *Rilke et la France*, Bruxelles, 1943 (a collection of essays, tributes, etc.).

# INDEX

PRINTED IN GREAT BRITAIN
AT THE UNIVERSITY PRESS, OXFORD
BY VIVIAN RIDLER
PRINTER TO THE UNIVERSITY